Edith Wharton in Context

Edith Wharton in Context

Essays on Intertextuality

Adeline R. Tintner

THE UNIVERSITY OF ALABAMA PRESS

Tuscaloosa and London

Copyright © 1999
The University of Alabama Press
Tuscaloosa, Alabama 35487-0380
All rights reserved
Manufactured in the United States of America
1 2 3 4 5 6 7 8 9 . 05 04 03 02 01 00 99

∞

The paper on which this book is printed meets the minimum requirements of American
National Standard for Information Science–Permanence of Paper for Printed Library
Materials, ANSI Z39.48-1984.

Library of Congress Cataloging-in-Publication Data

Tintner, Adeline R., 1912–
    Edith Wharton in context : essays on intertextuality / Adeline R. Tintner.
    p. cm.
  ISBN 0-8173-0975-6 (alk. paper)
    1. Wharton, Edith, 1862–1937—Criticism and interpretation. 2. Women and literature—
United States—History—20th century. 3. Influence (Literary, artistic, etc.) 4.
Intertextuality. I. Title.
  PS3545.H16 Z8786 1999
  813′.52—dc21
                        99-6206
British Library Cataloguing-in-Publication Data available

Contents

Illustrations

Preface

This collection of essays was written sporadically from 1972 through 1997. Now and then, in the past twenty-five years, my attention was drawn to solving certain problems of meaning in various stories and novels by Edith Wharton. My following of the literary relations between Wharton and James all grew out of my concentrated study of James's late short fiction. It began by my close study of James's tale of 1908, "The Velvet Glove," on which, after many rereadings, I realized that the Princess in that tale could be none other than Edith Wharton herself. Wanting corroboration, I sent my paper to Leon Edel, who promptly accepted unequivocally my "discovery," which I had hit upon just from reading James's tale. He had come to the same conclusion through documentary evidence and was at that very moment writing his chapter on the connection for the final volume of his life of James. I published my paper in 1971–72 just before that final volume came out of Edel's *Life* in *Modern Fiction Studies*. Then, encouraged, I read just as carefully the rest of the *Finer Grain* tales, which had all been written by James within a week's time in the winter of 1908–09 in response to a single request for a tale for *Harper's Monthly Magazine*. Each tale seemed to have Edith in it! The clues popped out, but only to someone alerted to their existence. By now, though, I felt that this could be part of a dialogue in which Edith Wharton herself took part. So I read her collected tales, which had been published just at that time, and, for the rest of the 1970s and 1980s, I found that this connection between the two writers, which their fiction caused to take place, had continued. My reading of James's late tales led me to see that "Julia Bride" (1909) supplied a source for Chapter 9 of Wharton's *The Custom of the Country*.

The Bourget literary relationship also began with work I was doing in connection with the French writer's close friendship with and admiration of Henry James. I read everything he wrote and one tale, "L'Indicatrice," contained a figure that seemed to me very close to a portrait of Edith. This was established as a matter of fact by a passage in Percy Lubbock's *Portrait of Edith Wharton* quoted from a letter from Charles Du Bos, the translator of *The House of Mirth* into French, stating that Bourget had written a short *nouvelle* and told Du Bos, "He had thought of Edith in writing it" (L, 98). However, Du Bos could not remember the title of the tale, the plot of which corresponded very closely to that of "L'Indicatrice." I could now identify it.

The identification of John Esquemeling's *The Buccaneers* was easy, once Maggs and Co., considering me a possible purchaser of the library of Edith Wharton, sent me a complete list of the titles of those books they were offering for sale. And there it was, just as so many elements in *The Buccaneers* corresponded to Consuelo Vanderbilt's review of her marriage to the Duke of Marlborough in *The Glitter and the Gold,* her autobiography.

The relations between Tiepolo's ceiling fresco in the Church of the Scalzi and *The Glimpses of the Moon* would never have revealed themselves to me if I had not attended a lecture given by my friend, the distinguished professor of American Literature at the University of Venice, Rosella Mamoli Zorzi. From the projected lantern slide I could see what this no longer existing ceiling painting was all about and consequently my seeing it and interpreting its iconography gave a new and crucial dimension to thoughts about *The Glimpses of the Moon,* which, up to this revelation, had not been taken seriously by any critics and had not been understood by me.

How did I get into Auchincloss's four original reconstructions of Edith Wharton's life? I read the first in "The Arbiter," a chapter in *The Winthrop Covenant* of 1976, and I saw the tale as a partial reinvention of the Edith-Teddy marriage. I asked Mr. Auchincloss if I had any right to see it as such, and he not only said it was a correct view, but that he had done another fictive version, of a part of Wharton's life, in another tale published a decade after "The Arbiter." So ever since, after he directed me to "The 'Fulfillment' of Grace Eliot," I watched Auchincloss's yearly production of tales or novels and found two more versions, the last in 1995 containing the "Real" Edith, dominating the conversation as Edith Wharton, under her own name, in her French home.

My other adventures in tracking down Edith Wharton in the fiction or poetry of other writers happened by simply reading. Her personality and her figure have been captured at least by seven authors, beginning slowly in the 1970s and 1980s, but developing steam by the 1990s. The last section of this collection of essays, called *The Legacy of Wharton's Fiction,* shows attempts by writers at bringing in her work itself. This shows a characteristic that apes the legacy of Henry James, which has so burgeoned in the 1990s that in one year, 1997, eleven pieces of fiction and two movies brought his work into postmodern literature and film. Edith Wharton is sure to follow soon, for with the film versions of *The Age of Innocence* and *Ethan Frome,* both shown in the 1990s, we have now up to eight popular versions of her figure or her work. The divide between high art and pop art is getting narrower and narrower. The popularity Wharton enjoyed in her own lifetime (in contrast to Henry James's) is reasserting itself in her importance as an icon for the end of this century.

However, the "discovery" that gave me the most pleasure was the finding on the back flyleaf of a book from the library of Henry James a five-line poem written in the handwriting of Edith Wharton. When I was examining the book a bookseller was offering me for sale, I turned to the back and saw this poem. I owned one or two samples of Wharton's handwriting—two short letters and a few inscriptions—and suddenly it dawned on me that it *might* be (please let it be!) her hand! I said nothing to the bookseller, for I knew that he had not noticed the poem or he would have upped the price of the book, which was not exactly cheap. I also was not sure it was Wharton's hand, but I went home, made Xerox copies of the poem, and sent copies to all the experts, who said it was her handwriting! I then went into the question of whether the lines were of her own invention or whether they were a quotation from another poet. I still don't know. But what I do know is that Walter Berry, James himself, as well as those who owned the book after both of them, also never turned to the back of the book. The book presents a mystery, and a possibly heartbreaking situation for Edith herself, whose words were ignored by this group of men so closely connected with her own life. Someone who will read the appendix included in this collection will perhaps solve this mystery for all of us.

As one who has for a quarter of a century been fascinated by the interliterary (and interartistic) relationships of two of our greatest American authors, I may be forgiven if I engage in such a relationship, even if minor, with one of them. In this introduction to my collected essays, I have been influenced by the example of Henry James's Prefaces to his New York Edition. Their purpose was to record "the *accessory* facts in a given case" (LCFW, 1039) and to provide the author with an opportunity to take "his whole unfolding, his process of production, . . . almost for a wondrous adventure" (LCFW, 1040). The very circumstances in which any kind of creative production takes place can be indeed "a wondrous adventure," and I agree with James that the moment and the place when and where one comes upon a new idea is such an experience.

Acknowledgments

I wish to thank Nicole Mitchell, Director of the University of Alabama Press, and Curtis Clark, Assistant Director and Editor-in-Chief, for their encouragement and editorial assistance; I am grateful to the staff of the Press for expertise in all departments. I also wish to thank Mark Piel, Chief Librarian at the New York Society Library in New York City, for his fine collection of Paul Bourget's novels and short stories unobtainable in other New York libraries. I am especially grateful to Annette Zilbersmit, the Editor of *The Edith Wharton Review*, for having made room in her journal for nine of the articles enclosed in this book. I profited by having heard Professor Rosella Mamoli Zorzi, Professor of American Literature at the University of Venice, speak on "Tiepolo References in the Travel Essays of Henry James and Edith Wharton" on March 16, 1997, at the Metropolitan Museum of Art in New York City. I am grateful to Helen Killoran and Kristin Lauer for their helpful suggestions.

I also wish to thank Louis Auchincloss for his candid discussion of the elements that went into his fictive portraits of Edith Wharton and for his helpful suggestions regarding my interpretations of his interpretations.

The author acknowledges the original publication of the following chapters, which are republished by permission:

Chapter 1. " 'The Hermit and the Wild Woman': Edith Wharton's 'Fictioning' of Henry James," *Journal of Modern Literature* 4, no. 1 (September 1974): 32–42.

Chapter 2. "James's Mock Epic, 'The Velvet Glove': Edith Wharton and Other Late Tales," *Modern Fiction Studies* 17, no. 4 (Winter 1971–72), pp. 483–501.

Chapter 3. "The Metamorphosis of Edith Wharton," *Twentieth Century Literature* 21, no. 4 (December 1975): 355–79.

Chapter 4. "Jamesian Structures in *The Age of Innocence*," *Twentieth Century Literature* 26, no. 3 (Fall 1980): 332–48.

Chapter 5. "Mothers versus Daughters in the Fiction of Edith Wharton and Henry James," *A. B. Bookman's Weekly,* June 6, 1983, pp. 4324–28.

Chapter 6. "Wharton and James: Some Literary Give and Take," *Edith Wharton Newsletter* (Spring 1986): 3–5, 8.

Chapter 7. "Henry James's 'Julia Bride': A Source for Chapter Nine in Edith Wharton's *The Custom of the Country*," *Notes on Modern American Literature* 9 (Winter 1985): Note 16.

Chapter 8. "Edith Wharton and Paul Bourget: Literary Exchanges," *Edith Wharton Review* 8, no. 1 (Spring 1991): 16–18.

Chapter 9. "The Portrait of Edith in Bourget's 'L'Indicatrice,'" *The Edith Wharton Review* 7, no. 1 (Spring 1991): 10–12.

Chapter 11. "Two Novels of 'The Relatively Poor': George Gissing's *New Grub Street* and *The House of Mirth*," *Notes on Modern American Literature* 6, no. 2 (Autumn 1982), Note 12.

Chapter 13. "Mother, Daughter, and Incest in the Late Novels of Edith Wharton," *The Lost Tradition: Mothers and Daughters in Literature,* edited by Cathy N. Davidson and E. M. Broner (New York: Unger, 1980), 147–58.

Chapter 14. "Wharton's Forgotten Preface to Vivienne de Watteville's *Speak to the Earth:* A Link with Hemingway's 'The Snows of Kilimanjaro,'" *Notes on Modern American Literature* 8, no. 2 (Autumn 1984): Note 10.

Chapter 16. "Consuelo Vanderbilt and *The Buccaneers*," *The Edith Wharton Review* 10, no. 2 (1993): 15–19.

Chapter 17. "*False Dawn* and the Irony of Taste-Changes in Art," *Edith Wharton Newsletter* 1, no. 2 (Fall 1984): 1–8.

Chapter 18. "Pre-Raphaelite Painting and Poetry in Edith Wharton's 'The Buccaneers' (1938)," *Journal of Pre-Raphaelite Studies,* 2, n.s. (Fall 1993): 16–19.

Chapter 19. "Tiepolo's Ceiling in the Church of the Scalzi and *The Glimpses of the Moon:* The Importance of Home," *The Edith Wharton Review* 14, no. 1 (Spring 1997): 22–28.

Chapter 20. "The Figure of Edith Wharton in Richard Howard's Poem *The Lesson of the Master*," *The Edith Wharton Review* 9, no. 2 (Fall 1992): 11–14.

Chapter 21. "Justice to Teddy Wharton in Louis Auchincloss's 'The Arbiter,'" *The Edith Wharton Review* 7, no. 2 (Winter 1990): 17–20.

Chapter 22. "Punishing Morton Fullerton in 'The "Fulfillment" of Grace Eliot,'" *Twentieth Century Literature* 38, no. 1 (Spring 1992): 44–54.

Chapters 23 and 24. "Louis Auchincloss's 'Four Edith' Tales: Some Re-arrangements and Reinventions of Her Life," *The Edith Wharton Review* 13, no. 2 (Spring 1996): 9–14.

Chapter 27. "Louis Auchincloss Rewrites Edith Wharton's "After Holbein," *Studies in Short Fiction* 33, no. 2 (Spring 1996): 301–303.

Appendix. "An Unpublished Love Poem by Edith Wharton," *American Literature* 60, no. 1 (March 1988): 98–103.

Edith Wharton in Context

Introduction

In the midst of the current preoccupation of critics and scholars with Edith Wharton's life and psyche, it is easy to forget that this intense interest arises from a genuine desire to understand the fiction of this important American woman writer of novels and short stories. But we also need to remember that Wharton's creative imagination operated as well in a literary context with her contemporaries. To fill a need in Wharton's scholarship, this collection of some of my essays, old and new, attempts to explore Wharton's give-and-take with authors whom she knew well, especially Henry James, as well as Paul Bourget, whose European context in her work is yet to be investigated fully. Included in this group of personal friends are F. Marion Crawford and Vivienne de Watteville. Not to be dismissed are those Wharton knew only through their writing, such as Grace Aguilar, George Gissing, and Hugh Walpole. Although Walpole and Wharton never knew each other, Wharton was aware of Walpole's last stories, as is evident in her redoing of "The Silver Mask" from his *All Souls' Night* in her "All Souls'."

Within her literary context should be considered those writers who, after her death, inherited her legacy. The most interesting part of that legacy for current writers seems to have been her life and her "figure." The poet, Richard Howard, and the novelist, Louis Auchincloss, wrote their own reconstructions of her life in poems and short stories, while others, like Carol de Chellis Hill and Cathleen Schine, extended her life in their fiction; Hill's figure of Wharton is based on her character and personality, as known from her biography. Schine's is based on the publication of Wharton's love letters to Fullerton.

When we first turn to her closest contemporary, Henry James, and look at their literary friendship beyond their personal relationship, we see it as a subtle game played by two intimates with a kindred sense of humor, something she herself mentions in her autobiography, but which is also characterized by some deep-seated differences. Wharton, as was once believed, was never really a James disciple, although she did adopt and adapt some of his fictional structures, but only in order to improve them and to convert them to her own uses. Although she admired him greatly as a person, I find that she seemed not to have been above using his figure as a starting point for her story, "The Eyes." In it, the figure of James, surrounded by his acolytes, dominates a tale in which a character, only partly dependent upon James, is the galvanizing center. Their references to each other in their work transcends an either-or position and only a detailed analysis, such as is contained in the enclosed papers, can do justice to the complexity of their interplay.

Whereas Wharton makes fiction out of Henry James in "The Hermit and the Wild Woman," as well as in "Ogrin the Hermit," Henry James retaliates by "fictioning" Edith in a series of stories written just after he had been visited by Wharton, who had carried him off in a whirlwind of social activity. The five tales included in the collection, *The Finer Grain,* contain Edith icons that clearly have a humorous reference to her vital yet domineering personality. Wharton herself seems to have plundered James's tale, "Julia Bride" (1909), for a chapter in *The Custom of the Country* (1913), but her recollections of James's fictional strategies and structures in *The Age of Innocence* (1920) appear as a form of homage, written in the midst of Wharton's involvement with Lubbock's editorship of James's letters rather than the influence of James as such on her Pulitzer prize-winning novel.

Edith Wharton did not have the same kind of kinship with Bourget that she enjoyed with James, as far as the subtle interconnection and well-concealed jokes are concerned, a form first exhibited by James and willingly engaged in by Wharton. With Bourget, she exchanges *données,* since both had an inexhaustible supply of plots ready at hand. In 1901, Bourget dedicated the title story of *Monique* in an eponymous collection of tales, to Edith Wharton. This tale was all about the making of fine furniture, for, to Bourget, Edith, at that time, was the furniture expert with her book, *The Decoration of Houses* (1897). He actually imitates Wharton's "The Moving Finger" in his tale "The Portrait." He bases a character, Alice Gray, on Wharton's figure, and Wharton, in turn, seems to have borrowed part of Bourget's *Idylle Tragique* for *The House of Mirth,* as well as Dorsenne's character from his *Cosmopolis* (1893) for the character of

Lawrence Selden. When Edith Wharton arrived in Paris as a celebrity after the success of *The House of Mirth* in 1905, Bourget created his character of Mrs. Edith Risley, which he admitted was based on Edith Wharton for her role in his tale, "L'Indicatrice."

In 1906 Wharton's *Madame de Treymes* shows Wharton tackling the theme of divorce, which in 1904 Bourget had castigated in his popular anti-divorce book, *Un Divorce,* a book that James had admired for its construction in a letter he wrote to Edith Wharton. Bourget sees divorce as creating a prison for Catholics. Wharton sees divorce as a prison for American Protestants married to French Catholics, and, as opposed to Bourget, she blames the Catholic church for creating the prison. However, it seems likely that Bourget's book is the chief source for Wharton's fine short novel that follows so closely on its heels and that apparently had been cause for discussion in her circle.

Two other authors have cross references with Wharton's work before 1910. George Gissing's *New Grub Street* (1891) contains the original phrase, "relative poverty," as opposed to absolute poverty. It is used as the main description by Edith Wharton of Lily Bart's financial condition. Also, the discussion of the meaning of success in life is engaged in *New Grub Street* by Jasper Milvane and Marian, his fiancée. It is imitated in *The House of Mirth* in the same kind of discussion between Lily and Selden.

The other author, the popular novelist, F. Marion Crawford, was closely connected to Edith Wharton because of her friendship with his half-sister, Margaret Chanler. After Edith Wharton wrote an article on Crawford's play, *Francesca de Rimini* (1902), Crawford may have sent her a copy of *The Heart of Rome,* published in 1903, just as she was writing *The House of Mirth*. Sabine, the heroine of *The Heart of Rome,* like Lily Bart, although accustomed to luxury, is suddenly impoverished and is put into the household of Baron Volterra, a Jewish financier. When Sabine's reputation becomes tarnished, he loses his interest in her, a plot structure we meet in Simon Rosedale's rejection of Lily in *The House of Mirth*. Sabine's economic plight is partially the result of the extravagance of her mother, the Princess Conti, and Lily Bart's is also conditioned by her mother's similar extravagance.

The intertextual relation of Edith Wharton to the next four discussed authors takes place in her late novels written in the 1920s and 1930s. The first group of novels, *The Mother's Recompense* and *Twilight Sleep,* finds support in Grace Aguilar, a novelist Wharton's grandmother read, as she tells us in the epigraph to *The Mother's Recompense,* named after one of Aguilar's most popular novels of guidance to how mothers and daughters should relate to each other. However, Wharton makes it clear that times have changed and what a mother's recompense is in a novel so named by herself, a writer of the 1920s, is the recovery of her own identity, not the happy marriages of her daughters.

In 1935 Wharton's preface to Vivienne de Watteville's *Speak to the Earth* created a link between the author and Ernest Hemingway, forged perhaps by Wharton herself, and her last tale, "All Souls'" (1937) appears to share certain clear-cut characteristics with Hugh Walpole's tale of 1933, "The Silver Mask," in his collection *All Souls' Night.*

For the past twenty years certain writers have found the details of Wharton's life with her husband, her lover, and her friends suitable for the creation of new fiction. Richard Howard's poem, *The Lesson of the Master* (1974), situates Edith in an automobile ride to bury the ashes of the man she loved, accompanied by a young man who reveals to her that her lover was a homosexual and, therefore, could not respond to her. Louis Auchincloss, from 1976 to 1996, rearranged facts known about Wharton's life with certain readjustments to create four different versions of that life. His last novel, *The Education of Oscar Fairfax,* brings her in as the real "Mrs. Wharton" in a cameo showing her as a hostess at her villa near Paris. Carol Hill's *Henry James's Midnight Song* also engages the "real" Edith Wharton in a comic mystery novel in which she protects Henry James and gets involved with Sigmund Freud. Cathleen Schine in *Love Letter* (1995) centrally incorporates an actual love letter from Wharton to Fullerton in a novel that justifies a woman's unconventional love affair.

Two writers have tried to redo some of Wharton's fiction itself: Auchincloss in a section of his novel, *The Partners,* rewrites Wharton's "After Holbein," and Daniel Magida plants recognizable names and situations from *The Age of Innocence* in his novel *The Rules of Seduction* (1992). Lev Raphael in his mystery novel *The Edith Wharton Murders* (1997) creates his suspense from focusing on the academic world's rival Edith Wharton societies and their meetings arranged to discuss the works of Wharton, a world to which Raphael as a Wharton scholar once himself belonged before his decision to write mysteries instead. We also find in an academic mystery in the 1980s (following the tradition of Amanda Cross) a heroine who, teaching in a London university, is in the process of "writing a book on Edith Wharton," all "part of a course on the influence of gender on style." It turns out that the aristocratic woman she is talking to has as "her favorite book" *The House of Mirth.*[1]

That Wharton continually exhibited her flair for art history in her travels and jaunts to both well-known and lesser frequented monuments throughout Europe is well documented; therefore, her inclusion of art in novels is not surprising, although not often closely investigated by scholars.[2] Her response to the original Italian Pre-Raphaelites and to the English Pre-Raphaelites of a generation before hers is analyzed here in three essays, one showing her sensibility to changes in art tastes and art collecting, the second to the inheritance of the revolution in Rossetti's paintings exhibited in Wharton's unfinished novel, *The Buccaneers,* which manifests other literary intertextual characteristics as well, and the third to the effect that Tiepolo's ceiling fresco in the Church of the Scalzi had on *The Glimpses of the Moon.*

Perhaps the most intriguing example of Wharton's complex relation with her three friends—Henry James, Walter Berry, and F. Morton Fullerton—exists in a poem clearly in her handwriting in a book that passed from the hands of Walter Berry to Henry James as a gift as James was about to sail for England in 1911 (see Appendix). Because Fullerton seems to have been the person for whom Wharton wrote the love poem on the back flyleaf of the book, one may surmise that he too had owned the book at one time. The book itself, Romain Rolland's *La Vie de Tolstoi,* remains a memorial to Edith Wharton and her three friends and is evidence of intertextuality on a physical rather than an abstract level.

The discovery of one author's work or figure planted in the work of another author may depend mostly on pure chance, in which case the reader may have come across many more than I have. However, since it is fairly recently that Edith Wharton has figured in the imaginations of other writers, outside of her contemporaries James and Bourget, we do not find the plenitude of novels and tales in which James appears, but her time will come. It is clear from the five novels of the 1990s, in which some part of her personality or work has been invoked, that the time is almost here.

Note: Seven essays have been written for this volume and previously unpublished: Chapters 10, 12, 15, 25, 26, 28, and 29.

A.R.T.

REFERENCES

1. Joan Smith, *A Masculine Ending* (New York: Fawcett Crest, 1987), p. 136.

2. Helen Killoran, *Edith Wharton: Art and Allusion* (Tuscaloosa and London: University of Alabama Press, 1996). This is the first book-length study to concentrate on art and literary allusions in Wharton's fiction.

PART ONE
Wharton and James

1

The "Fictioning" of Henry James in Wharton's "The Hermit and the Wild Woman" and "Ogrin the Hermit"

By detailed biographical investigation and stylistic literary analysis, both Leon Edel and I were the first to show that Henry James disguised Edith Wharton as the scribbling Princess in his mock epic, "The Velvet Glove" (1909).[1] It has not been recognized, however, that Edith had also disguised Henry James as the Hermit in her pseudo-life of a saint, "The Hermit and the Wild Woman" (1906), three years before and in her imitation medieval poem, "Ogrin the Hermit" (1909). (As late as 1934, she was to refer to Henry James's "hermit-like asceticism.")[2]

It is my purpose to show, from a close reading of the story and the narrative poem, both acknowledged autobiographical exercises, that the Hermit of both pieces can be identified with certain aspects of Henry James. This reading is borne out by what is known of the relations between Edith Wharton and Henry James. Indeed, Percy Lubbock links her, the "wild woman," with him, "the literary hermit," on the opening pages of *Portrait of Edith Wharton*.

R. W. B. Lewis, who has emphasized the biographical aspects of the tale, sees Walter Berry as the Hermit. It "becomes uncomfortably clear that the relation between the Wild Woman and the Hermit is an elementary version, at several kinds of remove, of the relation between Edith Wharton and Walter Berry during the period when she was escaping or trying to escape from her own convent, her marriage."[3] At this time the evidence for Fullerton's affair with Wharton had not yet emerged. Lewis quotes from Edith Wharton's diary: "I feel that all the mysticism in me—

Originally published as "'The Hermit and the Wild Woman': Edith Wharton's 'Fictioning' of Henry James," *Journal of Modern Literature* 4, no. 1 (September 1974): 32–42.

and the transcendentalism that in other women turns to religion—were poured into my feeling for you,"[4] in order to show how this feeling has been translated into a religious allegory where the wild woman, a renegade nun, feels the need to "sleep under the free heaven and to wash the dust from my body in cool water" (CS, 582). The expression of her love for Berry-Fullerton in this parable of a woman's need for refreshing waters seems understandable, but I cannot agree with Lewis's reading of the story, which leads him to conclude that Berry, "like the Hermit, evidently recoiled in some dismay at these revealed longings" and that the outcome of the story "appears as an only too familiar act of self-consoling prophecy: too late, her sometime lover would appreciate the true value of what he had missed" (CS, xix). The Hermit shows no personal feelings for the woman and the identification with Berry breaks down when it becomes clear from the text that the Hermit was not the object of the woman's longings nor does he at the end regret not having loved her. His sole concern is for the salvation of her soul and for the protection of his own reputation as a holy man. Lewis claims he finds further confirmation of his identification of the Hermit with Berry-Fullerton in Edith Wharton's narrative poem, "Ogrin the Hermit," in which the Hermit reappears, although Lewis is aware that the introduction of Tristan as lover of Iseult makes the Hermit someone other than Walter Berry.

> This reading is confirmed in part by a narrative poem called "Ogrin the Hermit," which Mrs. Wharton wrote in the spring of 1909. The story, briefly, is this: Tristan and Iseult, fleeing Iseult's husband, King Mark, take refuge with the Hermit Ogrin. In the days that follow, while Tristan is away hunting, the Hermit pleads with Iseult to give up her sinful life with Tristan; but Iseult replies with an eloquent defense of the innocence, again almost the holiness, of pure and dedicated erotic love. The Hermit, despite himself, is convinced of the rightness of her course. The poem is rather better, as a literary exercise, than "The Hermit and the Wild Woman," and it is of still greater biographical interest, since a third figure (clearly not the husband) has been added. (CS, xix)

Since Lewis has identified the Hermit of the short story with Berry, he must continue to identify him with the Hermit Ogrin of the narrative poem, even though Tristan is a more reasonable analogue. Since Lewis's Ogrin is Berry, Tristan in his reading is simply an unidentified male. If, however, the Hermit of the short story is to be identified with Henry James, then the Tristan of the poem clearly becomes Berry, with whom Iseult is fleeing from her husband, Lord Mark (Edward Wharton).

I

"The Hermit and the Wild Woman" begins with references that could only apply to Henry James. His home is called "a cave in the hollow of a hill . . . and across the valley . . . another hill . . . raised against the sky . . ." and is immediately recognizable as Rye and Winchelsea, the two hill towns of the region where James lived. As a boy he had fled the civil war of the Guelfs and Ghibellines, as James may have avoided becoming involved in the American Civil War. Like James, the Hermit "had no wish to go back." Like James, the Hermit "would rather have been bred a clerk and scholar than knight's son." His father, his mother, and his sister were all dead, as were James's, and his "longing was to live hidden from life" (571). The Hermit loves pictures, as James did, especially pictures of angels, which may be a sly reference by Wharton to James's boyhood nickname of "Angel." He has a garden, as James did, over which he fusses. This kind of personality is very different from Walter Berry, an eminently sociable lawyer involved with people and life. The Hermit's chief pleasure is the composition of "lauds in honor of Christ and the saints," which corresponds to the great joy James took in his writing of fiction. What is more, as James was now dictating to a secretary, the Hermit dictates his lauds! Since he "feared to forget them . . . he decided to ask a friendly priest . . . to write them down" (CS, 573).

Given these analogical references to James, it is then easy to identify the Saint of the Rock who is such an example of holiness that the Hermit in emulation wishes to visit him even though he lives far away "in holiness and austerity in a desert place." Wharton seems to be saying with tongue in cheek that Henry has made a long ocean trip to see his brother, William, who lives in Vermont in order to ask his opinions about his work, only to be soundly criticized and upset. The Saint calls the Hermit "You fool" for coming all this way to praise solitude with him; "how can two sit together and praise solitude, since by so doing they put an end to the thing they praise?" (CS, 576). The Hermit finally is reduced to "tears" by the Saint's logic. The Hermit returns, as Henry had from his trip to America, to find his garden watered. Edith may mean two things by this: one, that the one solace Henry had had on his 1904–1905 trip to

America had been his visits with her at Lenox and New York and, two, that she fixed up his "unkempt flower borders," referred to in *A Backward Glance*.[5] He sees a woman "lean with wayfaring" (Edith and her travels) covered with "heathen charms" and "brown as a nut," with "nothing to please him in the sight" of her and therefore "he ran no danger in looking at her." This seems to fit Edith's relation with James much more closely than it does her relation with her lover. The renegade nun had fled her convent because she had been guilty of bathing in pools of water, a habit considered sinful, and is now hunted down. Lewis suggests with justice that the convent stands for Edith's marriage with Teddy Wharton from which at this time she was trying to escape (CS, xix). "The Hermit . . . was much perturbed" by her story and would have driven her forth, yet "remembering the desire that drew him to his lauds, he dared not judge his sister's fault too harshly" (CS, 582). Edith sees herself and James as brother and sister, since both not only write but also have equally strong passions. Nevertheless, Edith wants James to remember that when he judges her he should remember his own weakness and intense passion for his work, as intense in him as her lust for life is in her. In her story the Hermit keeps "reasoning with her in love and charity, and exhorting her to return to the cloister" (CS, 583). This may be a reference to James's advice to Edith to save her marriage. The Hermit's function is to encourage her to "endure the condition of her life," her marriage. (His later letter of 1908 advises her to do just that.) Her troubles with Teddy are believed to have come to a head in 1905. While James was visiting her in America she may have confided the general condition of her life to James, and he may have been sworn to secrecy. If we are able to take our cues from the story, the Hermit "promised not to betray her presence" to her hunters, for "her innocency of mind made him feel she might be won back to holy living if only her freedom were assured" (CS, 584).

The Wild Woman, like Edith, is forced to travel, since they may "drag me back to the cloister" (CS, 584). Millicent Bell tells us that Edith's "chief desire . . . was to get away [from Teddy] if she could."[6] The Hermit, nevertheless, criticizes her for this wish and suggests solitude (James has written many letters referring to her as "rushing, ravening," engaged in a "prodigious devil's dance," and so forth), but her answer is that she must bathe herself in the waters of life. A "stream flows in the glen below us. . . . Do you forbid me to bathe in it?" The Hermit says not he but "the laws of God" forbid it, and the Wild Woman, after a certain amount of argumentation on the Hermit's part, "agreed to embrace a life of reclusion" (CS, 585). After two years of their living a life of mutual prayers, a plague hits the land and the Wild Woman nurses the sick, thereby getting a reputation for saintliness. The Hermit still feels it "behooved him to exhort her again to return to the convent . . . and that now she had . . . tasted the sweets of godliness, it was her duty to confess her fault and give herself up to her superiors" (CS, 586). However, the Hermit had enjoyed working side by side with the Wild Woman, as he had with Edith Wharton when either of them stayed with the other. "And gradually it grew sweet to him to think that, nearby though unseen, was one who performed the same tasks at the same hours" (CS, 585). (At least Edith thought he liked the idea of her working while he did!) The Bishop comes to celebrate the Assumption in the Hermit's valley, as a response to the nursing of the plague-ridden inhabitants. The Hermit comes upon the Wild Woman's body lying in the sacred pool where she had been bathing in spite of his warnings just before the pilgrims arrive. At the moment he sights the Wild Woman's body, "Fear and rage possessed the Hermit's heart. . . . At that moment he could have strangled her with his hands, so abhorrent was the touch of her flesh" (CS, 588). When he realizes she is dead, "a great pang smote him; for here was his work undone. . . . One moment pity possessed him, the next he thought how the people would find him bending over the body of a naked woman, whom he had held up to them as holy, but whom they might now well take for the secret instrument of his undoing; and seeing how at her touch all the slow edifice of his holiness was demolished, and his soul in mortal jeopardy, he felt the earth reel around him and his eyes grew blind" (CS, 588). At this point in the story my reading differs sharply from Lewis's. These reactions are not those of a lover, but of a man fearful of his reputation. Edith paints James as disturbed by the moral dilemma; perhaps she surmised that he felt compromised by her behavior, although as far as I know there is no evidence for this feeling. Then when the Hermit realizes she is a saint a "fresh fear fell on [him] . . . for he had cursed a dying saint . . . and this new anguish . . . smote down his enfeebled frame." Edith, in her fantasy, makes herself a saint, kills the James figure for having doubted her holiness (which turns out to be holier than his since he does not become a saint in the story), but she holds out a consolation prize for him, the satisfaction of his passion for his work. As he lies dying he "heard a peal of voices . . . and the words of the chant were the words of his own lauds, so long hidden in the secret of his breast" (CS, 589).

Surely this is a caustic character sketch of James. If he recognized himself in this portrait, he can be exonerated from any imputation of malice in "The Velvet Glove." The Hermit has been concerned not with the Wild Woman, but with his own reputation for holiness and with his own glory as a creative writer of lauds, the medieval equivalent, perhaps, of James's New York Edition, which he was revising at this time. Edith shows that her feelings for her lover are holy, in spite of the breaking of her marriage vows, and that James, although he may be remembered for his writings, is simply not to be compared with her as a human being. The fable may be summarized finally as a justification of the way of Edith Wharton to Henry James, a justification that either actually took place, or that is here presented in fable. She shows James as pleading with her to restrict and confine her life to the accepted conventions; she fantasizes herself as having her cake and eating it, too. She dips into the forbidden water and comes out a saint. The Hermit (Henry James) is forced to accept her point of view, having been bribed with immortality as a writer, the secret passion of his life.

This daydream seems to be either a transcription of her discussions with James or a projection of the arguments she was preparing for him. Actually, the story is quite dull unless read as a *roman à clef,* in which case all the clever little innuendoes and all the changes in the plot become significant. The journey that the Hermit makes to the Saint of the Rock is meaningless until we see the Saint as a humorous projection of William James, and his behavior, critical and sarcastic, typical of his treatment of his younger brother, Henry. The latter's being reduced to tears and fatigue by his frustrating interview with his brother, whose good opinion of his work was so important to him, becomes touching and amusing, once we understand what it stands for. Wharton seems to be telling us to see the story as biographical from the very second sentence when the topography of Rye is sketched in, followed by the civil war analogue between the Guelfs and the Ghibellines, especially when she mentions the "steel-colored line of men-at-arms," which corresponds to the gray uniforms of the Confederate army.

Once we are willing to accept the story as biographical, the characters define themselves. We learn from the correspondence between them made available by Percy Lubbock, Millicent Bell, and Leon Edel of the close association, personal and confidential, between Edith Wharton and Henry James, from the time he visited her at The Mount in 1904–1905 through the next few years, ending only with his death in 1916. In 1906 by means of this mock medieval saint's legend she tries to tell him that she must satisfy her need for life (expressed in the Wild Woman's need to immerse herself in the waters of life) just as he needs to satisfy his passion for dedicated work, which Wharton allegorizes in the love of his "lauds." She points out that the Hermit in his excessive love for his own writing is as guilty of sin as she is in her excessive needs. In fact, she is indicating that at least she sins from an excess of the desire to live. She is the nurturing force, and her watering his garden, which has become dried, and her resurrection of his plants seem to point to her refreshing influence on James for which she thinks he should be grateful. She seems to be telling James that he who has written just a few years before in *The Ambassadors* "live all you can" should be able to apply that principle to her life as well.

II

The narrative poem, "Ogrin the Hermit,"[7] appeared three years after "The Hermit and the Wild Woman." During that interval, four events took place. Edith Wharton had consummated her love for Morton Fullerton. She had confessed her marital crisis to James. He had responded with his famous letter of sympathy and understanding of October 1908. His story, "The Velvet Glove," had appeared in March 1909, written the year before and revised at the end of 1908. If we see it as a story about Edith Wharton, we must see it in relation to "The Hermit and the Wild Woman." If James had read the latter, he must surely have recognized himself, for he, too, planted at least one of his friends in *The Golden Bowl*.

"Ogrin the Hermit" was published in the *Atlantic Monthly*, in December 1909, nine months after "The Velvet Glove" appeared in *The English Review*, March 1909, with an epigraph from what appears to be old or pseudo-old French, "*Vous qui nous jugez, savez-vous quel boivre nous avons bu sur la mer?*" Edith seems to be saying to the Hermit, "You who judge us, what do you know about love, who have never drunk of the philtre?" This time the Hermit tells the story of what took place when Tristan and Iseult, fleeing from the court of King Mark, "Sought hiding from their hunters." He had given them shelter in a small hut near him in the forest, "Their sin abhorring, yet not them with it," hoping that being near a "grey cross . . . Its shadow should part them like the blade of God" (Og, 844). Then Iseult, while Tristan is at the chase, makes a plea for her position. Stressing the pantheism of love, she tells how the lovers hear "the heart-beat of the world / And feel a sense of life in things inert" (Og, 845). They are able to feel "The inextinguishable flame of life / That girdles the remotest frame of things / With influences older than the stars." Rather than her argument, it is her sympathy with nature that wins over the Hermit. At the same time as his "long prayers / Sought to disarm the indignant heavens," he becomes aware that there are other "old gods that hide in these hoar woods" and that they are not evil "But innocent-eyed as fawns," especially the god of love, "the great god housed within / Who hides in his breast, . . . / The purposes and penalties of life" (Og, 846). Finally, the lovers know they must return to their world, and, the Hermit, realizing that "a great vision . . . / Had swept mine eyelids with its fringe of fire," buys Iseult beautiful garments to return to King Mark, "his hands grown tender with the sense of her" (Og, 847). He tells her, " 'Fare forth forgiven,' " and she goes "Crowned and forgiven from the face of Love." The Hermit has made her aware that after "the heart . . . / Swoons of its [love's] glory," it "Craves the dim shelter of familiar sounds, / The rain on the roof, the noise of flocks that pass, / And the slow world waking to its daily round" (Og, 848). Edith Wharton appears to be putting in the Hermit's mouth the words of advice Henry James wrote to her in his famous letter of October 13, 1908. "Only sit tight yourself *and go through the movements of life.* That keeps up our connection with life—I mean of the immediate and apparent life; behind which, all the while, the deeper and darker and unapparent, in which things *really* happen to us, learns, under that hygiene, to stay in its place. Let it get out of its place and it swamps the scene. . . . Live it all through, every inch of it—out of it something valuable will come—but live it ever so quietly."[8] The poem is a resolution of the earlier story. The Wild Woman, now Iseult, takes the Hermit's advice and returns to her convent (in this poem her husband, King Mark), and the Hermit recognizes that there is the ancient god of Love, that deep needs must be satisfied. Edith changes from a saint to a queen, and the Hermit, in spite of his austerity, learns how to shop for elegant apparel in order to deck out a queen, not a sinner. The prize Edith gives Henry in this poem is that his advice to return to the accustomed ways of life, to return to her marriage (at any rate for the time being), has been taken. This is the reward for his "tender friendship—the understanding, the participation, the *princely* (though I say it who shouldn't) hospitality of spirit and soul of yours more than ever, Henry James."[9] But the price he pays is to give up his belief in only one God, the dedication of the artist. If Edith had read "The Velvet Glove" with understanding, she would not have had to belabor her point. In that story James had made quite clear that life and lover were to be put before creative writing, for those who were lucky enough to have the gifts for life. It is more likely that this poem is a sequel to and a revision of her version of James's attitude to her sense of vitality in "The Hermit and the Wild Woman." She no longer pokes fun at the Hermit's (and James's) peculiarities, vanity, and fears, but shows him sympathetic to the idea that physical love is a holy thing, part of the worship of gods older than Christ. She makes him aware that "the old gods" of passion and love were not "evil . . . but innocent-eyed as fawns that come to drink," and that "Love is not . . . / a witch's filter, brewed to trick the blood" (Og, 845).

III

In addition to the personal relationship between the two authors, these writings suggest the possible literary exchange. The sequence of "The Hermit and the Wild Woman" (which appeared in 1906), "The Velvet Glove" (which appeared in March 1909), and "Ogrin the Hermit" (written in the spring of 1909 and published in December 1909) raises the interesting question of whether each author penetrated his disguise in the work of the other. I do not know whether James ever read "The Hermit and the Wild Woman";[10] the book was not on his shelves at Lamb House.[11] But "The Velvet Glove" appears to be a response to the position imputed to him in "The Hermit and the Wild Woman." The personal cross references in these works are complex. Leon Edel has seen Walter Berry in John Berridge's name, as I see allusions to William James and the Civil War in Edith Wharton's story. We know from letters that Wharton read "The Velvet Glove" as soon as it appeared in *The English Review.* If "Ogrin the Hermit" is her final word in this exchange, it then becomes a testimonial to her acceptance of James's change of attitude. In fact, since the message of "The Velvet Glove" was " 'Only live. Only be. *We'll* do the rest,'"[12] it is appropriate that Wharton's neo-medieval poem is put into the mouth of Ogrin, or Henry James. He "in old age" takes over the task of scribbling and leaves the living to her. In "The Hermit and the Wild Woman," there had been no lover, only the burning desire of the woman to have one. "Ogrin the Hermit" contains the emergence of Wharton's real lover, Fullerton, in the guise of Tristan.[13]

REFERENCES

1. Leon Edel, *Henry James: The Master* (Philadelphia: Lippincott, 1972), pp. 352–59, 574; Adeline R. Tintner, "James's Mock Epic: 'The Velvet Glove,' Edith Wharton, and Other Late Tales," *Modern Fiction Studies* 17, no. 4 (1971–1972): 483–99.

2. Edith Wharton, *A Backward Glance* (New York: Appleton-Century, 1934), p. 244.

3. Edith Wharton, *The Collected Short Stories of Edith Wharton,* ed. R. W. B. Lewis, vol. 1 (New York: Scribner's, 1968), p. xix. All page references are to this edition and are indicated by CS and page number. In 1968, when Lewis published and annotated Wharton's *Collected Short Stories,* her lover was assumed to be Walter Berry. It was not until 1975 that Fullerton was known to have been Wharton's lover.

4. Edith Wharton, *The Best Short Stories of Edith Wharton,* ed. Wayne Andrews (New York: Scribner's, 1958), p. xxii.

5. Wharton, *A Backward Glance,* p. 245.

6. Millicent Bell, *Edith Wharton and Henry James: The Story of Their Friendship* (New York: Braziller, 1965), p. 148.

7. Edith Wharton, "Ogrin the Hermit," *Atlantic Monthly* 104 (December 1909): 844–48. All references are indicated by Og plus page number.

8. Henry James, *The Letters of Henry James,* ed. Percy Lubbock, vol. 2 (New York: Scribner's, 1920), pp. 104–105.

9. Ibid., p. 105.

10. However, we know from Edith Wharton's *A Backward Glance* (p. 181) that James was intensely interested in her work, so it is probable he read the tale. The following passage indicates how he kept track of her publications: "At any rate I always tried to keep my own work out of his way, and once accused him of ferreting out and reading it just to annoy me—to which charge his sole response was a guilty chuckle. In the present instance, as usual, he instantly replied: 'Oh yes, . . . I've read the little work—of course I've read it.'" After these words appear five lines of severely critical remarks, ending with the shattering words that

all those defects should have "'led you to reject your subject as—er—in itself a totally unsuitable one.'"

11. Personal communication from Leon Edel.

12. Henry James, *The Complete Tales of Henry James,* ed. Leon Edel, vol. 12 (New York: Lippincott, 1964), p. 263.

13. These final lines have been added in 1996.

2

The Give-and-Take between Edith Wharton and Henry James

"The Velvet Glove" and Edith Wharton

In 1909 Henry James published "The Velvet Glove." I propose to show that this short story is a mock-epic with a meticulously worked out classical mythology understructuring the imagery, language, and characterization, all mounted to launch an elaborate literary joke. At once the heroine of the mock-epic and the butt of the joke is Edith Wharton who plays the dual role of Artemis and the Scribbling Princess. In fact, so "in" is the joke that no one, even Edith Wharton herself, who has written fully on her knowledge of the germ of the story, has "gotten" it! Moreover, the tale was too late for inclusion in the New York Edition and so eludes mention by James in the Prefaces. However, his silence in connection with the story in the Notebooks and Letters, in addition to the curious fact that he never mentioned to Edith Wharton with whom he was in close contact that he had ever written the story, seems to indicate a "cold artistic calculation"[1] on his part, a trait he admits to in writing the "Turn of the Screw." Might not then "The Velvet Glove" also be construed as "an *amusette* to catch those not easily caught . . . "?[2]

I also relate the tale to the six others written during this remarkable year (give or take a few months) just after the self-scrutiny of the Prefaces, all of which belong to what became late in life James's favorite genre, the fairy tale, with its twin, the nightmare. Even though on the surface "The Velvet Glove" is a sparkling bit of courtly comedy, it has at its core bitter realities.

Why has this story eluded the fine comb of exegetical criticism? Perhaps it is because, read along with its sibling tales, it seems at first glance

Originally published as "James's Mock Epic, 'The Velvet Glove': Edith Wharton and Other Late Tales," *Modern Fiction Studies* 17, no. 4 (Winter 1971–72): 483–501.

silly, exaggerated, and snobbish, or so Mr. S. Gorley Putt finds it: "He [the hero] reveals himself, later, as a megalomaniac if fumbling snob, like a low-grade Baron de Charlus whistling to keep his courage up, and vulgarly impressed (for so delicate a writer) by social 'Olympians.'"[3]

I

Attention both to the elements and to the tone of the story will show that the word *Olympian* (occurring fifteen times in the thirty-three-page story) is part of a carefully structured mock-epic that shows how absurd it is for those who are capable of living on a high romantic plane to yearn for the writer's art. Although the machinery of the mock-epic involves hyperbole and personification, it is intimately related to two of the serious recurrent themes of James's late oeuvre. First, it is necessary to live fully. Strether's advice to young Bilham in Gloriani's garden of *The Ambassadors* is repeated here, in Gloriani's studio, in the thoughts of John Berridge, the writer-hero. Second, a writer must maintain his integrity and standards no matter how strong the temptation may be to compromise them. These two themes are joined in the request made by a glamorous Princess for a literary puff for her worthless novel from John Berridge, an American author of current popularity. A new literary star "that had begun to hang, with a fresh red light over the vast . . . Anglo-Saxon horizon,"[4] he is the author of a "slightly too fat" volume, *The Heart of Gold* (a deprecation of the length of *The Golden Bowl*) made "into a fifth act too long play," which, unlike James's own plays, has been a great hit. By compressing his tale into three dense parts or acts, James humorously corrects the prolixity of his novel, *The Golden Bowl*. He continues this self-deprecation when he travesties the effect of the writer on the young Lord who approaches him on behalf of his novelist friend (an effect Mr. Putt sees as another evidence of snobbery).[5]

"Perhaps the very brightest and most diamond-like twinkle he had yet seen the star of his renown emit was just the light brought into his young Lord's eyes by this so easy consent to oblige" (235). Not snobbery, but the exaggerated gallantry of the James of the late correspondence is expressed by this special kind of joke—a parody of snobbery. The stage is thus set for a mock-epic in which the Olympian Diana or Princess descends to the earth to seek out her favorite shepherd, Endymion or John Berridge.

The tale begins its high exaggeration in the opening sentence when "poor John Berridge" (a term of endearment James reserves for the sympathetic "I"-heroes of the late stories) is placed as "the new literary star." The "red light" identifies him as an American (the Western star, Mars, is red) who is approached by a young aristocrat whom Berridge finds familiar in some way, for he "had wondered about him, had . . . imaginatively, intellectually . . . quite yearned over him" (236), but can't place him. He is aware of his superiority. "One placed young gods and goddesses only when one placed them on Olympus, and it met the case, always, that they were of Olympian race, and that they glimmered for one, at the best, through their silver cloud like the visiting apparitions in an epic" (238). This begins the references to Olympus and Olympians, mentioned six times in three pages, the music played at the party making "the whole of Olympus presently open," until an unknown beauty, "Olympian herself, supremely, divinely Olympian" (240), arrives, and John Berridge knows he has seen before both god and goddess together. "Who had they been, and what? Whence had they come, whither were they bound, what tie united them, what adventure engaged, what felicity, tempered by what peril, magnificently, dramatically attended?" (211). So closes Part One.

Part Two opens with Mme. Gloriani introducing John Berridge to a great French dramatist whose use for John is simply to ascertain who the "young woman might be . . . who wore the pale yellow dress, of the strange tone, and the magnificent pearls" (243). The "strange tone" of the dress is the color of the moon and is significant here because James will soon identify the Princess with Diana or Artemis. In this part of the story, the references to Olympians, Atlas, Hebe, and Diana, thicken and accumulate. We are prepared for it by the "Atlas-back of renown" belonging to the well-known dramatist who blocks out, temporarily, John Berridge's view of the glamorous couple. The allusion to Atlas who gathered the golden apples of the Hesperides for Hercules is related to the Princess making her way to our hero and telling him that she has read his *Heart of Gold* three times. "If she was Olympian . . . this offered air was that of the gods themselves: she might have been . . . Artemis decorated, hung with pearls, for her worshippers, yet disconcerting them by having . . . snatched the cup of gold from Hebe. It was to him, John Berridge, she thus publicly offered it; and it was his over-topping *confrère* of shortly before who was the worshipper most disconcerted" (244). This ties Hebe's husband, Hercules, to whom the cup of gold *should* have been given, to Atlas, who bears the weight of the world on his shoulder and is here the dramatist. In the next three pages, the word *Olympian* occurs seven times, mostly in relation to an Olympian career and what John Berridge would have made of it. "He should have consented to know but the grand personal adventure on the grand personal basis: nothing short of this . . . would begin to be . . . Olympian enough" (245). His revery is broken by the young Lord's giving him a copy of *The Top of the Tree,* an allusion to Wharton's *The Fruit of the Tree,* by Amy Evans, the novelist friend he had mentioned, whose book "represented an object as alien to the careless grace of goddess-haunted Arcady as a washed-up 'Kodak' from a wrecked ship might have been" (249). Then James quotes a passage from this book, which also contains classical references to Pheidias and Astarte but is written poorly, dominated by "which" clauses. John Berridge is in a daze when the Princess tells him that *she* is Amy Evans and that it is her latest book that she wants him to read. In fact, if he will forego supper at Gloriani's, she will drive him home. While "the perspiration on his brow might have been the morning dew on a high lawn of Mount Ida" (254), he joins her as Part Two ends.

Part Three opens with John ensconced in the Princess's "chariot of fire," her motor car. With her hand on his, while "the whites of her eyes . . . gleamed in the dusk like some silver setting of deep sapphires" (258) (silver is Diana's color), she reveals her desire that he write a puffing preface for *The Velvet Glove.* The effect on him is this: "It was as if she had lifted him first in her beautiful arms, had raised him up high, high, high, to do it . . . and then . . . setting him down exactly where she wanted him to be—which was a thousand miles away from her" (259). The iron fist shows itself under the velvet glove. Amy Evans now takes over from the divinity. He who had wanted to be loved for himself is loved for a preface. If, after this revelation, John should stop the car "that would be an answer . . . only to inanely importunate, to utterly superfluous Amy Evans—not a bit to his at last exquisitely patient companion" (260). She awaits his answer: "she quite bent over him, as Diana over the sleeping Endymion," and he realizes that "She *was,* for herself . . . Amy Evans and an asker for lifts, a conceiver of twaddle both in herself and in him" (261).

The enchantment is over. But she is unaware of his thoughts and kisses his hand to influence him further. He in turn kisses *her* hand, from which the glove has fallen, and tells the chauffeur to stop. He gets out and sees her through the open side window of the car "suspended, silvered over and celestially blurred, even as a summer moon by the loose veil of a cloud. . . . It was such a state as she would have been reduced to . . . for the first time in her life; and it was he, poor John Berridge . . . who would have created the condition" (262). So he puts her back in the moon, as Diana, and eliminates Amy Evans. He bids her goodnight and refuses her the preface. "Nothing would induce me to say a word in print about you. I'm in fact not sure I shall ever mention you in any manner at all as long as ever I live" (263). (This is also James's goodbye to the international theme, the last example of the genre he ever wrote.) The Princess does not understand and thinks John does not like her. He says he adores her but is ashamed for her. "You *are* Romance . . . so what more do you want? Your Preface . . . was written long ages ago by the most beautiful imagination of man" (263). "Here he may be referring to Homer, the poet of mythology who wrote about Diana as Artemis.) When she fails to understand, he tells her not to try. "Only live. Only be. *We'll* do the rest." And when still obtusely she urges him just to *try* the preface and he sees he cannot communicate with her, he decides on something else: "he'd, by the immortal gods, anticipate it in the manner most admirably effective" (264). He kisses her on the mouth, he breaks away from the car, and "he had no further sound from her than if, all divinely indulgent but all humanly defeated, she had given the question up" (265). The story ends "as she [the Princess] passed to disappearance in the great floridly-framed aperture whose wings at once came together behind her" (265), in true fairy-tale style. And the dual existence of divine goddess and silly scribbler, so admirably developed, sustained, and paralleled, is brought to a close.

The atmosphere of this wistful disillusionment of a mortal with a goddess's view of herself is densely poetic. The mythological references differ from the extended metaphors of the other late work in that they girdle the entire story from beginning to end and stem from the effect the two young aristocrats have on the writer-hero. They operate as metaphor, not simile, since the Princess is a double, both goddess and Amy Evans. Gloriani's party is also an Olympian entertainment. The story is dramatic in a mock-heroic sense. It is like a Greek epic in that slowly, bit by bit, John Berridge "discovers" that the Princess is only a hack writer, the complete revelation not taking place until the final tête-à-tête in the motorcar, so bedazzled is he by her Olympian aura. The divine goddess prefers to become a mortal, euhemerized into a vulgar lady novelist, but Berridge refuses to help her in her base transformation. He places her "suspended, silvered over, even as a summer moon" back in her divine role. He will play Endymion to a goddess for love, but he will not betray his literary standards for the ambition of an Amy Evans.

Throughout the story, James so sticks to the classical unities of time and place that from the hints of "ten minutes" here and a "half-hour" there we can time the story at just about two hours, almost exactly the time it takes to read it, for its density precludes skipping. The place is a few feet of standing room at Gloriani's studio party (remembered as the party scene in *The Ambassadors*) and, for Part Three, the close interior of the Princess's motorcar.

It is not only an epic, but it comes across as the most theatrical or dramatic of the last seven stories, with the drama focusing on the activity of the hero's consciousness, which is the machine making the mythological metaphor. Nevertheless, the physical actions that do take place—the personal encounters, the seating in the motorcar, the hand kissing, the leaving of the car by John Berridge followed by his kissing the Princess on the mouth (an action equivalent in a James story to an offstage murder in a Greek tragedy)—are all concretely realized. But they are small, restricted actions, as befit the rococo nature of this mock-epic, and are fashioned for the stage of the mind, not of the theatre. By 1909 James had loosened up about sex. The climax of Part One is not only the arrival of the Princess at the party but also Berridge's awareness that she is the "missing connection" to the young Lord, that she is equally Olympian, and that both are "preoccupied . . . with the affairs, and above all with the passions, of Olympus" (241). The small events of the plot all support the "discoveries" that John makes after the manner of Oedipus, but the truth dawns slowly, for it is impeded by the mythological apparatus of glamour that Part Two constructs after the Princess's arrival and introduction. Singling out John Berridge as Diana does the shepherd of her whim, she is the Olympian goddess tricked out by metaphor and glorified by remembered myth. Here James reverts to *Diana* and not *Artemis,* which seems to be in this tale the only example of the Roman rather than the Greek name of the goddess. He may be thinking of Keats's *Endymion.* In the third act, in her "chariot of fire," the intimacy of her close presence and the significance of her kissing John's hand could only be staged in the privacy of the prepared consciousnesses of both hero and reader. It is a light playful drama depending on interior rather than external action, the few overt gestures contributing intensity to the ironic situation.

The manner in which the mock-epic is mounted is very carefully worked out. John Berridge is placed as a star in heaven as the story opens. This permanently deifies him, for the gods have survived beyond classical periods in the heavenly bodies. Then the Olympian note with its "silver tone, implemented by the tenor's music. . . . It ruled the scene . . . while all the rest of consciousness was held down as by a hand mailed in silver" (239), ends Part One. Part Two is a mythologized account of the Princess's asking for John Berridge's goodwill where she is a snatcher of Hebe's cup and an "Artemis decorated for her worshippers" (244). She has chosen her shepherd, or so John thinks, in a note of divine whimsy. Part Three is the breaking of the illusion and the revelation of the true cause of the Princess's favor—her desire for John's preface. The divinity is bifurcated into Artemis and Amy Evans. John ends the mock-epic by driving Amy Evans out of the picture and sending Artemis back to her divine role. What carries the hyperbole along is the excitement accompanying the classical apparatus. For classical references in literature, art, and architecture were the stock in trade of the turn of the century. That James should use neoclassic tags to structure his story was much more natural then than it would be today. The World Columbian Exposition in Chicago in the 1890s brought to every person's eye what had been part of a well-educated person's background of the last half of the nineteenth century. Henry James's youth had been well stocked with neoclassic impressions of all sorts:[6] "the grand manner, the heroic and the classic, in Haydon, came home to us more warmly . . . than in the masters commended as 'old.'"[7] It was the romantic aspects of nineteenth-century classicism that excited a young boy who liked Paul Delaroche as well as Eugène Delacroix, and the Galerie d'Apollon in the Louvre gave him a general sense of glory, fostered by Prudhon's Cupid and Psyche and "David's helmetted Romanisms."[8] "The beginning in short was with Gericault and David."[9] All these impressions of the romantic neoclassicism of the early nineteenth century for him were "charged somehow with a useability . . . which would keep me restless till I should have done something of my own with them."[10] It was not until his trip to America in 1904 with the memories it stirred up (later to be reworked by him in his three autobiographies) that the details of classicism seem anything more than the clichés used by Amy Evans or followers of the Chicago White City. And it is only in "The Velvet Glove" that the trappings of classicism appear as humorously handled allegory. In "The Jolly Corner," a story probably written just before "The Velvet Glove," we are indirectly put into a mythological setting by the suggestion of the underworld in the descent of Spencer Brydon and the discovery of his alter ego in a figure almost blind like Pluto and, like Pluto, very rich.

II

We usually look to James himself for the "germ" of his fiction, but, in the case of "The Velvet Glove," there are no references either in the *Notebooks* or the *Prefaces* completed before the story was written. However, in his letters written at the same time, similar figures of speech recur as in the story. Allusions to the motorcar as a "chariot of fire," references to Olympians and Olympus, and "whirling Princesses" cluster in his letters of 1906–1909. The same classical hyperbole of "The Velvet Glove" reflects, as in the case of the letters, the new presence of Edith Wharton in the life of James, and her effect on him reads like the effect of the Princess on John Berridge. In fact, we must look thirty years after the story was written to Edith Wharton herself for the only clue to its origin. In her autobiography, she discusses the

> exquisite picture of Paris by night in the tale—perhaps the most beautiful of his later short stories—called "The Velvet Glove." He and I had often talked over the subject of this story, which was suggested by the fact that a very beautiful young Englishwoman of great position, and unappeased literary ambitions, had once tried to beguile him into contributing an introduction to a novel she was writing—or else into reviewing the book; I forget which. She had sought from him, at any rate, a literary "boost" which all his admiration and liking for her could not, he thought, justify his giving; and they parted, though still friends, with evidences on her part of visible disappointment—and surprise. The incident . . . lay unused for lack of a setting for he wanted to make of it, not a mere ironic anecdote—that was too easy—but a little episode steeped in wistfulness and poetry. And then, one soft spring evening, after we had dined somewhere out of town . . . knowing his love for motoring at night, I proposed a circuit in the environs, which finally brought us home by way of Saint Cloud; and as we hung there, high above the moonlit lamplit city and the gleaming curves of the Seine, he suddenly "held" his setting, as the painters say, and though I knew nothing of it till long afterward, "The Velvet Glove" took shape that night.[11]

At the time the story was published, in 1909, Edith Wharton writes to Charles Eliot Norton's daughter: "Read 'The Velvet Glove' . . . [a] delightful little story—a motor story!"[12] But she makes no comment to James about it, as far as I know. But since his letters do, at this time, refer to images and expressions used in this story, we cannot help but find that the source of the imagery is Edith Wharton herself, who from 1906 to 1909 made her first strong impressions on James. According to Millicent Bell, James, "already practicing the language of gallantry which it always amused him to assume to her," wrote letters to Edith Wharton in connection with her 1906 spring motor trip to England, and he refers to the Whartons in a letter to Gaillard Lapsley, as "rich, rushing, ravening."[13] James goes to France in 1907 at the end of March to visit the Whartons at their apartment at 58 rue de Varenne. He writes to Howard Sturgis in April 1907 that he was seeing France "in our friend's chariot of fire."[14] In a letter of December 1907 to W. E. Norris he says that "my ten weeks in Paris were, for me, on a basis most unprecedented: I paid a *visit* of that monstrous length to friends (I had never done so in my life before), and in a beautiful old house in the heart of the Rive Gauche . . . tasted socially and associatively. . . . of a new Paris altogether and got a bellyful of fresh and nutritive impressions."[15] The unique impressions of Paris account for the following enthusiastic and euphoric description of Paris in "The Velvet Glove":

> *That* was knowing Paris, of a wondrous bland April night; that was hanging over it from vague consecrated lamp-studded heights and taking in, spread below and afar, the great scroll of all its irresistible story, pricked out, across river and bridge and radiant *place,* and along quays and boulevards and avenues, and around monumental circles and squares, in syllables of fire, and sketched and summarized, further and further, in the dim fire-dust of endless avenues (256).

This is the Paris that Edith Wharton presented to him via her motorcar.

Following the trip, he seems to have had a spell of good health and splendid creativity. "I never have had such a sense of almost bursting, late in the day though it be, with violent and lately too much repressed creative (again) intention,"[16] he writes to Howells. In addition to the glamour of the Paris seen by motorcar, there is the glamour of the Faubourg St. Germain society which, as Percy Lubbock tells us, was "almost new to him."[17] A society formed by Edith Wharton's family connections and the Bourgets' writing set has been described at length in Mrs. Bell's book. Learning how to coalesce these worlds from the Countess Rosa Fitz-James, Edith Wharton provided the social aura that surrounds "The Velvet Glove."

Now, if we look for a prototype for the Princess and heroine in the tale, we find Edith Wharton herself supplying the physical details. James, in a letter to Sturgis, refers to her as one of "these whirling Princesses!"[18] and (to Walter Berry) as "The Lady of Lenox."[19] To Howard Sturgis, in 1908, he writes: "Delightful your letter with its wondrous glittering *reflex* of the most brilliant of women and of all the lights she sheds. . . . Truly you too are caught up, and the chariot of fire, I gather, causes you to flash, almost consort-like, at her shining side! . . . It all sounds glorious and godlike—almost too insolently Olympian."[20] The rich and fairly young American Princess, Edith Wharton, and her magic chariot surely are the prototypes for the Princess of the story and the chief social star of James's life during the years 1907–1909.

But although Edith Wharton in her paragraph on the origin of the story seems to have suppressed any memory of it, there is another association from the earliest connection between her and James that might very well provide the real germ of the story: the asking of a literary puff by a glamorous but bad novelist—without our having to resort to "a very beautiful young English-woman of great position" that Edith Wharton claims James used as the model. For a man who has documented so fully the sources of his tales, silence in his *Notebooks* on this origin is significant. However, James is not silent as to his attitude and judgment of Edith Wharton's fiction and, although he gradually comes to recognize her talent, we have enough evidence to know that he was very critical of her writing at the time of "The Velvet Glove." Edith Wharton herself tells how James "had begun . . . with the sincere intention of praising" a story of hers "but no sooner had he opened his lips than he was overmastered by the need to speak the truth, and the whole truth, about anything connected with the art which was sacred to him."[21] A 1902 letter to Mary Cadwalader Jones, Edith Wharton's sister-in-law and an old friend of James, shows that James, while saying he approves of two books of short stories by Edith Wharton, still wants "to get hold of the little lady and pump the pure essence of my wisdom and experience into her. . . . If a work of imagination, of fiction, interests me at all . . . I always want to write it over in my own way. . . . *That* I always find a pleasure in, and I found it extremely in the 'Vanished Hand' . . . " (a mistake for "The Moving Finger,"[22] which may have unconsciously given rise to the title "The Velvet Glove").

In 1907 Henry James had been approached by a journalist named Markeley to do a "personality paper" about Edith Wharton, apparently at her suggestion (although she denied this) and was waiting for the appearance of her *The Fruit of the Tree* before doing it. After reading this book, he writes to Edith Wharton, "I *want* to enthuse over you . . . , but I must wait for the right & harmonious occasion for so doing" (November 24, 1907), but he begs out of doing the 'personality' paper: "I shall probably *not* find myself at all well-advised to do that paper on your Personality. . . . I don't feel I can 'enthuse' over you in a hole & corner publication." He claims to like *The Fruit of the Tree,* but for every compliment he pays, he makes a critical remark, especially in regard to "the terrible question of the composition & the conduct of the thing."[23] To Mrs. Jones he wrote, "But it is of a strangely infirm composition and construction." [24]

Is it accidental that one of the bad novels of the Princess in "The Velvet Glove" is called *The Top of the Tree,* recalling the title, *The Fruit of the Tree?* Is not the name *Amy Evans* somewhat like the name *Edith Jones,* just as commonplace with its similar syllabic name? Unless "The Velvet Glove" was written before Markeley approached James in the summer of 1907 for the literary boost on Edith Wharton that he claimed she had suggested,[25] we do not have to strain to see that she could very well have supplied James with all the essential details of the heroine of his story, the dazzling, beautiful asker of literary lifts. However, it must be kept in mind that James is making a joke about the whole episode, writing in the exaggerated gallantry of a typical letter to Edith Wharton: "You are indeed my ideal of the dashing woman, and you never dashed more felicitously or fruitfully, for my imagination, than when you dashed, at that particular psychological moment, off to dear old rococo Munich."[26] When he asks her to wish him luck on his play, *The High Bid,* in 1908, he uses in comic fashion references to classical worship: "This is just a tremulous little line to say to you that the daily services of intercession and propitiation (to the infernal gods, those of jealousy and *guignon*) that I feel sure you have instituted for me will continue to be deeply appreciated." [27] In *A Backward Glance,* Edith Wharton refers to the pyramidal jokes that were part of James's conversation. "Henry James's memory for a joke was prodigious; when he got hold of a good one, he not only preserved it piously, but raised upon it an intricate super-structure of kindred nonsense, into which every addition offered by a friend was skillfully incorporated."[28] In light of this and the comic element in "The Velvet Glove," some of James's so-called pomposity appears rather as raillery.

Whether or not James wanted Edith Wharton to know how much she contributed to this story is another matter. We have seen that his criticism of her works was always somewhat disguised and his retreat from her "personality" paper lamely made. He very clearly did not wish to hurt her feelings, for he valued her as a person. In fact, it is this value that he exaggerates in the fable of "The Velvet Glove." Those who have the gifts for living should not bother to write. However, even James found that he was too old to handle the problems that were posed by living on the physical and emotional scale of Edith Wharton. After his second trip to Paris, he has had enough: "a small rude Sussex burgher *must* feel the strain of your Parisian high pitch, haute élégance, general glittering life and conversation" he writes to Edward Childe in 1909.[29] This reaction to the Paris experience takes place presumably after "The Velvet Glove" had been written in memory of the excitement.

REFERENCES

1. Henry James, *The Novels and Tales of Henry James,* vol. 12 (New York: Scribner's, 1908), p. xviii. Subsequent references are indicated by page number.

2. Ibid., p. xviii.

3. S. Gorley Putt, *Henry James: A Reader's Guide* (Ithaca, N.Y.: Cornell University Press, 1966), p. 237.

4. Henry James, *The Complete Tales of Henry James,* ed. Leon Edel, 1962–1964, vol. 12 (Philadelphia: J. B. Lippincott, 1964), p. 233. Subsequent references to this volume are indicated as page numbers in parentheses in the text.

5. Putt, *Henry James,* p. 237.

6. Henry James, *A Small Boy and Others* (New York: Scribner's, 1913), p. 28.

7. Ibid., p. 314.

8. Ibid., p. 350.

9. Ibid., p. 351.

10. Henry James, *The Middle Years, The Autobiography of Henry James,* ed. Frederick W. Dupee (New York: Criterion, 1956), p. 571.

11. Edith Wharton, *A Backward Glance* (New York: Appleton-Century, 1934), pp. 308–9.

12. Millicent Bell, *Edith Wharton and Henry James: The Story of Their Friendship* (New York: Braziller, 1965), p. 135.

13. Ibid., p. 114.

14. Henry James, *The Letters of Henry James,* ed. Percy Lubbock, vol. 2 (New York: Scribner's, 1920), p. 74.

15. Ibid., 85–86.

16. Ibid., 102.

17. Ibid., 5.

18. Bell, *Edith Wharton and Henry James,* p. 155.

19. Ibid., p. 156.

20. Ibid.

21. Wharton, *A Backward Glance,* p. 181.

22. Bell, *Edith Wharton and Henry James,* p. 247.

23. Ibid., pp. 257–58.

24. Ibid., p. 259.

25. Ibid., p. 257.

26. James, *Letters,* 2:142.

27. Ibid., 94.

28. Wharton, *A Backward Glance,* p. 179.

29. James, *Letters,* 2:121.

3
The Metamorphoses of Edith Wharton in Henry James's
FINER GRAIN *Stories*

The close friendship between Edith Wharton and Henry James, begun in 1904 and ending only with his death in 1916, has been amply documented by Millicent Bell and Leon Edel, as well as by Edith Wharton herself in *A Backward Glance.*[1] During the years from 1906 to 1909 when Mrs. Wharton began her frequent trips to Europe and finally settled in Paris, James wrote only one book of stories, *The Finer Grain* (1910). These stories are the fictional analogues of the complex, affectionate—at times contradictory, at times complementary—feelings that characterized this friendship between two extraordinary people.

A detailed study of all the stories included in the volume has brought to light what seems to be a carefully planned system of allusion to the "Lady of Lenox," her world, her environment, her virtues, and her foibles. Indeed, the entire suite of stories in *The Finer Grain* seems to be an Edith Wharton Suite. The recognition of certain icons as Whartonian helps the reader to interpret and understand some difficult passages that perhaps would remain opaque without the biographical information. To this information we must add the précis James wrote himself for the jacket of the first edition of *The Finer Grain,* unique in James's *oeuvre* because it is the only volume of stories, aside from the New York Edition, for which the author has written such an explanatory précis.

The original statement James prepared for his publisher appeared in an adapted version on the dust jacket of the book: "*The Finer Grain* consists of a series of five stories, the central figure in each is involved, as Mr. James loves his characters to be, in one of the tangles of highly civilized

Originally published as "The Metamorphoses of Edith Wharton," *Twentieth Century Literature* 21, no. 4 (December 1975): 355–79.

existence. By the 'finer grain' the author means, in his own phrase, 'a peculiar accessibility to surprise, to curiosity, to mystification or attraction—in other words, to moving experience.' It is needless to add that the book exhibits the most delicate comedy through-out."[2] Years later E. V. Lucas, who had come into possession of the original statement, published it in its entirety:

> *The Finer Grain* consists of a series of five tales representing in each case a central figure (by which Mr. Henry James is apt to mean a central and lively *consciousness*) involved in one of those greater or less tangles of circumstance of which the measure and from which the issue is in the vivacity and the active play of the victim's or the victor's sensibility. Each situation is thereby more particularly a moral drama, an experience of the special soul and intelligence presented (the sentient, perceptive, reflective part of the protagonist, in short), but with high emphasis clearly intended on its wearing for the hero or the heroine the quality of the agitating, the challenging personal *adventure*. In point of fact, indeed, it happens in each case to be the hero who exhibits this finer grain of accessibility to suspense or curiosity, to mystification or attraction—in other words, to moving experience: it is by his connection with and interest in the "grain" woman that his predicament, with its difficult solution, is incurred. And the series of illustrations of how such predicaments *may* spring up, and even be really characteristic, considerably ranges: from Paris to London and New York, and then back again, to ambiguous yet at the same time unmistakable English, and ultra-English, ground.[3]

Both versions indicate that *The Finer Grain* as a title had been chosen very carefully by James to indicate the predominant characteristic of the heroes in each of his tales. James's complete statement explicitly defines the kinship among the stories. Not only was the hero of each to be of "a finer grain of accessibility" to "moving experience," but "it is by his connection with and interest in the 'grain' woman," the woman who goes against the grain of the "central and lively *consciousness*," that he becomes the key figure in the ensuing "predicament."

I propose that "the 'grain' woman" in James's later years reflects the personality of Edith Wharton, who provided the basis in reality for these late fantasies of "the agitating, the challenging personal *adventure*." In the manner of "the silver-footed ironies, veiled jokes, tiptoe malices" that she herself noted in the conversation of the older James (BG, 178), her presence provided the Master with a ready-made heroine for a carefully articulated suite of stories. The perfect example of the new American woman whom James was to encounter in his American trip in 1904, she is no longer the doomed Milly Theale or Daisy Miller, a victim of society. The triumphant American queen reigning at Lenox, Park Avenue, or the rue de Varenne, Edith Wharton fills *The Finer Grain* with the penumbra of her existence—her problems, her décor, her fiction, and her idiosyncrasies. The volume presents Mrs. Wharton's persona, in a range from the mock-epic treatment of the Goddess-Princess of its first story to the woman in the final black comedy in which a ruined man is saved by the power of this woman who had destroyed his happiness.

The five women of the five stories are all transformations or transpositions of James's relation to Mrs. Wharton to which the hyperboles in his letters attest. The stories were, in fact, written in the winter of 1908 and 1909 (after his visit with Edith in her rue de Varenne flat in Paris in the spring of 1908), all within a few days except "The Velvet Glove," which was composed soon after the last visit. Miss Theodora Bosanquet, James's amanuensis, records in her diary that it "is almost literally true to say of the sheaf of tales collected in *The Finer Grain* that they were all written in response to a single request for a short story for *Harper's Monthly Magazine*" and that they were "written by hand" at a time when most of his writing was done by dictation.[4]

James at this time was trying to recover from the unmistakable failure of the New York Edition. The stories of *The Finer Grain* present in microcosm what he had exhaustively attempted in his Collected Edition but which had brought him neither money nor critical esteem. The vast example of Balzac, invoked in the first Preface as well as in the last and whose collected edition left its mark, as Leon Edel demonstrated, on the New York Edition (*The Master,* 333), is clearly visible in James's last attempt to gain fame as the writer of a contemporary *comédie humaine.* The stories are consciously distributed "from Paris to London and New York, and then back again. . . . English and ultra-English ground," to correspond to Balzacian divisions. They are filled with the "paraphernalia" of modern life, derived chiefly from the experience of it he had had at Edith Wharton's country house, the Mount, during James's visit to America in 1904–1905, at her flat in the rue de Varenne to which he made two trips during 1907 and 1908, from her fairly frequent descents on him at

Lamb House from 1906 on, and from the fairly frequent trips he made with her.

Each story is studded with more topical references than had ever appeared in his work previously—the motorcar, the Dreyfus case, flying machines, women smoking cigarettes, skyscrapers, the snapshot, the cinema, modern urban hotel life, apartment houses named after artists or writers, Wall Street machinations, a decaying resort. All show the Balzacian imprint brought up to date by James's attempt to root his scenes in known specific places through fresh data. "The Velvet Glove" corresponds to a *scène de la vie parisienne;* "Mora Montravers" to a *scène de la vie de Provence.* "The Bench of Desolation," a *scène de la vie de campagne,* could also be viewed as another *Les Paysans,* for it shows the decay of a borough (there is an allusion to Crabbe) and of the lower middle classes, just as Balzac's novel showed the decay of relations between the peasantry and the landed gentry.

James called Edith Wharton "the pendulum-woman" because she crossed the Atlantic each year (BG, 177). The " 'grain' woman," the woman who goes against the grain of a man of finer sensibilities but on whom the hero depends for his sense of life, is a phrase similar to "the pendulum-woman" in which a noun is used as a modifier and characterizes another aspect of Mrs. Wharton's personality that invaded James's existence. James wrote to Walter Berry while Edith was still in England in 1908, "But what a frame of steel, and what a way of arranging one's life. I have participated by breathless dashes and feverish fits, but then had to rush back to recuperate or meditate." He continues, "But I envy you great livers" (Bell, 157). On May 4, 1909, four months after Edith had left, James wrote to Gaillard Lapsley, "I have been motionless in this place [Lamb House] ever since I came back to it . . . after episodes on our wondrous friend E. W.'s eventual . . . departure for Paris—the prodigious devil's dance of which you saw but the first pass or two. . . . But it's too late now to pick up *those* smashed pieces before you & I meet again. . . . Suffice it that she had a social 'time' worthy of her general eagle-pounce or eagle flights, of her devouring or desolating, ravaging, burning or destroying energy. . . . *The angel of desolation* [emphasis mine] was the mildest name we knew her by" (Bell, 157).

Edith Wharton has called attention to qualities of James's talk that we recognize in his hidden references in *The Finer Grain.* His "silver-footed ironies, veiled jokes, tiptoe malices, were stealing to explode a huge laugh at one's feet" (BG, 178). E. V. Lucas mentioned how at Sidney Colvin's house James made malicious remarks about almost everyone there, and Jacques-Emile Blanche noted that James was responsible for words "uttered behind her [Edith Wharton's] back," as well as words behind Blanche's back.[5] The whole burden of the stories in *The Finer Grain* rests on the ambiguous feelings James entertained for Edith. He resolved them through a connected series of elaborate literary burlesques.

I have detailed in my chapter 2 how "The Velvet Glove" is a playful parody of Mrs. Wharton's many invocations of the gods because of its mock-heroic Olympian terminology. References to classical mythology appear not only in her poetry written in 1907 and 1908 ("Artemis and Actaeon," "Orpheus") but also specifically in *The Fruit of the Tree* (1907).[6]

Mrs. Wharton's story "The Lamp of Psyche" (1895) uses the myth of Cupid and Psyche to show how a young woman, happily married to a fine man and living in a beautiful house, is nagged by the fact that he did not fight in the Civil War. She forces her husband to admit his cowardice and so destroys her happiness. The Diana and Endymion theme of "The Velvet Glove" may be an allusion through an analogous myth to the Wharton story, and the identification of the Princess-Artemis or Diana with Edith Wharton herself is strengthened by James's letters to and about her, in which she is called a "pampered" or "whirling" Princess, driven by a "chariot of fire," a motorcar, as is the Princess of the story. The Parisian atmosphere is a memorial to the Paris of Mrs. Wharton's rue de Varenne flat.

The rejection of the Princess may be an analogue for James's refusal, after his second visit in 1908, to experience again the strenuous social life of the Wharton flat in Paris.[7] The very language of his fiction is echoed in James's subsequent letters when he writes about Mrs. Wharton. "All I want for the improvement is to be *let alone,* and not to feel myself far aloft in irresistible talons and under the flap of mighty wings—and about to be deposited on dizzy and alien peaks. 'Take me down, take me home!'" (Bell, 185). In every tale the image of a bird is used in some form; in "The Velvet Glove" the goddess is so winged: "It was as if she lifted him first in her beautiful arms, had raised him up high, high, high, to do it, pressing him to her immortal young breast while he let himself go, and then . . . setting him down exactly where she wanted him to be—which was a thousand miles away from her."[8] James thus describes Berridge's reaction to the Princess's desire for a literary lift. The figure of a bird's wings also occurs in the stories that follow. Mora, too, had "wide wings of freedom" (309), White-Mason's "wings" of imagination flopped "grotesquely at its sides" (344), and Monteith's "bruised spirit . . . folded its wings" (431), all earlier fictional analogues of the way James later wrote about himself to Edith Wharton. In his letters he saw himself "a poor old croaking barnyard fowl 'advising' a golden eagle," but he also mocks his terror of Mrs. Wharton's "great pinions . . . cold on my fore-doomed brow!" (*The Master,* 461). Finally, Herbert Dodd's "weak wings of his pride" that only "vaguely tremble" (417) develop the rhythm of the progressively weakened bird to parallel the weakening will of each hero of the tales. The finer-grained man gradually fails to hold his own against "the 'grain' woman" and ends up exhausted and in her power. In "The Bench of Desolation," the last tale, we are very far from the strong resistance put up in the first tale, by Berridge's artistic integrity, to the personal attraction of the goddess-like Princess.

The dazzling "Lady of Lenox" with her auto, the "chariot of fire," her goddess-like ambience, her personal attraction, and her glamour, lies behind the Princess who is conquered by her misconception of the area of her power. Berridge's artistic integrity produces the one victory for the finer-grained hero in the entire suite of stories.

"Mora Montravers," though placed second in the volume of *The Finer Grain,* was completed last. The story exhibits the "'grain' woman" transformed from the role of Princess Artemis into the "new woman." The basic situation facing Sidney Traffle and his wife, Jane, vis-à-vis their half-niece may constitute a sly reference to a story by Edith Wharton, "The Mission of Jane" (1904), in which a couple who are not particularly compatible adopt a baby girl named Jane (also Mrs. Traffle's name) whose difficult character reconciles husband and wife. It suggests the ironic situation, which characterizes Edith Wharton's stories. Sidney Traffle sets the stage by thinking about the irony of his and his wife's situation, "the famous, the provokedly vicious, 'irony,' the thing he had so often read about in clever stories" (267), a possible allusion by James to Wharton's stories.

Wharton's "cleverness" was a characteristic James had mentioned in his letters about her. He wrote to Mrs. Jones in 1902, "I take to her very kindly as regards her diabolical little cleverness" (Bell, 246). And later in 1913 to Edith herself he wrote (after he had read the first installment of *The Custom of the Country*) that he admired her "cunning . . . [her] devilish resource in the preparation of" her fiction (Bell, 280). As far as irony went, when James actually published criticism about the novels of

Edith Wharton in his essay, "The New Novel" (1914), he mentioned how great a part irony played in her fiction up to *The Custom of the Country.* "Mrs. Wharton's reaction in presence of the aspects of life hitherto, it would seem, mainly exposed to her is for the most part the ironic."[9]

There follows an allusion to Mrs. Wharton's story, "The Mission of Jane," by a *denial* of a resemblance, "their unspeakable niece, though not, absolutely not and never, as every one would have it, their adopted daughter" [268] (therefore, *not* the adopted Jane of Wharton's story).

While James was wrestling with this most intransigent of all the stories of the suite, Bernard Shaw wrote to him to redo his dramatization of "Owen Wingrave," *The Saloon.* Shaw deplored the passing on of the values of the father in the play and wrote that "Families like these are smashed every day and their members delivered from bondage, not by heroic young men, but by one girl who goes out and earns her living or takes a degree somewhere."[10] In "Mora Montravers" the influence of Shaw's statement appears as the story starts. "The joke was at all events in its having befallen *them* . . . to have to pick up again . . . the life that Miss Montravers . . . had smashed into smithereens by leaving their roof" (268). James wrote to Gaillard Lapsley after Mrs. Wharton's visit to England in 1908, "But it's too late now to pick up *those* smashed pieces before you & I meet again" (Bell, 157). Like Mora, whose name is an echo of Ibsen's Nora, Edith Wharton is the "New Woman." Since James always wanted to do over again any story that interested him, we may see him doing over Edith's little ironic anecdote in Shaw's terms.

Max Beerbohm had written a review of Shaw's *The Doctor's Dilemma* in November 1906, which James must have read, entitled "Mr. Shaw's Roderick Hudson," in which he points out that "Louis Dubedat, the central figure . . . is, essentially, just such another as Roderick Hudson." He distinguishes the minds of the two writers and goes on to compare the two heroes, giving the palm to Roderick, since, unlike Dubedat, "We believed in his genius."[11] It is possible that James is returning the compliment that Shaw paid him, by creating a character drawn from his colleague's work, and that "Mora Montravers" is the return salute of one artist to another.

Both Mora and Edith, working artists, defy the conventional moralities. The germ of "Mora Montravers" appears in the *Notebooks* nine years before it was written, in "the notion suggested . . . by the man with whom his niece had 'bolted' and was living . . . 'If I marry her I lose all control of her.'" The guardians insist they marry "and what he foretold happened—he lost all control."[12] The plot waited many years until James had found that Edith Wharton fitted the role of his heroine. James at the same time answers Shaw's objections and gives the victory to life and regeneration. Mora, paradoxically, marries to be free. Her suitor says that if he marries her, "I shall probably lose my hold of her" (270). In connection with Edith Wharton's difficulties with her husband, James appears at this time to take "the impartial, the detached, in fact—hang it!—even the amused view" (269) of Traffle in regard to Mora and Puddick. (Puddick, incidentally, is called Walter, Berry being invoked in this story as well as in "The Velvet Glove.") Both the writing of Edith Wharton and her character are combined to flesh out James's "veiled jokes." Mora, who is made to marry Walter Puddick, remains free after she has secured Jane Traffle's bribe of money for her impoverished painter. Sidney Traffle, conscious of Mora's having "tremendously the sense of life," asks his wife, "What do we know . . . when it breaks out with real freedom?" (274). Again, as in "The Velvet Glove," James repeats his favorite figure for Edith who spreads her "wider wings of freedom. . . . She was spreading her wings . . . like an angel in a vision" (309).

James's reference to the Dreyfus case in this story adds contemporary concerns to the Edith Wharton "matter." The case had been a source of friction among James, Mrs. Wharton, and the Bourgets, the latter violently anti-Dreyfus (Bell, 66). Millicent Bell reports how James was "repelled" not only by Bourget's work but also by his antisemitism, exhibited "by his reactionary stand during the Dreyfus affair . . . while Edith Wharton . . . argued with, but did not resent the views of her friend" (Bell, 66). From Mrs. Bell we learn that when Mrs. Wharton told James about a trip she made with the Bourgets in the summer of 1899, "she remembered, they had argued back and forth about the Dreyfus case" (Bell, 72).

In "Mora Montravers" there are three references to the case by way of the "new facts" associated with it. "I've only to go, and then come back with some 'new fact,' à la Dreyfus in order to make her sit up in a false flare that will break our insufferable spell" (302). Mora "exhaled a distinction . . . which was practically the 'new fact' all Wimbledon had been awaiting" (306–7). Finally, "It was hard . . . to be able neither to overlook her new facts without brutality nor to recognize them without impertinence" (307). The references all derive from the use of the term "new fact" or "new facts" that had been widely used in association with the drive for reopening the Dreyfus case. A random opening of one of the many books on the case will disclose the special use of "new fact" for designating the fresh evidence that made a retrial possible—"the unlikelihood of the Dreyfus family finding a new fact which might lead to the reopening of the case."[13] The "great difficulty lay in the fact that, to secure a retrial of Dreyfus by his peers, he [Ballot-Beaupré] must produce a new fact which threw doubt on the verdict of 1894. . . . He did not ask the court to find Dreyfus innocent, but to find that a new fact of a character to establish innocence had arisen. The audience could not restrain their applause, and Mazeau did not attempt to check it."[14] In other words, the reopening of the Dreyfus case depended on the finding of "new facts" or "facts too long withheld."

That James's view of the Dreyfus case was bound up with the Teddy-Edith relationship, as well as the Mora-Puddick relationship, is further implied in a letter James wrote to Gaillard Lapsley about it in 1911, asking "whether there is any definite 'new fact' . . . any new proposal" in regard to Edith's and Teddy's marital difficulties (Bell, 178).

James imbeds another Whartonian icon in the observation of Mora's talent for chic as well as for art. Like Edith, the well-dressed writer, Mora "exhaled a distinction . . . in her dress" although "she had always . . . had the genius of felicity there" (306).

As James had identified himself with Berridge, he now becomes Traffle, the spectator of the drama, leading "a life, exquisite, occult, dangerous and sacred" (332), that of ironic detachment, missing, however, the fun shared by the others. James puts "B. B.'s" initials in Sir Bruce Bagley's name, with the addition of "Bart" to allude to Bernard Berenson. Like the real "B. B." (who reappears in James's *The Outcry* in the combined Breckenridge Bender-Hugh Crimble), Sir Bruce, "the patron of promising young lives" (332), is interested in paintings and painters. James has Traffle wondering "about Sir Bruce, recalling his face and his type and his effect—his effect, so immediate, on Mora"; wondering "how he had proceeded, how he would still proceed, how far perhaps even they had got by that time. Lord, the fun some people did have!" (332–33). (A few months later Edith was to mimic Mora when she and B. B. became great friends.) Mora, like Edith, was "leading a life; but whatever she was doing it was clearly the particular thing she might best be occupied with" (304). As Edith had revitalized James's existence, so Mora had come into Traffle's life "so immensely to enrich and agitate it" (301). As James had been at the same time both devastated and thrilled by Mrs. Wharton, so is Traffle by Mora. He says to his wife, "If we're having the strain and the pain of it let us also have the relief and the fun" (279). The notion of desolation (308), appearing even in the idyll, "The Velvet Glove" (249), returns in "Mora Montravers" like a Wagnerian leitmotif to announce the devastation in the wake of "the 'grain' woman." He refers to Edith Wharton's "vertiginous abysses" that become here "a vertiginous view of a gulf; the abyss of what the ignoring would include for the convenient general commerce" (282). He repeats "abyss" twice more, and it is to occur in the other stories at least once. James's allusion to the retreat of Louis XVI from Varennes (276) might be an "inside" joke referring to Edith's rue de Varenne home. At the story's close, Traffle, by whose "original and independent measure . . . the whole case had become interesting" (328), was now left only with the "memory" of his secret meeting with Mora and her new conquest. Like James he can only "hug this treasure of consciousness, to make it . . . his very own" (329). By analogy, James reworks Edith's experiences into his own, by transmuting them into art.

In the third story, "A Round of Visits" (1910), James alludes to a tale by Edith Wharton and creates a fresh version of the "'grain' woman." Edith Wharton had written about financial embezzlement in America in 1899 in "A Cup of Cold Water," included in *The Greater Inclination*. Woburn, ruined financially and morally, goes to a ball knowing that his fiancée is unaware of his business crimes. Like "A Round of Visits," the story is set in New York on a frosty winter day. The hero makes a round of visits from the cold outside into warmly lighted social interiors just as James's Monteith does. The Wharton tale is told from the point of view of the criminal, not the victim, and it is the embezzler who comes into the warmth from the cold. The encounter with a policeman and the suicide attempt both occur first in Mrs. Wharton's story, but her hero prevents the suicide, whereas Monteith does not in James's "A Round of Visits." Having redeemed himself by saving a woman's life, Mrs. Wharton's hero can now face his punishment by giving himself up.

The resemblance to the James story is striking, although in the latter the similar elements have been altered to meet the demands of James's special preoccupations. From Berridge, who just manages to hold off the importunate Princess and Goddess whose whim must be satisfied, from Traffle, the onlooker who simply skirts with his irony the conventions smashed by the modern young woman of talent, the reader moves on to Mark Monteith, who is so exploited by two possible variants of "the 'grain' woman" that he is drawn in spite of himself into an unavoidable disaster. A self-absorbed, Europeanized American, returning to New York to investigate his having been defrauded by a relation and finding that two lady friends on whom he had depended for sympathy can think of nothing but their own problems, Monteith unloads his woes on an unexpectedly sympathetic embezzler who commits suicide after hearing how bitter an exploited client can be.

James implies that if both women had listened to Monteith, he would not have been put in the position of unwittingly causing a suicide. These two women, in different ways, resemble aspects either of Mrs. Wharton's personality or of her work. The first encountered, Mrs. Folliott, is a lady whose scale of living is much higher than the hero's, as Edith's was higher than James's. The second is Mrs. Ash, whose "life-style" in relation to her husband and whose use of Monteith as confidant mimic Mrs. Wharton's use of James himself in the years of her marital distress. Mrs. Folliott resembles more closely the incarnation of the hotel world, Mrs. Norma Hatch, whom Edith Wharton had made memorable in *The House of Mirth* (1905) and whose home is the Emporium, a luxury hotel in New York. It seems to me that James must have had in mind the following passage from the novel in which she appears:

> Lily found her [Mrs. Hatch] seated in a blaze of electric light, impartially projected from various ornamental excrescences on a vast concavity of pink damask and gilding, from which she rose like Venus from her shell. . . . The environment in which Lily found herself was as strange to her as its inhabitants. She was unacquainted with the world of the fashionable New York hotel, a world over-heated, over-upholstered, and over-fitted with mechanical appliances for the gratification of fantastic requirements, while the comforts of a civilized life were as unattainable as in a desert. Through this atmosphere of torrid splendour moved wan beings as richly upholstered as the furniture, beings . . . who drifted on a languid tide from restaurant to concert-hall, from palm-garden to music room."[15]

We find echoes of this passage in the following passages by James in "A Round of Visits": "the whole sprawl . . . of the great gregarious fireside . . . was a complete social scene in itself." Monteith "threaded the labyrinth, passing from one extraordinary masquerade of expensive objects, one pretentious 'period' of decoration, one violent phase of publicity, to another: the heavy heat, the luxuriance, the extravagance, the quantity, the colour, gave the impression of some wondrous tropical forest" (431). James follows with a description of Mrs. Folliott corresponding to Edith Wharton's description of Mrs. Hatch, only with a more comic thrust. "Mrs. Folliott . . . sat with him, under a spreading palm, in a wondrous rococo *salon,* surrounded by the pinkest . . . imitation Boucher panels. . . . She would herself have tumbled on a cloud, very passably, in a fleshy Boucher manner, hadn't she been overdressed for such an exercise" (432). Because Mrs. Folliott did not "have the benefit of a grain of *his* vision" (434), she goes against Monteith's grain, but she is not to be completely identified with Edith Wharton.

It is Mrs. Ash, however, next encountered by Monteith, who exhibits another aspect of Mrs. Wharton's character: her dependency on James's support and advice at the time of her marital crisis, which, as the Lubbock letters show, he freely gave. When Monteith goes to her for some sort of consolation, he remembers "the so prized custom of nine years before [James at the time of the writing of this story had known Edith for approximately nine years] . . . that of walking over the river to the Rue de Marignan" (437) (this is an amusing substitution, perhaps, for the rue de Varenne. The victory of François I at Marignano over the Swiss in 1515 has the same sort of historical function for the French as the arrest at Varennes). Then, instead of being allowed to tell her *his* troubles, Monteith "knew already, without the telling, that intimate domestic tension must lately . . . have reached a climax and that he could serve supremely—oh, how he was going to serve!—as the most sympathetic of all pairs of ears" (439). Mrs. Bell documents the role Henry James played at this time in Edith Wharton's life as "the witness and counsellor who stood at her side during a long period of emotional turmoil" (Bell, 9). The arrangement with her husband that Mrs. Ash describes is virtually that of the Whartons about this time. "Bob had had it from her . . . and it was absolutely final now, that they must set up avowedly separate lives—without horrible 'proceedings' of any sort, but with her own situation, her independence, secured to her once and for all" (439). If Edith Wharton read this story she would have recognized her own predicament, including the mention of Mrs. Ash's unfaithful husband's having "a regular 'bevy'" of women (439), as Teddy Wharton was supposed to have had.[16]

Even the French furniture of the rue de Varenne flat reappears intact. When Mrs. Ash receives Monteith in her New York apartment, there is "the little recognized marqueterie table between them (such an anciently envied treasure") [439] which recalls Edith's many little tables. (Her friends thought "her cable address could be *Little Tables*." There were so many of them that Sir Kenneth Clark knocked one over.[17]) Monteith's "very own tapestry *bergère*" (439) on whose mate ("the second, the matching *bergère*" [441]) Mrs. Ash sits is part of the furniture she had reconstituted from her Paris apartment. Lubbock mentions that "Edith sat in her *bergère*"[18] in the rue de Varennes apartment, and he comments on Edith's perpetual smoking, her "snapping perpetual cigarettes out of her little gold case."[19] In James's story, Mrs. Ash's flat was filled with "the faint sweet mustiness of generations of cigarettes" (438), as in fact the very name of the lady, Ash, shows the tendency in "high" James to the humorous use of freighted synecdoche. In this story James also introduces a definite association in a figure of speech to the *Androcles and the Lion* Mrs. Wharton and he saw together in 1907. Mrs. Folliott, who "pawed and tossed her bare bone" (433) is described as leonine and predatory. In a letter to Howard Sturgis, James hyperbolically pictured Mrs. Wharton as a beast of prey, "Our friend is a great and graceful lioness"; and he has himself "come in for many odd bones and other leavings of the Christians . . . who have been offered to her maw in this extraordinary circus" (*The Master*, 341).

If "the 'grain' woman" has declined from a pampered Princess to a free woman, Mora, and becomes a self-centered, unhappily married woman in need of a confidant in "A Round of Visits," she stands in the figure of Mrs. Worthingham in "Crapy Cornelia" for modernity in its most unattractive glaring light and for "the high modernity, as people appeared to have come to call it, that made her so much more 'knowing' in some directions than even he . . . could pretend to be" (342). James writes of Mrs. Wharton in such terms to Fanny Prothero: "Mrs. Wharton being due in her motor-car half an hour hence . . . designing, with a full intensity, to whirl me away for several days. . . . Nothing could suit me less. . . . Ah our complicated modernity" (*The Master*, 461). Edith, the "Shining One" (Bell, 159) has now become a "blinding light." Everything in the house of Mrs. Worthingham is greeted by her suitor, White-Mason, "with something of the grimace produced on persons without goggles by the passage from a shelter to a blinding light; and if he had . . . been 'snap-shotted' on the spot, would have struck you as showing for his first tribute to the temple of Mrs. Worthingham's charming presence a scowl almost of anguish. He wasn't constitutionally . . . a goggled person" (339). The figure of the blinding light and the repeated image of

White-Mason's need to wear goggles reappear in James's letters about Edith Wharton. When riding in her car he and all passengers had to wear goggles. When he writes about visiting her in 1908 he mentions minding to "face the Social Monster. . . . Let me come, please, utterly incognito & wholly masked in motor-goggles" (Bell, 141). Goggles are a Wharton icon. One wears goggles as protection from dust when riding with her in her motorcar and, in joking terms, as protection against Edith herself. His reactions to Mrs. Worthingham's house are echoes of his response to The Mount, the Whartons' house at Lenox. His ironic remark about it to Sturgis, "a delicate French chateau mirrored in a Massachusetts pond (repeat not this formula),"[20] shows how absurd he thought it to duplicate a European *maison de campagne* in a Yankee landscape.

In describing Mrs. Worthingham James speaks of "the attaching play of her iridescent surface, the shimmering interfusion of her various aspects, that of her youth with her independence—her pecuniary perhaps in particular, that of her vivacity with her beauty, that of her facility above all with her odd novelty" (342). In a letter of January 4, 1912, James writes, "Our great Edith has been with us—come and went, with a great flap of her iridescent wings" (Bell, 177), again showing how his fictive description stands for the real woman. James had described Edith to Margaret La Farge in June 1904 as "too pampered and provided and facilitated for one to be able really to judge of the woman herself" (*The Master*, 208). Again, in the story: "She was 'up' to everything . . . it was as if the suitability of the future to her personal and rather pampered tastes was what she most took for granted." She would "skip by the side of the coming age as over the floor of a ball-room, keeping step with its monstrous stride and prepared for every figure of the dance" (342). James writes to Gaillard Lapsley in 1908 about Edith's "prodigious devil's dance" (Bell, 157). Millicent Bell observes that "The metaphor of a dance upon the Aubusson carpet of the rue de Varenne apartment became one of James's favorite ways of describing the social activities constantly in motion there. . . . He could congratulate Walter Berry . . . on joining 'the sarabande'" (Bell, 139). Mrs. Worthingham is not only a light too blinding for White-Mason, but she represents money, with "the golden stream" (349) of her fortune, recalling James's lament to Lapsley "that an *intellectuelle*—and an Angel—should require such a big pecuniary basis" (*The Master*, 454). Poor, dim Crapy Cornelia surrounded by "sallow carte-de-visite photographs" (360), in contrast to the blinding Mrs.

Worthingham, could provide Mason-White with "the pitch and quantity of what the past had held for them" (356). As Mrs. Wharton stands behind Mrs. Worthingham, so her sister-in-law, Mrs. Mary Cadwalader Jones, stands behind the character of Cornelia Rasch. When James revisited the United States in 1904, he was put up in New York both by Edith Wharton and by Mrs. Jones. Although his main hostess was Mrs. Jones, he interrupted his stay at her Eleventh Street house for a week's visit to Mrs. Wharton's Park Avenue house uptown. Mrs. Worthingham's house in "Crapy Cornelia" is described as "a perfect bower of painted and gilded and moulded conceits" (340). James described Mrs. Wharton's house in a letter as "a *bonbonnière* of the last daintiness."[21] Mrs. Worthingham's "polished and prosperous little person" was surrounded "with exactly the right system of rococo curves and convolutions and other flourishes" (340), whereas in Cornelia's apartment the table "preserved the plain mahogany circle, with never a curl nor a crook nor a hint of a brazen flourish" (360). James had written of the "almost too impeccable taste of Mrs. Wharton's furnishings."[22]

The atmosphere in Cornelia's apartment house, called "The Gainsborough," recalled Howells's letter to James telling him of a house called "The Henry James," to which James answered that it should be named after a more successful writer and called "The Edith Wharton" (Bell, 245). James nostalgically remembered Mrs. Jones's place where he had spent "those Eleventh Street matutinal *intimes* hours, those telephonic matinées, as the most romantic of [his] life" (Bell, 52). White-Mason found Cornelia's shabby things "beautiful" (360), Mrs. Worthingham's expensive décor "awful" (361), just as James had found Mrs. Jones's Eleventh Street place agreeable and Mrs. Wharton's house uncomfortable. Edith Wharton herself records the discomfort that James felt in visiting her (which he did not feel in visiting Mrs. Jones):

> In New York James was a different being. He hated the place . . .
> but he was amused by the social scene, and eager to leave nothing of it unobserved. During his visits, therefore, we invited many people to the house. . . . But this mundane James . . . was a totally different being from our leisurely companion at the Mount. . . . I suspect that he was much happier . . . in Boston than in New York . . . where. . . . he found all sorts of old affinities and relations. . . .
> He had always clung to his cousinage . . . and I remember his once

saying "You see, my dear, they're so much easier to talk to, because I can always ask them questions about uncles and aunts and other cousins." (BG, 194–96)

In the more comfortable environment of Mrs. Jones's house, James could talk about his cousins, as White-Mason was to talk to Cornelia.

The contrast between Mrs. Worthingham and Crapy Cornelia, which reflects the contrast between Edith Wharton and Mrs. Cadwalader Jones, may also be heightened by James's recollection of the contrast between Lily Bart of *The House of Mirth* (with whom Edith Wharton in some ways sympathetically identified herself) and her cousin, Gerty Farish, as being also expressed in terms of intensity of light. "Such flashes of joy as Lily moved in would have blinded Miss Farish, who was accustomed, in the way of happiness, to such scant light as shone through the cracks of other people's lives."[23] Selden is unlike Monteith, since he is not in need of goggles: "But if the new light dazzled, it did not blind him."[24] James may be incorporating in his story the image of the two cousins of *The House of Mirth,* so opposite in effect, one brilliant and the other dim.

If Mrs. Worthingham represents some of those aspects of Edith that James found difficult to accept unless transformed into burlesque terms (the facilitation of her wealth, her modernity, her too-good taste, the lack of shadows and dimness and of history), Kate Cookham, in the final story, "The Bench of Desolation," becomes the angel of desolation and "devastation," to whom the hero must finally submit. She is the complete parodic embodiment of the extremes of Edith Wharton's persona. She manifests both the difficult as well as the saving aspects of her cleverness, generosity, and wealth.

An example of James's judgment that Edith was difficult comes not from a parodic exaggeration in his letters but from a sober estimate of her character and can be found in a statement he made to A. John Hugh-Smith in 1908 or 1909, according to Percy Lubbock: "Ah, my dear young man, you have made friends with Edith Wharton. I congratulate you; you may find her difficult, but you will never find her stupid, and you will never find her mean" (Bell, 190).

"The Bench of Desolation" contains the most telling aspects of the Wharton material, incorporating her fiction, her personal traits, her possessions, and her function in relation to her friends. The ambiguity of the other stories is replaced by specific allusions to the Edith ambience, as if James were underlining them to guarantee their recognition, at least by

Wharton. The most striking of the many topical references in the suite occurs in this last story and is based on an actual event in the life of Morton Fullerton, a member of James's circle, which Leon Edel had revealed in *The Master* (416–18). Since the publication of R. W. B. Lewis's biography of Edith Wharton, it is now known that Morton Fullerton was Mrs. Wharton's lover from 1907 through 1910. Since 1907 James knew that a woman now identified as Henrietta Mirecourt who lived in the same apartment house with Fullerton had been blackmailing him, with demands "that he come back to live with her; better, that he marry her at once; and in any case that he again provide financial support."[25] Edith Wharton offered to buy off the black-mailer and "so conspired" with James in the early part of January 1909. James wrote to Edith that "We can help him—we even can't *not*. And it will immensely pay" (*The Master,* 417). So it is hardly accidental that at the same time that James wrote about a breach of promise suit he was deeply involved in thinking about extricating Fullerton from his dilemma by means of Edith Wharton's help. Although the financial details were not to be worked out completely until later that summer, the January letters to Edith show that they had already decided on a plan. Mrs. Wharton had herself written a farce, "The Introducers" (1905–1906), which takes place also at a seaside resort on a bench facing the sea. Thus the title, "The Bench of Desolation," fuses a story by Edith with her role as the "angel of desolation" found in James's letters where he had called her "devouring and desolating, ravaging, burning and destroying" (*The Master,* p. 340).

The most telling link lies in the plot of the story. Herbert Dodd has been sued by Kate Cookham for 400 pounds because of a breach of promise to marry her. On December 26, just a week before he began the story, James had actually heard an anecdote he recorded in his *Notebooks* about a working-class man's being sued for 200 pounds by a woman whom he eventually marries, after his first wife died. Thus equipped with all the details for the plot of "The Bench of Desolation," James could concentrate on the woman. "What I seem to see in it," the *Notebooks* record, "is *her* life and behaviour—her subsequent action. . . . She *sees* him suffer . . . sees him pay for what he had done to her. . . . She has taken the money because she has known he would want money badly later on."[26] James now had the figure of Edith Wharton as the savior of Fullerton all ready as a model for Kate. From the person of Edith, James has made an interesting coalescence of an angel of mercy and an angel of devastation and desolation, a juxtaposition of opposites we have seen constantly reappearing comically in his letters about her. "Her powers of devastation are ineffable, her repudiation of repose absolutely tragic," he wrote to Mrs. Jones in 1911, and followed with "and she was never more brilliant and able and interesting" (*The Master,* 464). If we consider James's reaction to Edith's personality, we understand why Herbert Dodd, whose life has been wrecked by Kate Cookham, finally submits to her. Just as James wrote, "the being devastated [by Edith] has done me perceptible good," so the being devastated by Kate saves Herbert Dodd. His surrender to Kate Cookham is a transposition of James's metaphor about Edith in a letter to Goody Allen when he announces Mrs. Wharton's impending arrival from Paris. "I shall not get off without *some* surrender . . . one must go some little part of the way to meet her—even at the cost of precious hours and blasted labours and dislocated thrift and order" (*The Master,* 461). Any rather trivial encounter with Mrs. Wharton was presented in the baroque imagery of exaggeration.

We even recognize in Kate Cookham's "large, clean, plain brown face" (372) Mrs. Wharton's "Brown, much-wrinkled skin" (*The Master,* 365) and "browney-yellow" complexion described by Miss Bosanquet (*The Master,* 540). When Kate Cookham returns to Properley "in the sharp terms of her transformed state," she appears to be "simply another and a totally different person. . . . He had remembered her as inclined to the massive and disowned by the graceful; but this was a spare . . . almost wasted lady—who had repaired waste . . . with . . . a rich accumulation of manner . . . she had had a life, a career, a history" as Edith had had in the years between 1904 and 1908 (391–92). Another characteristic of Kate noticed by James in Edith was her "dryness" (*The Master,* 204) mentioned often in letters when he first meets her. He even incorporates it into his literary judgments of her work, referring to her "dry, or call it perhaps even the hard, intellectual touch."[27] The "harassed look" Miss Bosanquet saw in 1908 on Edith's face reappears in Kate's face, "a worn, fine face" (424), when she returns transformed into a fairy godmother with her "money in handfuls" (412). Kate's last name incorporates the last name of Mrs. Wharton's chauffeur, Cook, responsible for so many of the drives James enjoyed (just as White, Edith's butler, appears in White-Mason's name [Bell, 196]). What reason can James have had for mentioning that Kate has changed her rooms from the Royal Hotel to some lodgings "At the Mount, Castle Terrace" (422) other than the wish to plant another clue? "Oh, I *know* the Mount," Herbert says. "So that if it isn't . . . like the Royal, why, you're at least comfortable" (423). It would be but a slightly "veiled" joke for those in the know to read that lodgings were named after Mrs. Wharton's elegant house at Lenox, The Mount, and that it would be disguised as a place inferior to the epitome of vulgarity, a grand hotel at a watering place! When Kate stands before Herbert on her return, a "mature, qualified, important person" looking "at the limp, undistinguished . . . shabby man on the bench" (390), we recognize James's figure of speech when he writes to Howard Sturgis: "Our famous and invincible Fire-bird announces herself to me as flashing down here . . . and culling me, as she passes, to present me as a limp field flower that evening at Qu'Acre. I needn't tell you that I can only, for the occasion, be all predestined limpness, and where the devastating angel catches me up there I shall yield to my fate."[28]

The situation of Herbert Dodd, ruined and saved, hating and loving, devastated and protected by a unique woman repeats that of James's situation vis-à-vis Mrs. Wharton. To Fanny Prothero he writes, once again in the comic style he had established for his comments on Edith, "I clutch at anything to hang on by—Mrs. Wharton . . . designing, with a full intensity, to whirl me away for several days. . . . Yes, pray for me while I am hurried to my doom" (*The Master,* 461). In 1912, especially during Edith's visits to England, his reaction to her as a combination of wonder and horror is always mentioned in his correspondence (*The Master,* 462). The fictive Kate Cookham also combines seemingly irreconcilable attributes. She returns "a handsome, grave, authoritative, but refined and, as it were, physically rearranged person—she, the outrageous vulgarity of whose prime assault had kept him shuddering so long as a shudder was in him" (393–94). It is as if from having been the horrible woman who was blackmailing Fullerton in real life, she becomes Edith Wharton whose money saves him in real life. From a witch the fictive heroine turns into a loving fairy godmother. Herbert saw his fortune "confess itself at once a fairy-tale and a nightmare" (411), for he saw Kate offering a "pecuniary salve . . . for his wounds." In addition, James identifies himself with Dodd when he refers to the breakup of the Wharton marriage. He writes to Sturgis on May 13, 1913, that "Teddy is now definitely and legally 'put away'. . . . And now I both long and shudder (though that's a rude word) to see the great author, or authoress, of the deed!" (Bell, 188), a repetition of Herbert Dodd's submission to the inexorable Kate Cookham. So we see two polaric types fused in one person, based on the true story of two women (one, Fullerton's blackmailer in Paris, and the other, Edith Wharton, his lover and his savior), reinforced by the natural polarity of James's own strong personal feelings pro and con Mrs. Wharton—her intelligence and imperiousness, her powers of stimulation and possessiveness. The order of the stories has been arranged to present Edith moving from a goddess to an "angel of desolation," sitting on the bench of desolation with the hero whom she has first defeated and then succored. All the contradictions in Edith's personality as James felt them, the extremes of his attraction and his revulsion, are presented: "She rode the whirlwind, she played with the storm, she laid waste whatever of the land the other raging elements spared. . . . Her powers of devastation are ineffable, her repudiation of repose absolutely tragic, and she was never more brilliant and able and interesting" (*The Master*, 464).

The final question we must ask ourselves is: Did Edith Wharton perceive the hidden references to her work and character? She is not on record as having done so, but she has given us hints. She has indicated that she knew James read all of her work, and any reference to her stories in his work would not be accidental. Although she claimed to have found his late work less readable than his earlier, the evidence of *The Reef* and *The Writing of Fiction* testify to the fact that she studied it very carefully. Mrs. Bell sees "The Beast in the Jungle" behind the *Age of Innocence* (1920), Marcher behind Archer (Bell, 295). Edith admired "The Velvet Glove," although her comments show no indication that she was aware of her presence in it. Although Mrs. Wharton told Leon Edel that she could not have been the Princess because she would never have asked for a literary lift (*The Master*, 353), the evidence published by Mrs. Bell makes this statement suspect. Although Leon Edel writes in *The Master*, "Mrs. Wharton saw the joke [of "The Velvet Glove"] at once, it would seem, but apparently closed her eyes to the meanings that might be read in it." Although Edel has published no evidence to show that she *did* see the joke, we may assume she took it all in fun.

In *Men and Ghosts* (1910), stories Mrs. Wharton published just after the appearance of *The Finer Grain,* there seem to be enough references both to James's work and to his personality to show that she may have been engaging in a riposte to *The Finer Grain* stories. She had written that James gave his judgment of anyone's work "when they asked for it—and sometimes when they did not" (BG, 182). Her story, "Full Circle," reverses the relation of the writer and the young man in James's "The Great Good Place" in the persons of Geoffrey Betton and Duncan Vyse. "The Legend" (to which we automatically add "of the Master") tells about a writer, John Pellerin, who, like James, had been popular twenty-five years before but has lost his reading public and who, in appearance and in pseudonym (Winterman) like "the good grey poet" whom James had read to Edith's circle at The Mount, returns to find out what the pundits are saying about him. The feature Mrs. Wharton seizes on as characteristic of the writer was his "eye." "He hasn't used it to dominate people; he didn't care to. He simply looked through 'em all like windows." [29] We know that James's eyes were his most distinguished feature. Elizabeth Jordan and Alice Boughton, as well as Ezra Pound, were haunted by them. In "The Eyes" (1910), set in a framework like "The Turn of the Screw" (and which, like it, has, presumably, two ghosts), Andrew Culwin, like James, is the center of an admiring group of acolytes. Culwin, described as a "wise old idol," is remembered in his youth as "a charming little man with nice eyes." He is presented as homoerotic and "liked" his young men "juicy," but "his friendship was not a disintegrating influence"; on the contrary, it stimulated the current young man of talent. "Indeed, the skill with which Culwin had contrived to stimulate his curiosities without robbing them of their bloom of awe seemed to me a sufficient answer to Murchard's ogreish metaphor." [30] (One recollects Mrs. Wharton's "Ogrin the Hermit.") Edel's revelations in *The Master* about James's feelings in these years about a number of young men make it obvious, given Edith's intelligence and intimacy with the group, that Phil Frenham, the current favorite, could be identified with any one of them.

Edith Wharton's description of James's circle at Sturgis's home, "Qu'acre," in *A Backward Glance* suggests Culwin's circle in her story, "The Eyes":

> This inner group I see now, gathered around him [James] as the lamps are brought in at the end of a foggy autumn afternoon. In one of the armchairs by the fire is sunk the long-limbed frame of the young Percy Lubbock, still carrying in his mind the delightful books he has since given us, and perhaps as yet hardly aware that he was ever to put them on paper; in another sits Gaillard Lapsley, down for the week-end from his tutorial duties at Cambridge, while John Hugh-Smith faces Percy across the fireside, and Robert Norton and I share the corners of the wide chintz sofa behind the tea-table; and dominating the hearth, and all of us, Henry James stands, or heavily pads about the room, listening, muttering, groan-

ing disapproval, or chuckling assent to the paradoxes of the other tea-drinkers. And then, when tea is over, and the tray has disappeared, he stops his prowling to lean against the mantelpiece and plunge into reminiscences of the Paris or London of his youth, or into some elaborated literary disquisition. (BG, 231)

The opening of "The Eyes" also creates the mood of a group of men friends (including one whose "slender height" reminds the reader specifically of Lubbock), which seems to echo the "Qu'acre" group (although Mrs. Wharton extends the roster from the six of the actual group to eight of the fictive group). "There were eight of us" by "the drowsy gleam of a coal fire" sitting and talking, grouped around the equivalent of James, Mr. Andrew Culwin, who was "listening and blinking through the smoke circles with the cheerful tolerance of a wise old idol"[31] and who like James dominated the conversation. "His mind was like a forum, or some open meeting place for the exchange of ideas: somewhat cold and drafty, but light, spacious and orderly—a kind of academic grove from which all the leaves have fallen. In this privileged area a dozen of us were wont to stretch our muscles and expand our lungs; and, as if to prolong as much as possible the tradition of what we felt to be a vanishing institution, one or two neophytes were now and then added to our band."[32] The description of one young man Culwin encourages—"slender and smooth and hyacinthine, he might have stepped from a ruined altar—one to Antinous, say"[33] is a direct reference to the homosexuality of Hadrian, spoken by Culwin. Culwin's ghosts turn out to be his own eyes that haunt him twice when he performs acts that go against the grain of his own egotism: "They were a hallucination, then: that was plain. . . . I had gone deeply enough into the mystery of morbid pathological states to picture the conditions under which an exploring mind might lay itself open to such a midnight admonition."[34] This might suggest that Edith agreed with many modern interpretations of "The Turn of the Screw." "Those eyes hung there and drew me. I had the *vertige de l'abyme,* and their red lids were the edge of my abyss."[35] Mrs. Wharton here incorporates a direct quotation from "Crapy Cornelia" in which Monteith deliberates whether or not he could live the kind of life Mrs. Worthingham (or, by inference, Mrs. Wharton) could offer him: "He could have lived on in *his* New York . . . the sentimental . . . the more or less romantic visitation of it;—but had it been positive for him that he could live on in hers?— unless indeed the possibility of this had been just (like the famous *ver-*

tige de l'abyme, like the solicitation of danger, or otherwise of the dreadful) the very hinge of his whole dream" (354). It seems worthy of comment that Mrs. Wharton echoes this quotation from James's story at that point in her story where her hero is presented with the same problem of proposing to a woman he does not desire. However, the most striking recollections of James's fiction are in the theme of the man haunted by himself, recalling the recently published "The Jolly Corner" (1909), in which Spencer Brydon is haunted by his alter ego, a projection of his egotism, and "The Beast in the Jungle" (1902), in which the beast is also a "hallucination" of Marcher's egotism.

So in one way the stories constitute a private correspondence which the reader can intercept, an exchange in which the parodied exasperation that James often felt in Edith's presence merged with the great personal and social pleasure he derived from their relationship. Mrs. Wharton herself had insight into the basis for their compatibility: "Perhaps it was our common sense of fun that first brought about our understanding. The real marriage of true minds is for any two people to possess a sense of humour or irony pitched in exactly the same key, so that their joint glances at any subject cross like interarching searchlights" (BG, 173). *The Finer Grain,* however, also illustrates the *literary* use that James made out of the complexity of Mrs. Wharton's persona and life, and "The Eyes" shows her ingenious response to James's humor by an even sharper characterization of a man she deeply loved. The ultimate justification for paying attention to the biographical material (so involved with the genesis of these tales and so evident in the texture of the stories themselves) is that it has been transmuted into works of art by two masters of fiction.

References

1. Millicent Bell, *Edith Wharton and Henry James: The Story of Their Friendship* (New York: Braziller, 1965). Further references to this book are designated as Bell and page number. Leon Edel, *Henry James: The Master* (Philadelphia: Lippincott, 1972). Further references to this book are designated as *The Master.* Edith Wharton, *A Backward Glance* (New York: Appleton-Century, 1934). Further references to this book are designated as BG and page number.

2. Leon Edel and Dan H. Lawrence, *A Bibliography of Henry James* (London: Rupert Hart-Davis, 1961), p. 146.

3. E. V. Lucas, *Reading, Writing, and Remembering* (London: Methuen, 1932), pp. 184–85.

4. Theodora Bosanquet, *Henry James at Work* (London: Hogarth, 1924), p. 249.

5. Jacques-Emile Blanche, *Portraits of a Lifetime* (New York: Coward-McCann), p. 237.

6. Adeline R. Tintner, "James's Mock Epic: 'The Velvet Glove,' Edith Wharton, and Other Late Tales," *Modern Fiction Studies* 17, no. 4 (Winter 1971–72): 483–99.

7. Henry James, *The Letters of Henry James,* ed. Percy Lubbock, vol. 2 (New York: Scribner's, 1920), p. 121.

8. Henry James, *The Complete Tales of Henry James,* ed. Leon Edel, vol. 12 (Philadelphia: Lippincott, 1964), p. 259. All references to the stories included in *The Finer Grain* are indicated by page number only.

9. Henry James, *Notes on Novelists* (New York: Scribner's, 1914), p. 355.

10. Leon Edel, ed., *The Complete Plays of Henry James* (Philadelphia: Lippincott, 1949), p. 643.

11. Max Beerbohm, "Jacobean and Shavian," reprinted in *Henry James: Twentieth Century Views,* ed. Leon Edel (Englewood Cliffs: Prentice-Hall, 1963), pp. 18–20.

12. F. O. Matthiessen and Kenneth B. Murdock, eds., *The Notebooks of Henry James* (New York: Oxford University Press, 1947), p. 309.

13. Guy Chapman, *The Dreyfus Case* (New York: Reynal & Col., 1955), p. 141.

14. Ibid., pp. 262–63.

15. Edith Wharton, *The House of Mirth* (New York: Scribner's, 1905), p. 441.

16. Louis Auchincloss, *Edith Wharton* (New York: Viking, 1971), p. 93.

17. Grace Kellogg, *The Two Lives of Edith Wharton* (New York: Appleton-Century, 1965), p. 256.

18. Percy Lubbock, *Portrait of Edith Wharton* (New York and London: Appleton-Century, 1947), p. 80.

19. Ibid., p. 9.

20. Henry James, *The American Scene,* Introduction and notes by Leon Edel (Bloomington: Indiana University Press, 1968), p. 469.

21. Ibid., p. 472.

22. Ibid., p. 469.

23. Edith Wharton, *The House of Mirth,* p. 241.

24. Ibid., p. 247.

25. R. W. B. Lewis, *Edith Wharton: A Biography* (New York: Harper & Row, 1975), p. 198. There has been some confusion about the name Henrietta Mirecourt.

26. Matthiessen and Murdock, eds., *Notebooks of Henry James,* p. 331.

27. James, *Notes on Novelists,* p. 356.

28. Henry James to Howard Sturgis, August 2, 1910. (Leon Edel has generously permitted me to read the James-Sturgis correspondence and to quote this specific passage.)

29. Edith Wharton, *The Collected Short Stories,* ed. R. W. B. Lewis, vol. 2 (New York: Scribner's, 1968), 94.

30. Ibid., p. 116.

31. Ibid., p. 115.

32. Ibid., p. 116.

33. Ibid., p. 123.

34. Ibid., p. 121.

35. Ibid., p. 122.

4

Jamesian Structures in THE AGE OF INNOCENCE *and Related Stories*

Many critics have made the claim that *The Age of Innocence* is the most Jamesian of Edith Wharton's novels, whereas others have denied it. Millicent Bell wrote that the novel "contains some of the most obvious resemblances to James's works to be found anywhere in her writings,"[1] and Cynthia Wolff stated that its "central meaning grows out of the complex way in which the novel beckons" to James.[2] Yet Edmund Wilson saw her in relation to James "as a lesser disciple of whom she is sometimes pointlessly listed,"[3] and Irving Howe found that in her "most important novels it is hard to detect any *specific* influence of James."[4]

The claims for the Jamesian element are made either in large generalities or in specific instances that do not seem to hold. If we examine the novel from the point of view of very specific structures that repeat almost identical models found in James, it may become apparent to the reader that there is in this book a greater reference in a technical sense to the work of James than we had thought from previous criticism. This dependence not only is on James's early work but also extends to such late works as *The Golden Bowl* and to James's last completed novel, *The Outcry*, as well as to the New York stories that he wrote in the early years of the twentieth century. Despite Wharton's statement in *A Backward Glance* that she found James's late novels unattractive, they seem to have left their mark on other stories by Wharton that are associated in time with *The Age of Innocence* and were written when Wharton was greatly involved with thinking about James, surrounded by his circle of friends, and rereading his letters with a view to their publication by Percy Lub-

Originally published as "Jamesian Structures in *The Age of Innocence,*" *Twentieth Century Literature* 26, no. 3 (Fall 1980): 332–48.

bock, whom she had chosen as their editor. The year of this concentration on James, his work, and his friends was 1919–20, when she wrote *The Age of Innocence* and the short story called "Writing a War Story." During this time she also mapped out a group of four novellas published in book form in 1924, which she was to call *Old New York,* the title she had originally planned for *The Age of Innocence* but ultimately discarded. Critics have noted a family resemblance between *The Age of Innocence* and the four *Old New York* novellas because of their reconstruction of a past New York society (Edmund Wilson wrote that "*Old New York* was a much feebler second boiling from the tea-leaves of *The Age of Innocence*").[5] The Jamesian strain apparent in this group of stories as well as in the novel shows that Wharton used everything that could assist her archaeologizing habit, but it has resisted detection because the specific borrowings have not been excavated except in one or two cases where, as we shall see, they have not been properly located.

When Edith Wharton was about to write *The Age of Innocence,* the close circle of friends of Henry James had foregathered at the Pavillon Colombe, Wharton's home on the outskirts of Paris, to go over the publication of James's letters. R. W. B. Lewis tells us that "Edith felt strongly that someone needed to decipher the vast numbers of letters to her and to other members of the Queen's Acre constituency, 'someone,' as she wrote to Edmund Gosse, asking him to intercede in the case 'familiar with the atmosphere in which Henry and our small group communed together.'"[6] We know that for the "ritual opening of the Pavillon Colombe on August 7" in 1919 the group, including Lubbock and Lapsley, came "for a fortnight's stay, and Edith kept them up late discussing 'Henry questions.'"[7]

"Writing a War Story" is about Ivy Spang, a girl who acts as a tea-server in a big Anglo-American hospital in Paris during the First World War. She has been asked to write a short story for a magazine called *The Man-at-Arms,* and her photograph appears along with the story. Since she is pretty, all the soldier-patients want her picture but are not interested in reading her story. A famous novelist, Harold Harbard, who is one of the patients, gets hold of the magazine and the poor authoress overhears him laughing at her fictional effort. She is especially hurt because he too asks for her photograph.

In view of the fact that Wharton and James's friends were at this time going over James's letters to them and recalling his advice, it is not surprising to find Harbard, the writer in the story, commenting to the heroine, Ivy Spang, in almost the exact terms in which James had criticized *The Custom of the Country* in a conversation with Wharton. When Ivy asks Harbard why he is laughing at her story, he tells her it is very hard to explain it to her.

> He shook his head. "No; but it's queer—it's puzzling. You've got hold of a wonderfully good subject; and that's the main thing, of course."
>
> Ivy interrupted him eagerly. "The subject is the main thing?"
>
> "Why, naturally; it's only the people without invention who tell you it isn't."
>
> "Oh," she gasped, trying to readjust her carefully acquired theory of aesthetics.
>
> "*You've got hold of an awfully good subject,*" Harbard continued: "*but you've rather mauled it, haven't you?*" [italics mine][8]

In *A Backward Glance,* Edith Wharton quoted James:

> "But of course you know—as how should you, with your infernal keenness of perception, *not* know?—that in doing your tale you had under your hand a magnificent subject, which ought to have been your main theme, and that you used it as a mere incident and then passed it by?"

She then commented that after she tried to justify herself to James, "he could merely answer, by implication if not openly. '*Then, my dear child, you chose the wrong kind of subject*'" [italics mine].[9]

"Writing a War Story" is based on the idea that it is necessary for an author to have both a subject and the management of that subject well in hand—the "donnée" and its "treatment," about which James always talked and wrote. Both James and Edith Wharton kept notebooks of données. Edith began hers around 1900 and James did not get into contact with her through her sister-in-law, Mrs. Cadwalader Jones, until 1902, so we cannot credit him with that impetus. But his letters advising her to be "tethered in native pastures, even if it reduces her to a back-yard in New York"[10] and his praise for "her sharp eye for an interesting *kind* of subject" show that the subject was important for him, as well as the "treatment."

In his essay "The Art of Fiction" (1884), James had written:

"The story," if it represents anything, represents the subject, the idea, the data of the novel; and there is surely no "school" . . . which urges that a novel should be all treatment and no subject. There must assuredly be something to treat. . . . The story and the novel, the idea and the form, are the needle and the thread, and I never heard of a guild of tailors who recommended the use of the thread without the needle or the needle without the thread.[11]

James's advice to Wharton about writing her story is divided between Harbard and Ivy's old governess, "Mademoiselle," who tells Ivy to begin by "Thinking of a subject," and adds, "in writing a story, one has to have a subject. Of course, I know it's only the treatment that matters; but the treatment naturally would be yours, quite yours." She then offers Ivy her notebook in which she has recorded her données. "One notation was dated, 'Military Hospital No. 13. November, 1914. Long talk with Chasseur Alpin Emile Durand, wounded through the knee and the left lung at the Hautes Chaumes. I have decided to write down his story.'"[12] This is a reminder that in a letter of January 7, 1908, Henry James gave Edith Wharton a donnée of the story that she used in "Pretext" (1908).

Also, the persona of Henry James himself is clearly discernible behind the sketch of the wounded novelist, Harold Harbard (the last name an obvious disguise for Harvard). The first piece of evidence for this is that Harbard is cited as the author of a novel called *Broken Wings*. Henry James, too, was the author of the story, "Broken Wings," published in 1900, about an authoress who considers herself a failure.

It was not the first time that Edith Wharton had used Henry James, his figure, and his literary persona in her fiction. She seems to have used him and his role in her life, as I have already indicated, in her imitation medieval story, "The Hermit and the Wild Woman."[13] Further, as I have also shown, the short story, "The Eyes," presents stylistic evidence from which Henry James and the homoerotic group that met at Howard Sturgis's home can be recognized in the fictional characters.[14]

There are other elements in the Wharton tale that also point to a connection with the memory of James's advice about the writing of fiction. After Ivy Spang has been assigned to write for the magazine, she looks into *Fact and Fiction*, another magazine, and tries various kinds of opening sentences. She hits on one that satisfies her, "A shot rang out," only to realize it was also used as the opening sentence of one of the stories printed in the magazine.

The sentence was there—she had written it—it was the first sentence on the first page of her story, it *was* the first sentence of her story. It was there, it had gone out of her, got away from her, and she seemed to have no further control of it. She could imagine no other way of beginning, now that she had made the effort of beginning in that way.[15]

This sentence about *her* sentence recalls another one by Henry James about a sentence of *his* in "The Great Good Place." He

had left his phrase unfinished and his papers lying quite as if for the flood to bear them away on its bosom. But there still, on the table, were the bare bones of the sentence—and not all of those; the single thing borne away and that he could never recover was the missing half that might have paired with it and begotten a figure.[16]

On September 24, 1920, four years after James's death, Wharton wrote to Lapsley: "My longing to talk with you about Henry is getting *maladive*. No one can *really understand* but you and me." Thus she found herself, to quote Cynthia Wolff, "very much in the midst of her memories of James while she was engrossed with *The Age of Innocence*." Wolff continues that although the novel "borrows more extensively from the ambience of her childhood world than any other novel she published . . . perhaps the central meaning grows out of the complex way in which the novel beckons to Wharton's dearest friend, Henry James."[17] The evidence for this Wolff finds in the title, "The Age of Innocence," because, she writes, it is named after the portrait of a "little lady" by Sir Joshua Reynolds in the National Gallery in London and thus points to Isabel Archer, whose name resembles that of Wharton's hero, Newland Archer. Since Ned Winsett, a friend, tells Newland that he is "like the pictures on the walls of a deserted house: 'The Portrait of a Gentleman,'" the title of the book—the name of a picture—is presumed by Wolff to recall James's *The Portrait of a Lady*.[18] However, to this reader there is a much closer connection with James established by the title, "The Age of Innocence." It distinctly harks back to another novel by James, not *The Portrait of a Lady*, but *The Tragic Muse* (1890). By that title James invoked a famous picture by Sir Joshua Reynolds, "The Tragic Muse," known to every cultivated reader as a portrait of Mrs. Siddons. The title is closely related to James's theme in that novel, which is how the young actress, Miriam

Rooth, makes a choice between a career on the stage and the role of an ambassador's wife. She chooses to be a Mrs. Siddons, rather than a Lady Hamilton, who had often been painted by Romney and who later became the wife of the British ambassador to Naples. Wharton's title, "The Age of Innocence," thus imitates the title, "The Tragic Muse," because May Welland Archer is meant to personify the young girl representing innocence in Reynolds's picture, "The Age of Innocence." Of course, here the title is used ironically, since May, supposedly innocent, actually gets what she wants by lying and cheating to protect her own marriage. This strategy has been recognized by Millicent Bell[19] as also dependent on James's *The Golden Bowl.* However, the lie that Maggie Verver tells so that Charlotte Stant, her husband's mistress, may keep her self-respect is a virtuous lie, whereas May Archer tells an evil lie. She fabricates her pregnancy, knowing that the expected arrival of a child will force Ellen to give up Newland. The picture we have of May until near the end of the novel is that of the truthful child, the innocent child-wife, whom Newland must protect. Yet that May is the same May who changes the lives of the two lovers and whose lie separates them just before their planned union.

In addition, it does not seem too farfetched to find within *The Tragic Muse* by James a scene that appears as a model for an equivalent scene in *The Age of Innocence.* On the estate at Skuytercliff in *The Age of Innocence* was a small stone house of the original Patroon settler, dated 1612. It suggests, in the way it is treated by its owners, aesthetically and historically, and as a focus of erotic climax, the *tempietto* on the estate restored by Julia Dallow's deceased husband in James's *The Tragic Muse.* It was in the small temple to Vesta that Nick Dormer felt the physical appeal of Julia Dallow, embraced her, and proposed to her. (Early in her career Edith Wharton had written a story, "The Muse's Tragedy" [*Greater Inclination,* 1899] where she used the title of his 1890 novel in her own fashion to give an ironic twist to the title itself.)

Just as Julia Dallow had the little *tempietto* cleaned and ready for use when she should want it, so Mrs. Van der Luyden had opened and heated the house for Ellen. Newland is so passionately attracted to her in this "secret room" that we are reminded of Nick's having sworn away his career at that moment when he was under the spell of the small temple of Vesta on the Dallow estate, which was "a reminiscence of the small ruined rotunda which stands on the banks of the Tiber and is declared by *ciceroni* to have been dedicated to Vesta. George Dallow . . . had amused himself with restoring it."[20] There was "malice prepense in the temple," Julia had said. This same magic works in *The Age of Innocence*. As Mr. Hoppus's pamphlet had interfered with Nick and Julia's lovemaking and had cut into their erotic mood, so Julius Beaufort interrupts the growing idyll of Ellen and Newland's love. The small house of the past that was kept as a historic shrine is clearly modeled on the *tempietto* on Julia's grounds.

In Wharton's novel the figure of Julius Beaufort arriving at the Hudson River villa suggests the rotund figure of Mr. Caliph of James's "The Impressions of a Cousin" (1883), and like him he is involved in financial failure under a cloud of misappropriating funds. Like Mr. Caliph he is portly, wears a flower in his buttonhole, and has the magic of the East for the ladies. Like Mr. Caliph, he was loved by a woman of the ruling class in New York of the 1870s who remains, like James's Eunice, loyal to him.

There are two novels by James written in the 1870s, the period in which *The Age of Innocence* was supposed to have occurred: his first novel, *Roderick Hudson* (1875), and his second, *The American* (1877), which, with *The Princess Casamassima* (1886), supply a great number of Jamesian details that probably helped Wharton to construct her book.

The Age of Innocence opens with a performance of *Faust* at the Academy of Music in New York. In *The American* James for the first time had brought all his characters into the Paris opera house, where *Don Giovanni* is being presented. Having learned from Balzac how to present the play-within-the-play he expanded that technique in this novel to include the play-within-the-box.[21] In James's later story, "A London Life" (1888), the opera, *Les Huguenots,* points up the twofold drama of Selina and her lover and Laura and her young man, combining thereby the play-within-the-play and the play-within-the-box. In "Glasses" (1896), *Lohengrin* is the opera that underlines the theme of renunciation exemplified by the heroine, Flora, who, now blind, performs in her opera box. Although James had never invoked *Faust* as an opera, he alludes to it in a story, "Collaboration" (1892), and bases the story on the collaboration between Charles Gounod and Goethe that produced "Faust." In James's story the aspects of the temptation by Mephistopheles are emphasized rather than the loss of Marguerite, although that also figures in his tale. Wharton gives the Faustian analogy her own slant by making Marguerite into May Welland, who not only resists the unfortunate end of Goethe's Marguerite but emerges as victor. It is clear that Wharton thus has used a Jamesian technique from *The American,* in the opening scene of *The Age of Inno-*

cence. She has also borrowed from *The Princess Casamassima,* as well as from *Roderick Hudson,* for Ellen Olenska has been modeled on James's Christina Light (although Millicent Bell sees her formed on Eugenia from *The Europeans*), and others see her as a version of herself. The evidence for this can be seen when we consider James's earliest novel, *Roderick Hudson,* in which Christina makes her first appearance.

The connection of Ellen Olenska with Christina Light is supported by a number of scenes in *The Age of Innocence* that seem to repeat scenes in which Christina plays a role in the two novels by James in which she appears. There is a scene in *The Age of Innocence* that takes place at the Van der Luyden's dinner. The Duke and Ellen

> chatted together for nearly twenty minutes; then the Countess rose and, walking alone across the wide drawing room, sat down at Newland Archer's side.
>
> It was not the custom in New York drawing rooms for a lady to get up and walk away from one gentleman in order to seek the company of another. Etiquette required that she should wait, immovable as an idol, while the men who wished to converse with her succeeded each other at her side. But the Countess was apparently unaware of having broken any rule; she sat at perfect ease in a corner of the sofa beside Archer.[22]

The following scene from *Roderick Hudson,* which also includes Roderick's comments, is apparently its source.

> There was a long solemn pause before the music began, and in the midst of it Christina rose, left her place, came the whole length of the immense room, with everyone looking at her, and stopped before him. She was neither pale nor flushed; she had a dim smile.
>
> "Will you do me a favour?"
>
> "A thousand!"
>
> "Not now, but at your earliest convenience. Please remind Mr. Hudson that he is not in a New England village, that it's not the custom in Rome to address one's conversation exclusively, night after night, to the same poor girl . . . "[23]

"The next day" Rowland "repeated her words to Roderick" who replied:

"On the contrary, she has often said to me, 'Mind you now, I forbid you to leave me. Here comes that beast of a So-and-so.' She cares as little about the custom of the country as I do. What could be a better proof than her walking up to you with five hundred people looking at her? Is that, for beautiful watched girls, the custom of the country?"[24]

Wharton may have taken both the setting and the title of her novel, *The Custom of the Country,* from Roderick's speech. It seems very likely that Wharton came across the phrase in the scene that shows Christina committing the same kind of social act of independence that Ellen displays at the van der Luydens.

The other connections with Christina from *The Princess Casamassima* are equally convincing. Just as Hyacinth first meets Christina, now the Princess, in a box at a play, so Newland Archer meets Ellen in a box at the opera. Just as Christina had sent for Hyacinth to take tea at her own house, so Ellen sent for Newland to visit her at teatime and like Hyacinth he is kept waiting, so both men can absorb the surroundings of each American woman enobled by marriage to a member of the European aristocracy. As Hyacinth is overwhelmed by the tasteful and luxurious decorations of the Princess's house, so Newland is impressed by the way Ellen has tastefully converted an ugly little house into an aesthetically satisfying environment. Although he is more cultivated than Hyacinth, some of the pictures and books Ellen has on display are new to him, as the Princess's were to Hyacinth.

Both the James and the Wharton heroines send for their respective young men for the same reasons. The Princess, interested in the "people," needed Hyacinth to tell her all about the working class. In this regard she requires his aid: "I want to know them and I want you to help me."[25] Ellen also needed Newland to be her guide to New York life—"you'll explain these things to me—you'll tell me all I ought to know" (W, 76). Newland had read "Symonds, Vernon Lee's *Euphorion,* the essays of P. G. Hamerton and a wonderful new volume called *The Renaissance* by Walter Pater" (W, 71). Yet Ellen's pictures puzzled him, just as Hyacinth, able to talk about Titian's *Bacchus and Ariadne* and the Elgin Marbles, was mystified by some aspects of Christina's culture.[26]

Wharton describes Newland's reading much in the same way that James cites the books his characters read in *The Princess Casamassima.* Both Hyacinth and Newland read Michelet. It is significant that what

Newland reads usually turns out to be a book James reviewed in the 1870s or late 1860s. (For instance, he has read Swinburne's *Chastelard*, which James reviewed in the *Nation* in January 1866 [W, 85].) Archer thinks of "drawing rooms dominated by the talk of Mérimée (whose *Lettres à une Inconnue* was one of his inseparables), of Thackeray, Browning or William Morris" (W, 103). Mérimée's book was reviewed by James in 1874, and the other three authors were often subjects of essays or reviews by him, starting in the 1860s and continuing in the 1870s.

Newland opened a box of books that came from London, which contained "a new volume of Herbert Spencer, another collection of the prolific Alphonse Daudet's brilliant tales, and a novel called *Middlemarch,* as to which there had lately been interesting things said in the reviews. . . . Suddenly, among them, he came upon a small volume of verse which he had ordered because the name had attracted him: *The House of Life*" (W, 139). The volume by Herbert Spencer is the only one among these books which Henry James did not own or review. In the 1870s he had reviewed both Daudet and George Eliot in the *Galaxy.* One assumes he took the metaphor, "The House of Fiction," used by him frequently, from Rossetti's book, *The House of Life.*

The dependence of *The Age of Innocence* on James's novel, *The American,* the second novel he wrote in the 1870s, can be seen in the naming of Wharton's hero. "Newland" seems to suggest "Newman," the hero of *The American.* Also it seems likely that the scene very close to the end of *The American* is the model for the scene at the end of *The Age of Innocence.* Newman walks to the Carmelite convent where Claire has immured herself. "The day had the softness of early spring." He stands in front of the convent. "From without Newman could see its upper windows. . . . Newman stood there a long time; there were no passers; he was free to gaze his fill. This seemed the goal of his journey; it was what he had come for."[27]

One sees this scene repeated in the final scene of *The Age of Innocence.* Archer is in front of Ellen Olenska's house in Paris.

The day was fading into a soft sun-shot haze. . . . It was a modern building . . . many windowed. . . . Archer remained motionless, gazing at the upper windows as if the end of a pilgrimage had been attained. . . . He sat for a long time on the bench in the thickening dusk, his eyes never turning from the balcony. At length a light shone through the windows, and a moment later a man-servant came out on the balcony, drew up the awnings, and closed the shutters.

At that, as if it had been the signal he waited for, Newland Archer got up slowly and walked back alone to his hotel. (W, 361)

Like the scene in *The American,* it presents the lonely hero looking intently at the building that holds his beloved, the "goal" of his voyage. Both Newman and Newland came only to look and not to penetrate the building.

The connection with *The American,* a novel about a hero who also covets the European experience, appears in another structure in *The Age of Innocence.* Newland's intention is to take Ellen away from her European husband, just as Christopher Newman's intention was to take Claire de Cintré away from her corrupt family, the de Bellegardes. Both men fail and their surrender is expressed by both authors in the same way in the final chapters of their novels.

There is also an image of May Archer, Newland's wife, that, although seemingly trivial, suggests the figure of Catherine Sloper in *Washington Square,* just when Wharton wants to stress her seeming lack of energy. We see May "bent over her work [an embroidery frame] . . . and the right hand slowly and laboriously stabbing the canvas as she sat thus." Archer "said to himself . . . that never . . . would she surprise him by an unexpected move, by a new idea . . . a cruelty or an emotion" (W, 295). Compare this with a scene from *Washington Square.* Catherine "is always knitting some purse or embroidering some handkerchief." Her father, the doctor, continues in the same passage, "she hasn't much to say; but when had she anything to say?"[28]

James's late New York stories (1908–1910) have been plundered by Wharton for her "Jamesian" novel. The second chapter of *The Age of Innocence* seems to be built upon his late manner of treating certain feminine New York types. The description by Edith Wharton of the obese Mrs. Manson Mingott reads very much like the description of Mrs. David E. Drack, from "Julia Bride." Mrs. Mingott's "immense accretion of flesh which had descended on her in middle life like a flood of lava on a doomed city" had at its center "the traces of a small face survived as if awaiting excavation" (W, 28). Compare this with the James passage describing Mrs. Drack. She "presented a huge hideous pleasant face, a featureless desert in a remote quarter of which the disproportionately small eyes might have figured a pair of rash adventurers all but buried in the sand. They reduced themselves . . . to . . . a couple of mere tiny emergent heads."[29] Again, the description of Mrs. Mingott's dress—"around and below, wave after wave of black silk surged away over the edges of a capacious armchair"—seems to have its source in James's portrait of Mrs. Drack. James wrote, "the massive lady just spread and spread like a rich fluid a bit helplessly spilt. It was really the outflow of the poor woman's honest response."[30] Both women are viewed as overflowing liquefied masses. Could the reference to Pompeii in Wharton's "like a flood of lava in a drowned city" remind one of where John Marcher and May Bartram met?

The meeting of Ellen and Newland in that part of the old wing of the Metropolitan Museum where the Cesnola collection was kept repeats the same general setting as that of "Julia Bride." The technique of backing the rendezvous with the antiquities of the collection that "mouldered in the case" ("time blurred substances") (W, 309) may also come from James's "museum" story, "Julia Bride." In *The Age of Innocence* the museum guard walked "like a ghost stalking through a necropolis" (W, 311). This is a correlative of the doomed couple's lack of hope in the city of the dead. Edith Wharton is really using James's technique when he wrote that Julia "saw the great shining room with its mockery of art and 'style'"[31] in contrast to her own shabby future. The scene ends in *The Age of Innocence* with a gesture repeated from "Julia Bride." "When she [Ellen] reached the door she turned for a moment to wave a quick farewell" (W, 313). This gesture seems to reverse the beginning of "Julia Bride," where Basil French, also leaving the heroine in the museum, turned for "a last demonstration" and made a "cordial gesture."[32] When Archer goes home he views the objects in his own home "as if . . . from the other side of the grave" (W, 313). The theme of death and ruin extends beyond the museum scene. Edith Wharton has thus repeated the museum scene from "Julia Bride," even to its function as an aesthetic and moral fictional arch that covers the action symbolically. We know that Wharton admired this tale by James, as she wrote in a letter to Sara (Sally) Norton. (See Chapter 7.)

It seems also as if Wharton looked to James's "The Velvet Glove." Although the characters in her novel rode in carriages, not automobiles, in the 1870s, the final scene in "The Velvet Glove" seems to have been a model for the carriage scene in *The Age of Innocence* in which Newland and Ellen realize the hopelessness of their situation. When John Berridge of "The Velvet Glove" accompanied the beautiful Princess in the motorcar only to learn that she wants him to write a preface to her book, he "signified to the footman his view of their stopping short . . . the car pulled up at the edge of the pavement . . . Berridge . . . felt he had cut his cable . . . he leaned for farewell on the open window-ledge." The Princess is powerless, after being kissed through the open window, "All humanly defeated, she had given the question up, falling back to infinite wonder." [33] In *The Age of Innocence,* after Ellen resists Newland's invitation to be his mistress, Newland "pressed the bell, the carriage drew up beside the curbstone. "'Why are we stopping? This is not Granny's,' Madame Olenska exclaimed. 'No: I shall get out here,' he stammered . . . he saw . . . the instinctive motion she made to detain him. He closed the door and leaned for a moment in the window. 'You're right, I ought not to have come today,' he said, lowering his voice so that the coachman should not hear. She bent forward, and seemed about to speak; but he had already called out the order to drive on" (W, 291).

Another image that seems to derive its source from "The Velvet Glove" is the description of Mrs. Beaufort. "She was indolent, passive, the caustic even called her dull; but dressed like an idol, hung with pearls, growing younger and blonder and more beautiful each year, she throned in Mr. Beaufort's heavy brownstone palace" (W, 20). The possible source in "The Velvet Glove" is, "He felt for an instant as if he were speaking to some miraculously humanised idol, all sacred, all jewelled, all votively hung about, but made mysterious, in the recess of its shrine." [34] The borrowing becomes especially relevant when one considers the possibility that this story by James may be about Edith Wharton herself, who once asked James for a literary puff. These details I have discussed in Chapter 2.

The quartet of novellas called *Old New York,* written the year after *The Age of Innocence,* by its very format seems to have been suggested by the four late New York stories of James. In fact, the publication of each one of the four Wharton stories boxed together, *False Dawn, The Old Maid, The Spark,* and *New Year's Day* (dealing with the New York of the 1840s through the 1870s), although considered a very original format by Wharton's publishers, probably was modeled on the small volume published in 1909 of *Julia Bride,* a story printed for the first time in a volume of the *New York Edition* of James. In fact, it seems as if Wharton wanted her four novellas to appear as a miniature *New York Edition* of her own, frankly aping James.

The earliest in time of the four stories, *False Dawn,* although written second, is the best of the four and the most distinctly Jamesian in quality and aura. In fact, its first few pages, itemizing with succulent delight the pleasures of food and of the table of a country house supposedly based on that of Wharton's own family, seem to have been modeled on the early pages of James's *A Small Boy and Others* (1913), which Wharton would have been rereading in this period in which she was engrossed in the oeuvre of James. In this autobiographical volume the pleasures of taste, smell, and sight are exalted by the "small boy" in his visits to his relations. In spite of the fact that Wharton said in *A Backward Glance* that she did not enjoy James's late novels, *False Dawn* seems to owe something to *The Golden Bowl* (1904) and *The Outcry* (1911), James's last completed novel, for both are concerned with the art collector and with the art expert who is in advance of his time (Adam Verver is an example of the first and Hugh Crimble of the second). However, Bourget's books on art collecting might have also been models for Edith Wharton, as they were for James.

Making use of James's habit of referring to a painting well known to his readers in order to establish a character, Wharton has her young collector of the not-yet-appreciated masterpieces of Italian painters before Raphael meet the great critic of the avant-garde, John Ruskin, in an alpine location, recalling his well-known portrait painted by Millais in which he stands in front of a Scottish mountain and stream. The hero makes a trip to the small chapel in Venice in which the St. Ursula frescoes by Carpaccio show him a female type resembling his fiancée. James's hero in "The Great Good Place" describes his room as "a great square, fair chamber, all beautified with omissions . . . in which he was vaguely and pleasantly reminded of some old Italian picture, some Carpaccio or some early Tuscan."[35] A cultivated reader of the time would instantly recognize, once he had been clued in by the name of the painter, the fresco of the bedchamber in the Carpaccio series in which little St. Ursula sleeps. In *False Dawn* the ironic destiny of the marvelous masterpieces acquired by a taste too much in advance of its time reminds us of the end of *The Spoils of Poynton* where the "spoils," passing into the hands of a philistine woman, are burned through her neglect, just as the Angelico, Mantegna, and Piero della Francesca of *False Dawn* are converted by mercenary New Yorkers of the early twentieth century into pearls and Rolls Royces and are lost to the family.

The evidence of all these echoes of James's fiction in Wharton's later work on old New York points to a conscious effort on Wharton's part to write either a parallel to a James novel or one worthy of James. With attention the close reader of James can recognize in *The Age of Innocence* transpositions of important scenes or situations from his fiction. R. W. B. Lewis has suggested that Newland is really Wharton herself ("Newland" suggesting "Newbold," part of her own name),[36] but when we recollect the resemblance between the scene at the close of *The American* and the scene at the end of *The Age of Innocence,* Newland's identification with Newman, as another American also frustrated in his love for the beauty of Europe personified in a woman, seems to be more likely than his identification with Edith Wharton. At any rate, one association does not necessarily preclude the other.

One may speculate that Edith Wharton was attempting in this book to answer some of the criticism James had made about her work. Since he had early encouraged her to be "tethered" to her "back-yard," this novel tethers her.[37] Her research, with which Mrs. Cadwalader Jones helped her, involved James's own life in New York in the 1870s. Lewis tells us that writing *The Age of Innocence* was "much more than an act of a historical imagination alienated from the present hour,"[38] the aftermath of the First World War. She had written to Lapsley that "the happy few must 'get together' whenever they can and never let go again." The center of her close circle of friends had been Henry James, and one way of never letting him go again was to incorporate the artifacts of his genius in her own work, just as medieval architects (whom Wharton so deeply appreciated) incorporated pieces of ruined classical sculpture and architecture into their own structures, thereby enhancing their own appeal, offering at the same time a tribute to the quality of the antique and, incidentally, profiting from its juxtaposition. *The Age of Innocence* is homage to Henry James, and not an imitation of a Jamesian novel or tale.

REFERENCES

1. Millicent Bell, *Edith Wharton and Henry James: The Story of Their Friendship* (New York: Braziller, 1965), p. 294.

2. Cynthia Griffin Wolff, *A Feast of Words* (New York: Oxford University Press, 1977), p. 312.

3. Irving Howe, ed., *Edith Wharton: A Collection of Critical Essays* (Englewood Cliffs, N.J.: Prentice-Hall, 1962), p. 20.

4. Ibid., p. 8.

5. Ibid., p. 28.

6. R. W. B. Lewis, *Edith Wharton: A Biography* (New York: Harper & Row, 1975), p. 426.

7. Ibid., p. 426.

8. Edith Wharton, *The Collected Short Stories of Edith Wharton,* ed. R. W. B. Lewis, vol. 2 (New York: Scribner's, 1968), p. 369.

9. Edith Wharton, *A Backward Glance* (New York: Appleton-Century, 1934), pp. 182–83.

10. Henry James, *The Letters of Henry James,* ed. Percy Lubbock, vol. 1 (New York: Scribner's, 1920), 396.

11. Janet Adam Smith, ed., *Henry James and Robert Louis Stevenson* (London: Rupert Hart-Davis, 1948), p. 77.

12. Wharton, *Collected Short Stories,* 2:364.

13. See Chapter 1.

14. See Chapter 3.

15. Wharton, *Collected Short Stories,* 2:362.

16. Henry James, *The Complete Tales of Henry James,* ed. Leon Edel, vol. 11 (Philadelphia: Lippincott, 1964), p. 15.

17. Wolff, *A Feast of Words,* p. 312.

18. Ibid.

19. Bell, *Edith Wharton and Henry James,* p. 294.

20. Henry James, *The Tragic Muse* (New York: Dell Publishing Co., reprint, 1961), p. 203.

21. Adeline R. Tintner, "Hyacinth at the Play," *Journal of Narrative Technique* 2, no. 3 (September 1972): 171–85.

22. Edith Wharton, *The Age of Innocence* (New York: Scribner's, reprint, 1970), p. 63. Future references to this novel will be indicated by W plus page number.

23. Henry James, *Roderick Hudson* (Boston: Houghton Mifflin, reprint, 1977), p. 199.

24. Ibid., p. 200.

25. Henry James, *The Princess Casamassima* (New York: Harper & Row, A Perennial Classic, reprint, 1971), p. 200.

26. Ibid., p. 198.

27. Henry James, *The American* (New York and Toronto: New American Library, A Signet Classic, reprint, 1963), p. 321.

28. Henry James, *Washington Square* (New York: Crowell, reprint, 1970), p. 153.

29. James, *Complete Tales,* 12:171.

30. Ibid., 174.

31. Ibid., 167.

32. Ibid., 151.

33. Ibid., 262–65.

34. Ibid., 263.

35. See Chapter 2.

36. Lewis, *Edith Wharton,* p. 459.

37. James, *Complete Tales,* 11:33.

38. Wharton, *Collected Short Stories,* 2:424.

5

"Bad" Mothers and Daughters in the Fiction of Wharton and James

In the long list of her eighty-seven short stories,[1] Edith Wharton has only a handful that deal with mothers and daughters, and all with one exception were written after 1900. Herself a daughter but not a mother, Wharton has even fewer tales in which there is any significant relation between daughter and mother.

But the really striking fact is that in the seven stories that deal seriously with this relation, the mother shows herself to be regularly "bad" and she affects her daughter malevolently. Either she produces a daughter in her own image, an equally "bad" daughter cloned in the mother's image, or a daughter victimized by the badness of the mother.

In Wharton's first story, "Mrs. Manstey's View" (1891), the heroine has a daughter who lives far away and with whom she shares nothing in common. In "Friends" (1900) a mother is totally unconcerned with what happens to her daughter and gets upset by having her plans changed. The daughter in "April Showers" of the same year has a bad mother and a good father. This peculiar attitude to mothers and to their lack of feeling for their daughters is semantically denied by a favorite expression older women use constantly in these tales in relation to young women. This expression, "my child," remains only a locution, not a representation of fact or of feeling.

The most acute example of a bad daughter is to be found in "The Mission of Jane" (1904). The daughter here is adopted, and her repulsive personality provides a "mission," which is to bring together (in their dislike of her) a husband and wife who have become estranged. Jane is ty-

Originally published as "Mothers versus Daughters in the Fiction of Edith Wharton and Henry James," *A. B. Bookman's Weekly,* June 6, 1983, pp. 4324–29.

rannical, unmotivated by any sin except that of not being a biological daughter. The adopting mother is cleared of blame because she is not the biological mother.

How can the reader account for the striking emphasis on this relationship between mother and girl-child? Millicent, for instance, in an early story, "The Line of Least Resistance" (1900), is the bad mother who has had an affair. Her two little girls are exactly like her, spoiled and deceitful. The husband, from whose point of view the story is told, does not divorce his wife, even with the incriminating evidence he has, because of "the children," who are clearly not worth it.

In 1930, after Wharton had further developed the mother-daughter relationships and their peculiarities in three novels, *The Old Maid* (1924), *The Mother's Recompense* (1925) and *Twilight Sleep* (1927), in which the biological mothers come off very badly in her usual fashion, she does write a tale, "Roman Fever," in which she focuses on two mothers and two daughters. But the daughters never appear in the tale, and their function is that of pawns used by the mothers, who have in the past been rivals for the love of the future husband of one of them, Mrs. Slade. The latter reveals how she sent off her rival to the Coliseum with a note falsely signed by her fiancé in order to have her catch the "Roman Fever," which gives the title to the story, a title that is ironical because the two lovers met there and the passionate result was the birth of a child who becomes the brilliant débutante, while the supposed victor in this husband-chase, Mrs. Slade, produces a child who is socially colorless. That daughter is merely the offstage victim of her mother's "badness."

This tale is a strange distortion of the basic plot of Henry James's story, "The Wheel of Time" (1892), in which a father's plain daughter is likewise involved; she and her father both have to pay in a similar fashion for the relative badness of her father for having rejected a plain girl as *his* fiancée.

Wharton has one exception to this general principle, the mother and daughter in "Autre Temps . . . " of 1916. Here a divorced and disgraced mother returns to the States to visit her recently divorced daughter who, unlike herself, has been now accepted by society, for customs have changed in the intervening years. It is gradually revealed to her by the behavior of her daughter that her own conduct will never be revaluated, since she has been condemned forever by the standards of her earlier time. Here neither the mother nor the daughter is "bad" or to blame; only society is. But this seems to be the only mother-daughter story by

Wharton in which the mother is the victim, not of her daughter but of social custom. Her daughter, however, does not rise to her defense as does Rose Tramore, the young daughter of the divorced and disgraced mother in Henry James's "The Chaperon" (1891).

Daughters in Wharton's tales do not go out of their way for their mothers; it is abundantly clear they do not get along. In the period from 1904 to 1908 in "Les Metteurs en Scène" (1908) a mother and a daughter become rivals for the same suitor; the girl dies of pneumonia and the mother marries the girl's boyfriend. The role of mother-to-daughter has become transformed to the role of woman-to-woman.

The reader can attempt several explanations of this tendency. First, there are the facts revealed in Lewis's biography uncovering Wharton's hatred of her mother and her incestuous feelings for her father that emerge in the fiction, partially concealed in the later novels but revealed in the "Beatrice Palmato" fragment.[2] The antagonism to her mother is clearly shown in *Life and I*.

But there is another literary reason for this. Her early stories were greatly influenced by the stories of Henry James in whose shadow she served her apprenticeship and who was not above distinguishing between his "Good Heroine" and his "Bad Heroine."[3] Wharton's treatment of the mother–daughter theme is very much like his. In the twenty novels by James there are ten mother–daughter relationships, and except for Madame Vionnet (and the victimized mother in the short story "Fordham Castle" [1904]) every mother is bad, and, as in Wharton's tales, the daughter is either bad or a victim.

In James's one hundred and twelve short stories,[4] there are five tales concentrating on this kind of relationship. A silly mother like Mrs. Miller, who is bad in her own way, produces a daughter, like Daisy, who inherits her lack of social sense and dies because of it. In "The Pension Beaurepas" (1897) we have a savage set of bad mothers: Mrs. Ruck, the spendthrift killer of husbands, with her daughter created in her image, and Mrs. Church, the culture-vulture, who produces a daughter who schemes to get away from her mother.

There are also mothers who, bad in themselves, recognize their daughters as being worse, as in "Louisa Pallant" (1888), or a bad mother like the one in "Mrs. Temperly" (1887) who treats her daughter like a step-daughter, a "Cinderella," and prevents her from marrying because the other daughters must make good matches first. Victims both girls are, but not so cruelly victimized as those in "Europe" (1899) where the worst of the mothers keeps her daughters in a virtual prison because of her own jealously kept monopoly of European travel. One might argue that such a consistent series of bad mothers together with James's authority for the young Wharton may have struck a resonant note and reinforced a pattern fitting in so well with her own mother phobia.

There is one exception to the pattern in James's "The Chaperon" (1891). It serves as a model in reverse for Wharton's novel, *A Mother's Recompense* (1925), which turns out badly for both mother and daughter. In James's tale Rose Tramore not only successfully launches her bad mother by means of her own charm but also marries herself to a loving and protective husband. This outcome shows how James could never touch the deeper psychology of the mother-daughter drama, being neither a daughter (in spite of the quasi-daughter role Edel suggested James adopted in the late nineties) nor a mother.

Wharton did wrestle with this double role, part of which she experienced and part of which she projected herself into, in her late fiction when the struggle between mother and daughter for the father is at stake.[5]

REFERENCES

1. Edith Wharton, *The Collected Short Stories of Edith Wharton,* ed. R. W. B. Lewis, vols. 1 and 2 (New York: Scribner's, 1968). The stories referred to may be found in these volumes arranged chronologically.

2. R. W. B. Lewis, *Edith Wharton* (New York: Harper & Row, 1975), Appendix C, pp. 545–48.

3. *The Notebooks of Henry James,* ed. F. O. Matthiessen and Kenneth B. Murdock (New York: Oxford University Press, 1947), p. 140. "My Bad Heroine . . . my Good Heroine."

4. Henry James, *The Complete Tales of Henry James,* ed. Leon Edel, vols. 1–12 (Philadelphia: J. B. Lippincott, 1961–1964). The stories referred to may be found in these volumes arranged chronologically.

5. See Chapter 9.

6

Wharton and James

Some Additional Literary Give-and-Take

"Genius," says Peter Sherringham in *The Tragic Muse,* "is only the art of getting your experience fast, of stealing it, as it were,"[1] a point of view to making the most of hints from writings of others that James was quite open about all his life. In 1902 when he received from Edith Wharton's sister-in-law, Mrs. Cadwalader Jones, a copy of *Crucial Instances* (1901) and *The Touchstone* (1900) he wrote that in addition to having "extracted food for criticism from both," he always found that "If a work of imagination, of fiction interests me at all (and very few alas, do!) I always want to write it over in my own way, handle the subject from my own sense of it. *That* I always find a pleasure in, and I found it extremely in 'The Vanished Hand'. . . . I take liberties with the greatest."[2] At the moment he was taking liberties with Shakespeare (see "The Papers" as a redoing of *As You Like It*), Shakespeare who himself took liberties with the writings of others.[3] The letter to Mrs. Jones was written August 20, 1902, and James apologizes for not having answered her right away. Leon Edel has very neatly given us a schedule of what James was working on during the summer of 1902. During that time he was writing simultaneously (in addition to "The Beast in the Jungle") "The Papers" and "The Birthplace," both of which were finished by October and November.[4] "The Birthplace" shows signs of having been helped along by one of the Wharton tales in *Crucial Instances,* "The Angel at the Grave."

Both tales concern themselves with the perpetuation and care of the birthplace of a famous writer. James's is about a man who takes care of Shakespeare's birthplace but who gets so disgusted with the lies he has to

Originally published as "Wharton and James: Some Literary Give and Take," *Edith Wharton Newsletter* (Spring 1986): 3–5, 8.

tell about the origins of the Bard that he finally gives up. Although James records the "germ" in his notebooks, the development of the tale (on which he wrote sporadically in between the other tales) he may have learned from "The Angel at the Grave." The Wharton story concerns a woman's care of the birthplace of a once famous writer related to her. The detail seemingly helpful in solving James's problem was her introduction of a young man who encourages the woman caretaker to revive an interest in the now forgotten writer. James, by introducing a young American couple into "The Birthplace," Mr. and Mrs. Hayes, who appreciate what Morris Gedge, the curator, is doing in his curatorship, seems to reflect Wharton's similar intruder into the shrine in her tale. Her young man tells the lady, "Why this, you know, . . . is simply immense!" Mr. Hayes in James's tale also congratulates Gedge for " 'you renew so the interest,' " when he remarks on what Gedge has done with the paucity of material known about "The Birthplace."[5] It surely is consistent with the timetable of the writing of James's story that after having received *Crucial Instances* James got back to "The Birthplace" and rewrote Edith's story "in my own way."

But this is not the whole story. In "The Recovery," another of her tales in *Crucial Instances,* Edith shows signs of having borrowed, to redo *her* way, from James's "The Tree of Knowledge" just published in 1900 in *The Soft Side.* In both tales the wife's knowledge of her artist husband's lack of talent (a talent in which he supremely believes) is the issue, but Wharton in her version takes an independent tack. For James the point of view is that of Peter Brench, the family friend, who has been in love with the wife of the bad sculptor, Morgan, and who wishes to spare her the knowledge of the low quality of her husband's productions because he erroneously thinks she will stop loving him if she knows.

For Wharton the point of view is that of the wife, Claudia, who, after ten years of marriage to a greatly admired painter, Keniston, realizes he is a fraud, yet he, like Morgan, has complete "satisfaction" with his own "achievement." In "The Tree of Knowledge" her husband's lack of talent is no deterrent to Mrs. Mallow's love for him, and her chief aim in life is to keep him from knowing that she knows. James's tale is a remarkable exercise on the way each one of the quartet of characters learns to understand the state of affairs in regard to himself. Knowledge and its process of knowing in relation to the talents of both Morgan and his son Lance as received by each member of the family circle is the reason for the story's title. Wharton's tale, nevertheless, is an original variation on the theme, done from the viewpoint and psychology of the wife alone. It is concerned solely with Claudia's disillusionment with her husband's gifts and with her testing of his ability to see how lacking in talent he is. Unconcerned with protecting his ego, as the loving wife in James's tale is, Claudia has an obsession to measure his extreme egoism and his stupidity about himself. When exposure to the great masterpieces of European art shows him how he does not measure up to them, he plans to "stay out here till I learn how to paint" decent pictures. His wife "could have wept at his exquisite obtuseness."[6] Wharton's point is that although Keniston passes part of her test by realizing how badly his own pictures compare with great paintings, he fails the whole test by thinking he *can* learn to paint like them. Compared to James's tale of knowledge gained but concealed to protect the feelings of people who love each other, Wharton's tale shows an unpleasant woman who regulates her love for her husband according to whether or not he will face up to his inadequacy. It is Keniston we feel sorry for, not his heartless wife. Whereas James's tale is one of a good marriage, Wharton's is one of a bad marriage; it shows how the discovery of a husband's "obtuseness" in regard to his own capacities can destroy a wife's "ardor," not intensify it, for it never was really love. That "ardor" gradually spent itself against "the dense surface of her husband's complacency."[7] (Vide Edith and Teddy!)

In the same volume her playlet story, "Copy," contains two now mature writers who reenact in Edith's way the tale of a similar couple in James's "Broken Wings," which had appeared in the December issue of the *Century* (1900). James's tale is a touching one of a woman writer and an artist who, meeting at a country house weekend, confess they have avoided each other after an aborted love affair because each one thought the other was too successful to be approached. The truth is that their "wings" have been "broken" and they are failures. Recognizing this and their feeling for each other they decide to join their forces and work seriously together, without catering to the heartless society that has exploited their talents.

Again, as in "The Recovery," there is both a similarity to "Broken Wings" as well as a fundamental change in Wharton's playlet, "Copy." A woman novelist who has written "Winged Purposes" (which recalls the title of James's tale) and who has also written *Pomegranate Seed* (which Wharton herself will publish in the future) meets again her old lover, a successful poet, but, unlike the couple in James's tale, they are out to exploit their previous love affair by using their letters as "copy" for their memoirs. Their wings have not been broken, but their hearts have become hardened. It is only in a last minute memory of their previous love that they give up their plans and they burn the letters. Mrs. Dale is a woman made bitter by the loss of love, and Paul Ventnor has been made an exploiter by his success. James's story has been corrected in Wharton's way.

In "The Moving Finger" (1901) by Wharton (which James had confusedly recalled as "The Vanished Hand") is a reminder of James's stories about painters in which he presents the notion that the painted model can act as a substitute for the person himself. Written and published a few months apart in 1900, James's "The Special Type" and "The Tone of Time" both revolve around a portrait treated as a person. "The Special Type" concerns a fine woman who, used as a corespondent in a divorce case, wants to keep the portrait of the man she was servicing so that scandal would be kept from the woman he plans to marry and who does not deserve him. The picture will, for the loving corespondent, be "him," the man himself, to "make up" for her never having seen him "alone." In "The Tone of Time" a woman portrait painter executes on commission an idealized portrait of a gentleman who will stand for the buyer's deceased lover painted with the "tone" of fifty years ago.

In Wharton's version of the theme in "The Moving Finger" the portrait of the beautiful Mrs. Grancy is fought over after her death by the two men in love with her—its painter Claydon and her husband. The painter was accused of visiting Mrs. Grancy when alive only to see her portrait. For him "the portrait *was* Mrs. Grancy."[8] After her death her husband has Claydon age the portrait to keep up with his own aging. Claydon paints her as if she "knows her husband is dying," which hastens Grancy's death, after which Claydon obtains possession of the portrait. He explains his attitude to the portrait by contrasting himself with Pygmalion who "turned his statue into a real woman; *I* turned my real woman into a picture. . . . you don't know how much of a woman belongs to you after you've painted her!"[9] With her own cleverness in creating an original plot Wharton has redone the themes of the two tales by James, for in "The Special Type" the portrait of the man Mrs. Dundene loves "will be *him* for me. . . . I shall *live* with it, keep it all to myself."[10] In "The Tone of Time" like Claydon the woman painter whose love had been taken from her by the picture's purchaser sees that the latter "Unwittingly gives him back"[11] by refusing to give her the portrait.

In *The Touchstone* (1900) (in addition to the Jamesian names "Armiger" and "Touchett") one can find the traces of a dialogue from James's "The Given Case," a tale that appeared in *Collier's Weekly* at the end of December 1898. There the final words between Philip Mackern and Margaret Hamer may have had something to do with the format of the final dialogue in *The Touchstone* between Alexa Glennard and her husband who has published for money a great dead woman novelist's love letters to him. James's heroine Margaret has finally broken her engagement to her fiancé to marry Philip whom she loves, but she feels guilty about the pain she will cause the jilted man because he "trusted" her. "'But I pity him so that it kills me!'" When Philip says, "'And only him?'" he implies he should be pitied for his sufferings. "'It shall be the one you pity most.'" She responds with "'Pity *me*—pity *me!*'" And the tale ends with "it was perhaps the deepest thing in his gratitude that he did pity her."[12] At the very end of *The Touchstone* Glennard says, as he regrets his publication of Mrs. Aubyn's letters, "'Don't you see that the worst of my torture is the impossibility of such amends?'" But when Alexa pities the dead novelist, "'Ah, poor woman, poor woman'" he answers, "Don't pity her, pity me!"[13]

James, in turn, if he had perhaps read *The Touchstone* when it was first published in 1900, might have found something nutritive in its last pages for *The Wings of the Dove,* published the day after he wrote his letter of thanks to Mrs. Jones for the two books. Kate is telling Densher that, although he was not in love with Milly while she lived, he was after her death; "'she died for you then that you might understand her. From that hour you *did.* . . . And I do now. She did it for us.'"[14] Although Wharton's ending has a different significance, the presentation of a dead, betrayed woman who has transformed the character of her betrayer after her death is the same. We read in *The Touchstone,* "'Don't you see . . . that that's the gift you can't escape from . . . ? Don't you see . . . that. . . . she's made you into the man she loved? . . . *That's* worth suffering for. . . . —that's the gift she would have wished to give!'"[15] In other words, like Kate and Densher, Alexa and Glennard "'shall never be again as we were!'" (WD, 405). Their transformation anteceded Kate and Densher's, but again, we do not know whether James had read *The Touchstone* before or while writing *The Wings of the Dove.*

If the give-and-take between Wharton and James was a conscious game they played with each other (and we find reason for this possibility in *A Backward Glance*—her relish for the "forces of malice and merriment" that went into his jokes, and his love of "abstract fooling") or if it was in both of them an appetency for devouring anything that could further the machinery of their narratives, the answer may be irrelevant, for the interaction of their talents has simply enriched their fiction for those for whom it was essentially made, their readers.

REFERENCES

1. Henry James, *The Novels of Henry James,* vol. 8 (New York: Scribner's, 1908), p. 127.

2. *Henry James Letters,* ed. Leon Edel, vol. 4 (Cambridge: Harvard University Press, 1980), p. 237.

3. Adeline R. Tintner, "'The Papers': Henry James Redoes *As You Like It.*" *Studies in Short Fiction* 17, no. 2 (1980): 165–70.

4. Leon Edel, *Henry James: The Master* (Philadelphia: Lippincott, 1972), p. 128.

5. Henry James, *The Complete Tales of Henry James,* ed. Leon Edel, vol. 10 (Philadelphia: Lippincott, 1964), p. 456.

6. *The Collected Short Stories of Edith Wharton,* ed. R. W. B. Lewis, vol. 1 (New York: Scribner's, 1968), p. 274.

7. Ibid., p. 263.

8. Ibid., p. 303.

9. Ibid., p. 312.

10. James, *Complete Tales,* 10:191.

11. Ibid., p. 215.

12. Ibid., p. 380.

13. Edith Wharton, *The Touchstone* (New York: Scribner's, 1900), p. 153.

14. Henry James, *The Wings of the Dove,* vol. 2 (New York: Scribner's, 1902), p. 403.

15. Edith Wharton, *The Touchstone,* p. 253.

7
Henry James's "Julia Bride"

A Source for Chapter 9 in Edith Wharton's *The Custom of the Country*

Chapter 9 in Edith Wharton's *The Custom of the Country* (1913) bears a striking resemblance to Henry James's "Julia Bride," a tale first published in magazine form in *Harper's Monthly Magazine,* March–April 1908. Since James was Wharton's house guest in Paris from April 24 to May 9 she undoubtedly read it as a courtesy, especially since they read each other's work when it appeared. But even before that date she had written to Sara Norton that she had read it and had liked it: "Yes,—I've read Julia Bride, & found it living & vivid, and all the things *you* don't."[1] When in May Wharton sailed for the United States she continued the novel she had started six months before, "making a start on the seventh chapter."[2] Deep into her passionate affair with Morton Fullerton, she decided when she arrived at Lenox, her country home, that she could no longer stand her husband. Pulling herself together after a month of suffering she worked on her novel, which is centered on divorce, but then stopped, for the possibility of her own future divorce was at this time a distracting problem. But since Lewis tells us she did "a hard month's work in July" on the novel (L, 233) she must have finished Chapter 9. Completion of the whole novel and its serialization in *Scribner's* were delayed until 1913, the time of her own divorce with its attendant traumas, but by then "Julia Bride" had long since appeared in volume 17 of the New York Edition (which James gave her) in 1909, accompanied by his preface to the tale.

"Julia Bride" concerns a young woman's attempt to obtain guarantees of respectability from one of her mother's three divorced husbands as

Originally published in *Notes on Modern American Literature* 9 (Winter 1985), Note 16.

well as from one of her own six fiancés so that she may appear to be a suitable match for New York's most eligible bachelor, Basil French. It is part three of the tale in which Julia meets with Murray Brush (one of her ex-fiancés) in Central Park in an attempt to get him to "lie" for her, an incident that is lifted almost intact by Wharton for her Chapter 9. The unusually pretty Undine Spragg—"There's mighty few women as well worth looking at"[3]—like Julia Bride—"the prettiest girl any one had ever seen" (CT, 154)—meets her first husband, Elmer Moffatt, in Central Park in a virtually similar attempt to get him to lie for her in concealing not only their marriage but even their social acquaintance. A bargain is struck between Undine and Elmer, like the one between Julia and her ex-fiancé, where Murray will "fling" over her "the biggest kind of rose-coloured mantle" when she asks him to "lie for me like a gentleman."[4] In return she is to introduce his new fiancée and himself to the prominent Basil French for their own social advancement. "Couldn't you just simply make us meet him, at tea, say, informally; . . . and then see what we'd *make* of that?" (CT, 190). Elmer in like fashion responds to Undine's request to help her marry the equally socially prominent New Yorker, Ralph Marvell, when she pleads that "If any of his folks found out [about her first marriage] they'd never let him marry me—never! . . . And it would *kill* me, Elmer—it would just kill me!" (CC, 114), for he too suggests a bargain. "*I* ain't going to interrupt the wedding march. . . . I only just want one little promise in return. . . . if ever it should come handy to know any of 'em in a business way, would you fix it up for me—*after you're married?*" (CC, 115). Then like Julia who with "a long lonely moan of her conviction of her now certain ruin" (CT, 191) retreats to her own small room, so Undine, "with tears already on her face ("'You've been crying!'") "hoped to steal into her room." However, unlike the unlucky Julia, she is met by her passionately devoted fiancé who notices her desperation and allows her to leap at his suggestion for an immediate wedding, thus forestalling any threat to her plans.

Wharton thus changes the direction of her novel by converting the failed Julia to the successful Undine, only to expand the ironies that enrich James's short tale into a six-hundred-page novel with an ending just as ironical. Undine's first husband becomes the last and fourth husband, and although it seems as if she gets what she wants (as Julia did not), she is throughout her four marriages, one engagement, and one affair actually deprived of her desired role, in spite of the final billionaire husband. The last line reads: "She could never [as a divorced woman] be an Ambassador's wife, and . . . she said to herself that it was the one part she was really made for" (CC, 594).

The dependence of Chapter 9 on James's tale extends to the very details copied from part III of "Julia Bride." The self-arranged Central Park rendezvous of each girl reads alike. "Two days later" Julia met Murray "for he had promptly . . . replied, keeping . . . the appointment she had judged best to propose, a morning hour in a *sequestered* alley of the Park" (CT, 176) (italics mine). In *The Custom of the Country* "Undine, late the next day, waited alone under the leafless trellising of a wisteria arbour on the west side of the Central Park" (CC, 107), for the "habit of meeting young men in *sequestered* spots was not unknown to her; the novelty was in feeling any embarrassment about it" (italics mine). She remembers "similar meetings . . . with the romantic Aaronson," her riding-master (CC, 107), like Julia who was "risking . . . a recall of ancient licence in proposing to Murray such a place of meeting" (CT, 176). Just as Julia does not expect to meet Basil French in the Park because she never had a rendezvous with him there—"Mr. French, by good luck, had never been with her in the Park" (CT, 177)—so Undine knew there was an "unlikely chance of an accidental encounter with Ralph Marvell" (CC, 107), the rich and socially well-placed young man Undine wants to marry. As Murray Brush "isn't a gentleman" (CT, 170), so also "in the Marvell set Elmer Moffatt would have been stamped as 'not a gentleman'" (CC, 108). Like Murray Brush, in "his form of being more civilized" (CT, 178), Elmer also is changed "and Undine's heart sank at the thought of what the change implied" (CC, 108). As Murray now has a "new superiority" (CT, 181), so does Elmer, for his look that "had formerly denoted a somewhat desperate defiance of the world and its judgments, . . . now suggested an almost assured relation to these powers" (CC, 108). As Julia depends on Murray "for the innocence it was actually vital she should establish" (CT, 181), so too Undine depends on Elmer to keep the pact that no one in the Marvell family is "to know anything" about her connection with Elmer. She wanted to "wring from him some definite pledge of safety" (CC, 115). Almost the same word and the same concept had appeared in James's tale when Murray Brush appeared to Julia as a "ledge of safety" (CT, 185). As Murray patronizingly twice calls Julia "my dear child," so Elmer refers to Undine as the popularly known "child-bride," illustrating the Jamesian echoes in Wharton's language and in the picture of her heroine. Elmer's recalling to Undine her engagement to Millard Binch seems simply another reminder of James's tale through the similarity of Undine's former fiancé's name to that of Julia's former fiancé, Murray Brush.

The clue to this expansion of the basic situation in "Julia Bride" can be found in James's preface to his tale. He had admitted that his Julia is "foreshortened . . . to within an inch of her life; but I judge her life still saved and . . . its depicted full fusion with other lives that remain undepicted, not lost. Those other lives . . . press in . . . but, restricted as the whole thing is to implications and involutions only, they prevail at best by indirectness" (AN, 263). About Julia he wrote: "I really didn't take her for particularly important in herself . . . and would in fact have had no heart for her without the note . . . of multitudinous reference."[5] Julia's "case might lose itself promptly enough in a complexus of larger and stranger cases—even in the very air, by what seemed to promise, of the largest possibilities of comedy" (AN, 263–64).

Wharton's long novel may be considered, therefore, a fulfillment of this promise and an answer to James's question as to Julia's possibilities: "What if she were the silver key, tiny in itself, that would unlock a treasure?—the treasure of a whole view of manners and morals, a whole range of American social aspects?" (AN, 264).

His final word in the preface probably gave Wharton her artistic sanction for redoing his tale. Using the figure of a recipe for making a broth, James describes his creating the tale as if he were a cook, working in "a tablespoon of the due display of responsible consciousness," although he suspected that the outcome would promise "a much stronger broth . . . than I had engaged to prepare" (AN, 265). "The fumes . . . were the gage . . . of twenty more ingredients than I had consciously put in; and this means . . . I make out a residuum of admirable rich 'stock' which . . . must again certainly serve." Since James never himself used this rich stock again, by 1913 Wharton would view it as nutritive for herself. *The Custom of the Country* can be considered an amplification of James's metaphor by her own narrative mixture. Undine develops from being a victim like Julia into a conqueror who nevertheless is defeated by the same type of social irony.

This use by Wharton of a story by James provides some material for answering the constantly debated point of whether and how Wharton used James. It may also shed light on what he said to Wharton about her novel. " 'But of course you know . . . that in doing your tale you had under your hand a magnificent subject, which ought to have been your main theme, and that you used it as a mere incident and then passed it by?'"[6] "He meant by this," she claims, "that for him the chief interest of the book, and its most original theme, was that of a crude young woman, such as Undine Spragg, entering, all unprepared and unperceiving, into the mysterious labyrinth of family life in the old French aristocracy." She explained to James that her "task was to record her ravages and pass on to her next phase." She continues, "he could merely answer, by implication if not openly: 'Then, my dear child, you chose the wrong kind of subject'" (BG, 183). In the light of the insertion of some elements from "Julia Bride" into Chapter 9 of *The Custom of the Country* we may wonder whether it was not the subject of the much engaged and much divorced American woman that James wanted her to focus on, rather than the French episode, especially since he suggested a decade earlier that she "*must* be tethered in native pastures."[7]

However, in "The New Novel," when discussing Wharton's *The Custom of the Country,* James, to avoid offending Wharton, wrote "with *worlds* between the lines" as he had once defended in a letter to Fullerton his hypocrisy in praising Mrs. Ward's novels.[8] In "The New Novel" he judged *The Custom* as "almost scientifically satiric, and indeed the satiric light was doubtless the only one in which the elements engaged could at all be focused together." It is the "dry light" that creates "an effect of a particular fine asperity."[9] He seems to be saying in his characteristically cautious way when dealing with his friends' fiction that it is the authorial dryness that saves the book from being just a series of satiric episodes.

REFERENCES

1. *The Letters of Edith Wharton,* ed. R. W. B. Lewis and Nancy Lewis (New York: Scribner's, 1988), p. 140. Future references are indicated by LW and page number.

2. R. W. B. Lewis, *Edith Wharton: A Biography* (New York: Harper & Row, 1975), 233. Future references are indicated by L plus page number.

3. Edith Wharton, *The Custom of the Country* (New York: Scribner's, 1913), 109. Future references are indicated by CC and page number.

4. *The Complete Tales of Henry James,* ed. Leon Edel, vol. 12 (Philadelphia: Lippincott, 1964), p. 184. Future references are indicated by CT and page number.

5. Henry James, *The Art of the Novel,* ed. R. P. Blackmur (New York: Scribner's, 1934), p. 263. Future references are indicated by AN and page number.

6. Edith Wharton, *A Backward Glance* (New York: Appleton-Century, 1934), p. 182. Future references are indicated by BG and page number.

7. *Henry James Letters,* ed. Leon Edel, vol. 4 (Cambridge: Harvard University Press, 1980), p. 237.

8. *Henry James Letters,* ed. Leon Edel, vol. 3 (Cambridge: Harvard University Press, 1980), p. 405.

9. Henry James, *Literary Criticism: Essays on Literature: American Writers-English Writers* (New York: Library of America, 1984), p. 338. Future references are indicated by LC and page number.

PART TWO
Wharton and Others

8

Edith Wharton and Paul Bourget

Literary Exchanges

These remarks on Edith Wharton and Paul Bourget are based on seren-dipitous findings. While I was reading Bourget's fiction for other reasons, I was struck by signs of Edith Wharton appearing in one way or another, even though I was looking for something else. A good introduction to the personal relationship between Edith Wharton and Paul Bourget can best be found in her article *Souvenirs de Bourget d'Outre-mer* in 1936 af-ter Bourget's death in 1935. She remembers how excited she was when Bourget arrived at Newport in 1893 with his bride Minnie with an in-troduction for the Whartons from Teddy Wharton's relation, Henry Ridgway. Bourget was the first distinguished writer whom she had ever met, who, two years later, would become one of the youngest members of the French Academy. *Outre-mer,* the book Bourget wrote in 1895, after his trip, records, as we all suppose, his impression of Edith Wharton, al-though unnamed, the "intellectual tomboy" who "ordered her intellect somewhere as we would order a piece of furniture, to measure, with as many compartments as there are branches of human knowledge . . . may she make a blunder! in vain. A mind may be mistaken, a mind may be ignorant, but never a thinking machine!" This rather tough estimate changed when, in 1899 and 1900, the Whartons visited the Bourgets in Italy.

In *her* essay of 1936, Edith Wharton speaks about the technical ideas of Bourget. "They were completely opposed to mine. Having discovered that our theories did not agree, we made the wise resolution never to

Originally published in *The Edith Wharton Review* 8, no. 1 (Spring 1991): 16–18. Included are the author's translations of Wharton's essay on Bourget and Bourget's preface to Charles Du Bos's translation in French of *The House of Mirth.*

speak of our respective works but in revenge we never tired of relating to each other the subjects of our future books. The irony and sadness of a human life were both envisaged in the same manner. Each incident furnished for us, for him as well as for me, a new *donnée,* and we passed hours telling each other about them."

We see the result of these hours swapping *données* or ideas, for there seems to have been a kind of mutually penetrating interplay of texts during 1900–1908, the period of their most intense friendship. Edith Wharton published her playlet "Copy" in *Scribner's* in June of 1900 before Bourget wrote a story called "Le Dernier Poésie" in November of 1900. He always dated his work so we know when it was written, and he seemed to have read all the American periodicals. There is a curious similarity between both. Her story, as I have already indicated, is about a man and a woman, he a great poet and she a great novelist. The man comes to the woman to get back the love letters he sent to her years ago so he can use them for his memoirs, as she plans to do with his letters to her. At the end, they both decide that the whole idea to capitalize on their love affair was a mistake. It is presented from the woman's point of view. Bourget handles the story differently in "Le Dernier Poésie," but the plot is basically the same. His famous writer goes back to visit a young woman to whom he wrote love poems many years ago for he needs them for his memoirs. But finding her an overworked, little bourgeois housewife with children, his heart is touched and he gives up the idea. It clearly has the same plot as "Copy" but done in the context of French life, and by a repentant "male chauvinist," as some might call him today.

During this time, Edith Wharton, Bourget, and Henry James were writing stories based on similar themes, as if they were all taking a writing course and a teacher told them to write a story on a specific theme, each one doing it differently.

In 1901, in a collection of short stories called *Monique,* Bourget dedicated the title tale to Edith Wharton and one can see when one reads "Monique" why he did so. Edith had published her *Decoration of Houses,* with Codman, in 1897, and Bourget saw her at this time as an expert on fine furniture. In "Monique," he invents a character, Hippolyte Franquetot, who repaired fine pieces of eighteenth-century furniture with a true artist's genius. And then Bourget gives an essay on all the great furniture makers of that period—Riesener, Boulle, and Cressent—to show Mrs. Wharton that he too was knowledgeable. This was part of his character, which James called his "omnivorism," and Monique is the name of a little girl whom Hippolyte trained to carry on his artistic expertise in the tale.

In 1903, Bourget writes a story called "Le Portrait," clearly based on Edith's "The Moving Finger." As we have already seen, in Mrs. Wharton's tale, the painter Claydon, in love with Mrs. Grancy, is forced by her husband after her death to paint her as aging. In revenge, the painter paints in her eyes the message that her husband is dying and, getting the message, her husband does die. But the painter disavows any responsibility for this. "She had a message for him," he said, "and she made *me* deliver it." Bourget's tale, "The Portrait," concerns a painter who has been having an affair (and the concealed attachment is Bourget's specialty) with a married woman who, because he has thrown her over to become engaged to a rich American woman, then commits suicide by taking an overdose of chloryl. His fiancée, Mrs. Alice Gray, sees the portrait and then breaks off her engagement to the painter. Why? Because she read the message in the dead woman's eyes that she had killed herself for love of the painter. "You have put your remorse" for her death, she tells him, "in her eye." Clearly the message in Mrs. Grancy's eyes appears once more.

But to reinforce his indebtedness to Mrs. Wharton for her idea, if not for her treatment, it seems he put into the figure of the rich American fiancée certain recognizable features of Mrs. Wharton herself. Mrs. Alice Gray is American, rich; she drives around in an automobile, wears marvelous clothes, and has a taste for eighteenth-century furniture. She is clever and independent in mind. Surely this is Edith. Then, in 1905, Mrs. Wharton does a little dipping into Bourget. She shows that in *The House of Mirth,* her first novel, she has availed herself of fictional structures from two of Bourget's novels. One is from *L'Idylle Tragique,* 1896, the presentation copy of which one finds in Maggs's list of her library. This cosmopolitan novel is about a *femme du monde,* Ely de Carlsberg, married to a cruel archduke but having affairs serially with two best friends. But what I want to call attention to is that the main setting is on a yacht owned by Dickie Marsh, a financier and entrepreneur from Marionville, Ohio. He and his niece Florence, or Flossie, Marsh, are the only Americans on board where there is a pair of lovers, Andreana Bonnacorsia and the Vicomte de Corancez. But since Andreana's brother is against their marriage, they are supposed to be living in sin. However, they have been married secretly in the chapel of the Fregozo palace, although word has gone round that Flossie was an accomplice in a rendezvous between illicit lovers. Therefore, her fiancé, Verdier, begs off his engagement to her. Then Ely becomes a heroine since she tells the archduke and Verdier, armed with a letter as a document and with herself as a witness, that Andreana was respectably married. Flossie's fiancé is consoled, and it all ends happily for them.

What Edith Wharton does is to make a yachting party also the central crisis for *The House of Mirth* from which point Lily Bart's luck changes for the worse. In her yachting society, in her case made up of Americans, there is also a Bertha (a "Berthe" had appeared in the Bourget novel) who becomes the villainess of the tale, Bertha Dorset. Mrs. Wharton, though, has developed her plot further from the point which Bourget makes. In his novel, a young woman has her reputation tarnished for marriage if she is a guest on a yacht that shelters an affair. Mrs. Wharton's point enriches the plot. In her novel, the really guilty Bertha Dorset turns the tables on Lily and implies by a very clever maneuver that Lily was the lover of Bertha's husband.

Selden, whose warning Lily had not taken to get off the yacht, is himself a character based on another novel by Bourget, the very widely read *Cosmopolis* of 1893. Not only is he like the passive hero, Julien Dorsenne, but Selden's relation to Lily is very much like Dorsenne's relation to Alba Steno, the young girl who wants him to marry her to take her away from her mother's immoral cosmopolitan circle. He resists her appeal and she commits suicide. Like Lily's suicide, hers is also equivocal. She exposes herself to marsh fever and does not die until a protracted illness from the exposure kills her. However, Mrs. Wharton gives Selden dimensions and a depth of feeling we do not meet in Bourget's hero, who is a pedantic writer, a "restless analyst." And Mrs. Wharton is not guilty of one of Bourget's besetting sins, as she explains well in her memorial essay. "Bourget used to complain often to me that in my books I did not explain the characters enough and I answered that he underestimated the intelligence of his readers in supposing that he had to dissect in advance the motive power of every act, almost of each word, instead of allowing it to reveal itself by the words and actions of the characters."

Mrs. Wharton arrived in 1905 in Paris as a huge success after *The House of Mirth*'s phenomenal sales. Bourget then launched her in his exalted social circle of the Faubourg St. Germain. When Charles Du Bos's translation of *The House of Mirth* called *Chez les heureux du monde* was published, it appeared with a preface by Bourget that is a first-rate critical piece for Wharton's book. Bourget explains that *The House of Mirth* is a study of high life in the United States about which Mrs. Wharton, born and living among these self-appointed aristocrats, is an expert. The book had already become a best-seller in the United States, and the chief reason for this lies in the fact that in "this strange civilization" there are two seemingly irreconcilable characteristics. The first is that everything here breathes the spirit of equality; the second is that the differences in the social distinctions there are more implacably demarcated than in any European country. "If you take a walk in Central Park, you are struck by the appearance of the strollers whose clothing seems to indicate a minimum of differences in the manner of get-up. If you go on a train and it isn't a Pullman, you would swear there was only one class and all travelers belong to it, from the millionaire to the lowest employee." But "no prince of the Italian Renaissance has indulged his fantasies as the oil magnate does in his ball in New York hotels and his wife has a bigger budget than a princess royal. This is where the almighty Dollar [these words are in English] rules." One must understand the secret logic of the surprising paradox if one wants to understand the worldly life in the United States of America, and *The House of Mirth* is "the best key to this enigma," which explains the success of the novel. This aristocracy is open to all who have money and, in that, it is democratic, but you are not allowed to lose your money in this society. If you do, you are ruined, and ruined people must be ejected, for money rules.

Mrs. Wharton's memorial essay on Bourget in 1936 takes off, in a sense, from where Bourget left off in his preface to the translation of her first novel. She explains the structure of her aristocratic American background to the French reader and goes from that to Bourget, who is fixed on a worldly life and has tremendous respect for the cosmopolitan titled world to which he devoted his fictional canvas. She reviews her long friendship with him. She describes his growing rigidity of ideas and loss of an earlier wit and expertise at "talk" as he ages. It is a fine estimate of what was admirable in his character and personality. We see from the essay what a brilliant and engaging figure he was and why she continued to be his friend, even after his nationalistic and proto-fascist attitudes made him insupportable to others, among them Henry James. She tells us that his anti-Dreyfusard position was due, not to anti-Semitism, but to a disbelief that the French army could do any wrong. The essay was a final coda to a friendship of forty years, a relationship that was reflected in the work of both. Whether or not Mrs. Wharton made a portrait of Paul Bourget in Paul Ventnor, the great poet of "Copy," a tale that reflects their fondness for each other yet preserves their independent points of view, we see in Bourget inarguable signs that Edith Wharton lent her personality to one, if not two, characters in his stories and her plots to at least two of his tales. This section does no more than touch the tip of the iceberg. The whole of their friendship and how it affected their work, can no longer be ignored by Wharton scholarship.

9

The Portrait of Edith in Bourget's "L'Indicatrice"

A further interplay between the two authors became apparent when I read Bourget's *nouvelle, Les Détours du Coeur* (a form in which he was an acknowledged master). In that volume, I came across a tale, "L'Indicatrice" (1905), in which the main character, a rich American woman staying in a hotel in Paris, is the prey of a young thief.[1] His mistress, the temporary maid of the American, is to coordinate the plan to rob her employer of her valuable jewels, chief among them pearls. The maid, who has been brutally treated by her lover, is so impressed by the goodness of her employer that she reveals the plan to her and they both avert the disaster. The American lady wants the young woman to go back to America with her, but, at the last minute, she decides to stay with her lover, for she is incapable of leaving him. As the story proceeds it becomes clear that the American woman is a portrait of Edith Wharton created by the French novelist and essayist who, at this time, 1905, had renewed and made permanent his earlier friendship with Mrs. Wharton formed when he had visited the States in 1893 to write his book *Outre-mer.*

These are the telling details. When Adele, the young woman posing as a maid in order to be an informer or "indicatrice" (a "finger" woman for Jules Bélière, her lover-thief), enters the Hotel Beausite where Mrs. Edith (sic!) Risley is stretched out on a chaise lounge, we are treated to a full description of the interior and its creator. "She had during this winter transformed her hotel suite into a kind of 'home' " ("transformée en une espèce de *home*") (DC, 210). "All the things around her carry the imprint of her gracious personality whose charm would alone have

Originally published in *The Edith Wharton Review* 7, no. 1 (Spring 1991): 10–12.

explained why the confederate of Bélière had hesitated so many weeks" to start the plans for the robbery. "Edith was one of these Americans who seem to carry over to the area of refinement that strong will that the men of their country carry over into the area of money-making. There were in the *salon* bits of antique material spread over pieces of furniture, and chic bibelots placed on tables. Orchids bloomed in vases. Two paintings, one by Maes representing a little girl eating a wafer near her cat, the other a halberdier by Bronzino, were placed on two easels. The mistress of this improvised sanctuary had fought over them with cheques as ammunition in a resounding auction sale a few days before. Books in English and German, Italian and French, abounded in the library. This other sign attested to the cosmopolitanism of this exquisite creature whose fragile beauty was as if devoured by an excess of intelligence and sensibility." Edith Risley, the substitute for Edith Wharton, had very pale ash blond hair. "She had eyes of a clear brown, and a complexion of a flower, scarcely colored and of a delicate shade. In her dressing gown, of a supple lavender silk trimmed with lace, with the slenderness of her figure, her frail arms appearing from the light loose sleeves, her hands with their tapering fingers and her slender feet, she resembled one of the infantas of the Prado Museum. Although one has mocked, and rightly so, certain Americans for their ancestral snobbery, it is no less true that a great number of them seem just as smitten with less democratic atavisms. Edith was a member of the Van Alstyn family. She was descended from an *emigré* originally from the low countries in the seventeenth century who passed for a bastard of one of the last Spanish governors. Edith's friends, all of whom had, in the classic manner of Yankee millionaires, galleries crammed with more or less authentic masterpieces, called her *The Velasquéz*. She was also, in spite of the advantages of a too full existence, or perhaps because of it, one of those women one finds overseas who wants everyone around her also to be spoiled, also to lead a full life, so that she becomes profoundly, intimately kind. It signifies a goodness, a benevolence always active, going for important little things . . . which creates above all an atmosphere of sweetness. This grace of the heart has been—O irony!—the cause for Mrs. Risley's having chosen the mistress of the Apache [the thief] to work for her. Her usual maid, a German woman, in her service for ten years, had been called away . . . Mrs. Risley had hastily chosen a replacement, and had picked Adele at first sight under the pseudonym of Aurélie Brissaud. 'I believe it is sympathy or antipathy', she said, 'and I yield blindly'" (DC, 212).

Mrs. Risley was supposed to have visited her old governess, and the robbery was to have taken place while she was out. Mrs. Risley wants Adele to come back with her to the United States since she pleases her so. Adele feels guilty about this and tells Mrs. Risley, who has been so kind to her, about the planned robbery. At that moment there is a turning of the knob of the door. Adele tells Mrs. Risley to speak out and the latter says, " 'Who is there?' " "She found herself again the daughter of a race of energy in the presence of a real danger." She tells Adele, " 'You have saved me from this man and I will save you in my turn. You will come with me to America, change your name, and he will not follow you.' " But the next day she reads a note from Adele telling her she has gone back to her lover. She asks Mrs. Risley to pack her trunk and to include a photograph of herself. "She put in her portrait, in an envelope, five bills of a thousand francs each. Those who know her will recognize that trait, but will they recognize the finger girl of thieves, the mistress of a professional Apache, in this other trait? For Adele sent back the 5,000 francs in the same envelope. This disinterestedness in such degradation . . . together perhaps with remorse, rendered insupportable a crime committed against a benefactress" (DC, 214).

Before 1906, when she began her rental of the first rue de Varenne apartment, Edith Wharton stayed at hotels as Mrs. Risley did in the story. Her benevolent tyranny over the objects in the hotel suite was well known, so the fact that the whole apartment "carried the imprint of her gracious personality" is a trait in her Bourget recognizes when he gives to her the same dominant "will" found in the workers in Wall Street. Her money allowed her to outbid all others in any sale or auction in which she had an interest, as Mrs. Risley did. Nicolas Maes has been chosen as an artist to represent the Dutch School in which maids and servants are treated with compassion and tenderness, and Bronzino is chosen to show Mrs. Risley's, like Edith's, taste in a painting appreciated only by the *cognescenti* in 1905. Edith was considered *the* cosmopolitan figure in American society, with her international education as a child, her international travels as an adult, and the leisure which she did not waste but combined with it a working career as a novelist and short story writer. The books in Mrs. Risley's library in her hotel apartment ("English and German, Italian and French") attest to this cosmopolitanism, as does a peek into Wharton's own library. Her hair is of the right color, although Wharton seems to have been more "russet-gold."[2] The Rhinelanders, Edith's family, were Huguenot émigrés, according to Lewis (L, 10). Mrs.

Risley's forebears are the Van Alstyns, a name which Wharton had used for some of her characters, descended from a Spanish governor of the Netherlands. We know that Wharton had "brown skin" as reported by Theodora Bosanquet, James's amanuensis, who also attested to her "fairish-bright hazel eyes,"[3] that is, brown, agreeing with "clear brown" here. Her skin, Bosanquet repeated later, was "browny-yellow" (M, 540). This brown and dark complexion may have made the Spanish connection a reasonable fiction for Bourget to apply to Wharton. Charles Du Bos records that Bourget calls her *le Velásquéz*.[4] The attention to Mrs. Risley's kindness refers to that trait everyone recognized in Edith Wharton. Just at this time she was negotiating with Scribner's to bring out an American edition of Howard Sturgis's *Belchamber,* and her monetary kindnesses to Fullerton and James are well known, so that the 5,000 francs Mrs. Risley puts into the envelope for Adele, her maid, amounted to a customary gesture of Edith Wharton's; as Bourget writes "those who know her will recognize her traits." Muller, the German maid of ten years in Mrs. Risley's service, surely stands for Gross, Edith's maid, also German, who was with her until her death. Wharton's dressing gowns with sleeves that revealed her good arms seemed to be always in the range of pink or lilac. Bosanquet describes visiting her at her hotel, dressed in "a very elegant pink negligée wearing her cap of ecru lace trimmed with fur." She wrote, "her arms are very much displayed, coming from very beautiful frills of sleeves, and they were good arms . . . just the right plumpness and ending up in hands most beautifully manicured" (M, 540). "I believe in sympathy or antipathy" is a characteristic the reader of Edith Wharton's letters will recognize as a truth about her personality, and the description of her fictional *alter ego*'s wish to have "'everyone around her to also be spoiled, to also lead a good life'" as she was leading one, "'again signifies a goodness . . . going from important to little things.'" This portrait of Edith is a kind of recompense for Bourget's earlier portrait which everyone assumes was that of Edith based on the three weeks he saw much of her at Newport in 1892 where, in *Outre-mer,* he describes the "American intellectual tomboy." Over ten years later he has learned to appreciate her humanity, her kindness, and her generosity, characteristics that dominate her portrait in this story.

After building up my case to show that the character of Edith Risley is really a portrait of Edith Wharton, I was pleased to find, in reading Charles Du Bos's letter to Percy Lubbock included in his *Portrait of Edith Wharton,* this passage: "It must have been about the same time that

Bourget wrote a short *nouvelle,* of which the title now escapes me—you must remember that I am writing here far from all my books: the *nouvelle* was not much, but Bourget himself told me that he had thought of Edith in writing it: it bore upon the relation of a rich American woman with her maid, who had become the accomplice of a robbery at her expense, and it had at least the merit of bringing out most accurately that side of Edith's character which struck all who knew her—her inexhaustible and delicate kindness, understanding, pity and mercy for those who were in any way dependent upon her" (PEW, 98). We now have Bourget's word for it. What I have done is to identify the story and to spell out for the first time the actual parallels between the two Ediths and the details of the plot. The story contains so accurate a picture of Edith Wharton that one recognizes it without having Bourget's admission that he planned her to be the model behind his character. Unlike Henry James, whose transformations of Edith into his fictional characters are more acidulous,[5] Bourget's Mrs. Risley is an act of pure homage to his model.

REFERENCES

1. "Indicatrice," a tale included in the collection of short stories by Paul Bourget, *Les Détours du Coeur,* n.d. [1908?]; this story is dated 1905. Future references are indicated by DC and page number. My translation from the French.

2. R. W. B. Lewis, *Edith Wharton: A Biography* (New York: Harper & Row, 1975), p. 92. Future references are indicated by L and page number.

3. Leon Edel, *Henry James: The Master* (Philadelphia: Lippincott, 1972), p. 365. Future references are indicated by M and page number.

4. Percy Lubbock, *Portrait of Edith Wharton* (New York: Appleton-Century, 1947), p. 97. Future references are indicated by PEW and page number.

5. See my "The Metamorphoses of Edith Wharton in Henry James's *The Finer Grain,*" *Twentieth Century Literature* 21, no. 4 (December 1975): 355–81, or chapter 3.

10

MADAME DE TREYMES *Corrects Bourget's*
UN DIVORCE

The Whartons went to Paris on March 10, 1906, and stayed at the Hotel Domenici, which may have been the setting for "L'Indicatrice." During that period for a number of weeks, Bourget came over to the hotel with his aristocratic and intellectual friends, among whom were Anna de Noailles and Charles Du Bos, a young man now given Wharton's *The House of Mirth* to translate into French. In August of 1906, *Scribner's Magazine* published *Madame de Treymes.*

Considering how close Edith Wharton was to Paul Bourget at this time, while she was writing this novel in the midst of his French aristocratic social life, *Madame de Treymes* seems a correction of and a rewriting of his novel, *Un Divorce* (1904). When Bourget's book came out, Henry James wrote to Edith Wharton, "It is a subject so fraught with possible interest—nay rapture—on the whole, . . . The strange thing is that *any* dramatic interest survives it. But sometimes it doesn't, alas, at all! In this last, *Un Divorce,* it quite remarkably *does.* It does, however; it is his best thing since long—in spite, too, of the so large mechanical element." He criticizes Bourget for having "put the cart of the conclusion before the horse of the presentation which is one of the oddest intellectual helpnesses I have ever known—especially in a man who still has as *much* as B[ouget] has."[1] James wrote to Wharton about this book when it appeared, and it is unfortunate that he burned her letters, which may have revealed a discussion of it. On November 17, 1906, he warned her, "Don't go in too much for the French or the 'Franco-American' subject—the real field of your extension is *here*—it has far more fusability [*sic*] with *our* nature and primary material; between which & French elements there is, I hold, a disparity as complete as between a life led in trees, say, & a life led in—sea-depths, or in other words between that of climbers & swimmers—or (crudely) that of monkeys & fish" (*EW & HJ*, 67). We know from his comments that she was working on her novella during the period of the two months when she lived in proximity to the Bourgets and that the subject was really French even though its two major participants were American.

Bourget's novel, *Un Divorce,* is a long book of 363 pages, each of whose ten chapters is logically named in regard to the matter it presents.[2] That Edith's short book should also be divided into ten chapters is a little startling because the entire novelette occupies only fifty-nine pages in the Library of America edition. However, it seems to be a clue to the reader to see this numbering of chapters as a parody of the chapters separating the lengthy, repetitive, and didactic prose of Bourget. However, in spite of his wordiness, which Edith Wharton herself never liked, there is a very logical presentation of this particular divorce case, a presentation that shows how divorce for the Catholic French ends up not as freedom but as a prison for the applicant. In like manner, the plot of *Madame de Treymes* shows how a non-Catholic American married to a Catholic Frenchman also ends up in a metaphorical prison.[3] Divorce for heroines of both end in disaster, but for different reasons.

Let us begin first with the Bourget novel. In Chapter One, named "An Inextricable Difficulty," the heroine, Gabrielle Darras, is asking the advice of a famous priest-mathematician, Father Euvrard, to solve her dilemma. She has had a civil divorce many years ago from her first husband by whom she has a grown-up son. Her problem is that her daughter by her second husband (a freethinker, but one who has allowed her to be brought up as a Catholic) is going to have communion, and her mother wants to share it with her, for she has actually regained her faith. She is told that an annulment of her first marriage is impossible.

In Chapter Two, called "A Stepfather," Darras hears that the girl his stepson Lucien is in love with, Bertha, a medical student, has had an illegitimate child by a previous lover. Lucien confronts her with this information, which he has learned from his stepfather and which he wishes is false, but Bertha explains that it is true. She makes clear that she has been treated abominably by the young man with whom she thought she was having a free and loving relationship, since she herself does not believe in marriage.

Each chapter involves a further complication in the situation where a woman, like Gabrielle, who has obtained a civil divorce, finds religion once more and wishes to be received by the Church. Chiefly, she wishes that her daughter, who in the Church's eyes is illegitimate, be properly received also.

In the next section, Lucien asks permission from his mother to marry Bertha, but she refuses, confessing to her husband that she cannot condone the nonreligious elements in the marriage and that she cannot accept her own civil marriage with her second husband ("we are not married!") since she has regained her religion. Each chapter concerns itself with a new revelation. In the next, Gabrielle admits that she has seen Father Euvrard, and in the following one, we learn that Lucien's biological father, M. Chambault, wishes to grant permission for Lucien, who is underage, to marry Bertha, but that he is on his deathbed and may not live to grant it. The stepfather, Darras, goes to see Lucien's father. But since the latter does die, his permission for Lucien's marriage is invalid and the mother refuses to give it to her son. However, Darras's sense of justice makes him admire Bertha, whom he realizes is not what gossip would have one believe, but someone who shares his scientific attitude toward life.

In Chapter Ten, "The Prison," Gabrielle begs her husband to be married to her in a religious ceremony, since her first husband is now dead. This is a hypocritical action he will not accept. She threatens to leave him. He says that if she goes, "I shall keep our daughter." He reminds her that when she engaged "to become my wife, . . . I on my part engaged that if we had a child I would consent to its being baptized and brought up in the Catholic faith. You are now pleased to denounce the agreement. So be it. . . . You say you are not my wife? You speak of going away? So be it. But I am free again of my engagement. I take Jeanne back. She belongs to me. The code gives her to me. The agreement is cancelled, so I educate her after my own ideas" (D, 329). When he comes back from his office that night, he finds that Gabrielle has left their house and has taken Jeanne with her. When he gets a summons from Father Euvrard to visit him, he tries to put the case before him. However, when his wife finally returns to him, he is so happy he figures that once they live together again some kind of compromise with the forms of Catholicism will be reached by himself in time.

Bourget himself was clearly against divorce and believed in the Catholic supremacy of the family. He had behind him a history of scientific free thought, yet he also had his Catholic upbringing, which would, at the end of his life, dominate. He puts the kind of conflict he had within himself very convincingly into the arguments of the freethinking father and, typical of Bourget's method, presents his own authorial comment on them: "By this sophistical argument, he sought to quiet a scruple which was bound up with the sum total of his social ideas, which was singularly contradictory, as happens with moralists of his type who combine concern for the general good with the principles of complete anarchical individualism" (D, 341). He continued "to vex his heart with regrets and his mind with uncertainties" (D, 342). The novel is chiefly a dialogue between the husband and the wife.

At the end of Bourget's novel, Father Euvrard says that Albert Darras is a man of "absolute honesty" (D, 358). But Darras is lost by "his proficiency in science, whose misdirected energies are one of the great failings of our age" (D, 359). "He has never verified his religious prejudices. . . . I hope he will." Bourget, after so many pages, feels he must restate the case in the Father's advice to Gabrielle: "it is not so easy to escape from certain paths. Divorce is one of these paths. You are its captive, even now when it makes you shudder and when you have beheld all its fatal consequences. . . . The rule is absolute: you are not married to this man. . . . If you do not go back, no more religious education for the child. . . . and you, if you return? Ah, it is to prison, to prison" (D, 360).

As for Gabrielle, "feeling herself the prisoner of this divorce . . . [she] cursed once more the impious law, to whose seductions her feminine weakness had succumbed. Destructive of family life, subversive of religion, the source of anarchy and revolution, this law had promised her freedom and happiness, and all she found, like so many of her sisters, was captivity and wretchedness" (D, 363). This is how the novel ends, with an unnecessary summation typical of Bourget's didactic supererogation.

The conflict within Monsieur Darras and within Bourget himself is reflected in the character of Madame de Treymes in Wharton's novella. It is a dialogue chiefly between Madame de Treymes and John Durham, Fanny de Malrive's lover. Edith Wharton's response to the Bourget novel is that she makes the problem the same as Bourget's. The crux of the matter is the upbringing and education of a child of a marriage in which a divorce is desired.

But her changes are these. The chief potential victims of this divorce are two Americans: one is Fanny de Malrive, who is married to a French aristocrat but who is now being courted, after a separation from her husband, by another American, John Durham. One of the requirements of the separation from her husband is that she must live in France because of her son. Not a Catholic herself, she has enjoyed meeting Durham's mother and sister because of their Americanisms. In the next short chapter of six pages, Durham, her suitor, says that when her son is grown up she can leave him, since she will not be important to him. But she says she will want the boy always. The only member of the French family who is sympathetic to her desire to remarry (and therefore to her need of a divorce) is her sister-in-law, Madame de Treymes. But the latter tells Durham that it is fruitless for Fanny to ask for a divorce, so he says that he himself will try to obtain it for her.

The next two chapters, the center of the book, describe the meetings of Durham with Fanny's sister-in-law, Christine de Treymes. His friends tell him that Madame de Treymes is also unhappily married and in love with the Prince d'Armillac for whom she has sold her jewels to pay for his gambling debts. In Chapter Six, Madame de Treymes tells Durham that "my family will not hear of the divorce," but, if he should lend her a large sum of money, she will try to convince them. "She was ready to sell her influence." She tells him after he refuses to do so that he can tell Fanny how she has tried to blackmail him. However, he does not tell Fanny.

In Chapter Seven, Madame de Treymes informs Durham that Fanny's husband will not oppose the divorce, so he thinks he has succeeded in getting it. In the next chapter, Durham thanks Christine for what she has done about facilitating the divorce, and he wants to repay her. She says, "It is in the contemplation of your happiness that I have taken my reward" (MT, 47). In Chapter Nine, believing her report, Durham leaves for England and returns at the end of the summer expecting to have the divorce made final. He is complimented by Christine for his not having told Fanny about her attempt at blackmail, and she admires his sense of honor. She makes a confession: "I knew there was horrible misery in store for you and that at that time I was waiting to feast my eyes on it" (MT, 53). As Chapter Nine ends with her question, "Have you never asked yourself why our family consented so readily to a divorce?" (53), a question answered in Chapter Ten. Christine admits she concealed the fact that "on the remarriage of the mother, the courts instantly restore the child to the father." She knew that, if the innocent Fanny should get her divorce, she would surely lose her child. The whole situation changes once there is the question of another marriage. When that happens, the child automatically goes back to the father, no matter how brutal he may have been, but that is the law. Durham asks her why she has admitted this deceit: "I could not bear to have you say that I had deceived you twice" (57).

In spite of the differences in the details of the plot, the situation links both Bourget's novel and Edith Wharton's novella. The outcome is the surrender by non-Catholics involved in both divorces to the dictates of the Catholic Church. The non-Catholic Albert Darras of *Un Divorce* is broken by the Catholic Church. As soon as his wife takes on again her religious faith, he has no recourse to any kind of freedom within the marriage. Bourget believes that such a civil marriage should never have taken place because divorce is a prison and therefore should not exist, certainly when a Catholic ceremony has been entered into originally.

In Wharton's novel, if John Durham marries the American Fanny, he will deprive her forever of her son and that he will not, as a man of honor, do. Madame de Treymes, who is the spokesperson for the family and yet also a woman capable of understanding the good that is in people and their equally good motives, is moved both by her official role as spokesman for the family and by her repentance for this role in the light of the fact that Fanny and John Durham are "good people." Divorce, if you marry a Frenchman, if you have a child, and if you are going to remarry, becomes a prison and there is no exit. Wharton, unlike Bourget, does not believe this is good.

The very shortness of these chapters and the succinctness with which Wharton presents the arguments and the situation indicate a clear protest to the didactic verbosity of her good friend, Paul Bourget, whose novels she never really could read. This novella ranks among her very best because of its clarity and its tightness. (She wrote it while she was trying to finish *The Fruit of the Tree*.) Even though most critics see the influence of Henry James in this novella in echoes of *The American,* "Madame de Mauves," and even to a certain extent *The Ambassadors,* a familiarity with Bourget's novels and some knowledge of the conditions under which Edith Wharton wrote this novella—her living in France at the time and her introduction to an aristocratic group of French people—hastened the maturation of her new idea. It is engineered to repeat and to correct Bourget's novel of divorce and to show how divorce is the prison that he claimed it was, but now seen from a non-Catholic point of view. She learned from him how to plot such a novel, for *Un Divorce* is well argued, and the dialogue between Gabrielle Darras and her husband controls the interesting parts of the novel. But in Wharton's version she showed that the most interesting part, the dialogue concerning the case itself, was the heart of Bourget's book. In her reposte to Bourget's novel, she protested his treatment of the subject, as well as criticizing the disastrous effect of the French Catholic Church and the well-meaning Americans in her novel, both of whom are trapped by Catholic French laws regarding divorce. Further digging into Edith Wharton's literary relationship with Paul Bourget is sure to reveal additional interesting parallels.

References

1. *Henry James and Edith Wharton: Letters: 1900–1915,* ed. Lyall H. Powers (New York: Scribner's, 1990), p. 38. Future references are indicated by EW & HJ and page number.

2. Paul Bourget, *Un Divorce,* 1907. Future references are indicated by D and page number.

3. Edith Wharton, *Madame de Treymes,* in *Novellas and Other Writings* (New York: Library of America, 1990), pp. 1–60. Future references are indicated by MT and page number.

11

Two Novels of the "Relatively Poor"

George Gissing's *New Grub Street* and *The House of Mirth*

Since C. S. Collinson has called attention to the parallels between George Gissing's *The Whirlpool* (1897) and *The House of Mirth* (1905),[1] it may be pertinent to point out the parallels that exist between *New Grub Street* (1891) and *The House of Mirth*. The key to the fact that Edith Wharton was influenced by *New Grub Street* lies in the repetition of Gissing's phrase "the relatively poor" in her novel about financially insecure members of New York society. The theme of Gissing's novel is poverty in all its phases—relative and absolute. The term "relative poverty," apparently original with Gissing, appears early in the novel in striking salience: "the relatively poor," he wrote "(who are so much worse off than the poor absolutely)."[2] It occurs later on in the novel when Reardon's child comes "between him and the mother, as must always be the case in poor homes, most of all where the poverty is relative" (N, 133).

Wharton repeats Gissing's phrase and applies it to the situation of the unmarried Lily Bart, who sets her cap for a young multimillionaire to "free" her forever "from the shifts, the expedients, the humiliations of the *relatively poor*" (my italics).[3] The existence of this phrase in *The House of Mirth* surely argues for the author's close reading of *New Grub Street*.

What supports this argument is the presence in Wharton's novel of other factors from *New Grub Street*. The profusion of classical literary references to underline the inappropriate education ("To the relatively poor . . . education is in most cases a mocking cruelty" [N, 38], which keeps Gissing's Reardon from accommodating himself to the new London journalism) reappears in *The House of Mirth* in frequent invocations

Originally published in *Notes on Modern American Literature* 6, no. 2 (Autumn 1982), Note 12.

of the "Furies," which Lily feels pursue her; she once read a translation of *The Eumenides,* her only reading outside of the copy of Omar Khayyám she carries when she travels. Selden, like the people in *New Grub Street,* is also given his special book, the *Caractères* of La Bruyère, to indicate his interest in seventeenth-century French neoclassical literature with its satirical emphasis. This parallels the neoclassical satires of Johnson, Dryden, and Shadwell, the favorite topics of Alfred Yule in *New Grub Street.* Also, Selden's combination of Stoicism and Epicureanism is partly modeled on Jasper Milvain's philosophy of life.

This appears in a scene on the meaning of success that follows closely a similar one in *New Grub Street.* In Gissing's novel it takes place between Jasper Milvain, the opportunist, and Marian, his fiancée. She asks, "What do you understand by success?" He answers, "My aim is to have easy command of all the pleasures desired by a cultivated man. I want to live among beautiful things, and never be troubled by a thought of vulgar difficulties. I want to travel and enrich my mind in foreign countries" (N, 350).

In *The House of Mirth* Selden asks Lily, "Success—what is success?" She answers, "Why, to get as much as one can out of life, I suppose. It's a relative quality after all. Isn't that your idea of it?" He answers, "My idea of it? God forbid . . . My idea of success is personal freedom . . . freedom from everything—from money, from poverty, from ease and anxiety, from all the material accidents. To keep a kind of republic of the spirit—that's what I call success" (H, 108).

In each novel Gissing's hero and Wharton's heroine share a fatal flaw, an inability to do the right thing at the right time. Although Reardon is excused by his temperamental sensitivity, his spoiled wife who cannot bear poverty, and his inelasticity in the face of changing standards in Grub Street, Lily's weakness lies in a conflict between her emotional needs and her financial needs, which force her always to miss the opportunities that present themselves. Reardon's weakness lies in his maintaining standards appropriate to authors in ancient Greece or Rome rather than to the denizens of New Grub Street, and his tragic marriage takes place because of his innocence about social distinctions rather than to a lack of insight.

Wharton does not use poverty as Gissing does, for, compared to his eighty-odd invocations to poverty in some form as it permanently damages the three families affected by it, Wharton mentions it only ten times, even though it is crucial to her book, especially in its "relative" sense. She tends to restrict it to its analogic meaning, for Lily sees "the poverty of her friend's achievement" (H, 88) and like Amy Reardon "she was not made . . . for the squalid promises of poverty" (H, 39). It is "the abstract conception of poverty" (H, 243) that finally becomes a fact in her life, "dreadful" to her (H, 249) in her "old incurable dread of discomfort and poverty" (H, 478). Only once does Wharton tend to imitate the personification of poverty that Gissing resorts to when she admits that "Poverty simplifies book-keeping" (H, 514) almost at the end of Lily's life. Then poverty becomes absolute. But Wharton has not made the same kind of artistic use of poverty as Gissing has, for her story is not as complex or formal. There are in her novel no controlled networks of mythological and historical references to which Gissing ties the anxieties of his characters. Wharton's novel is closer to the naturalism of the French, and the trajectory of Lily's life follows the requirements of Zola rather than Gissing.

Is there any evidence that Wharton knew the works of Gissing or that she admired them? She never mentioned them in *The Writing of Fiction* or *A Backward Glance,* but she covered up certain parts of her life, as R. W. B. Lewis's recent biography has revealed. The evidence in favor of her having paid close attention to Gissing comes from Lord Clark who was a close friend of hers and to whom she left part of her library. In a communication to me in November 1979, Lord Clark wrote that he cannot "remember everything we talked about" since Edith Wharton "died forty years ago," but he does add the significant clause: "but I seem to remember her talking with admiration about George Gissing."[4]

Other evidence is provided by what we know about the conditions in which she wrote *The House of Mirth.* R. W. B. Lewis writes that, although the novel was begun at the end of the summer of 1903, Wharton stopped writing it. "It was Edward Burlingame," her editor at Scribner's, "who drew Edith back to it in August, 1904, by begging her to have the novel ready to begin serialization in *Scribner's* the following January. . . . After a period of 'black despair' the novel began to go with a rush; by early October, Edith could tell Brownell that she was 'fatuously pleased' with it. She managed to have enough of the narrative in shape by the time requested, and *The House of Mirth* ran through eleven issues from January to November, 1905."[5]

An important presence around Wharton while she was writing her book was Henry James. In May 1904, she met him on a visit to Lamb House and when he came to the United States in August of that year, he visited her at The Mount, her country house at Lenox, from October 17 to 31,[6] and they rapidly became intimate friends. Wharton was working again on *The House of Mirth,* while James was a house guest, for she had been drawn back to working rapidly on that novel in August, just when James arrived in the States, and she had a deadline for January 1905. She was to replace another novel in *Scribner's Magazine;* "the first chapters of my tale would have to appear almost at once, and it must be completed in four or five months," as she herself reports in *A Backward Glance.*[7] Her climax and her story were all planned, but she had "the intervening windings of the way" to write and was being "asked to gallop over them before I had even traced them out!" (BG, 208).

Because she lived for two weeks in the same house with James and had a tendency to talk constantly with him about literature, one may conclude that he encouraged her to read or reread Gissing's work. Also, since she read everything that James wrote at this time, she undoubtedly knew his "London Notes" in *Harper's Weekly* (summer 1897), in which he mentioned how "ever since reading 'New Grub Street'" he had "a persistent taste" for his works.[8] Inasmuch as he also called attention there to *The Whirlpool,* it might have been the locus for Wharton's interest in Gissing's work.[9] She also declared in her autobiography that when "the first chapters of her novel appeared," beginning in January 1905, "I had written hardly fifty thousand words: but I kept at it, and finished and delivered my novel on time" (BG, 208). Since so little was written by January, perhaps James helped her out again, for James stayed with Edith while she was writing her book in New York for two weeks from December 21 to January 9, 1905.[10]

The channel to Gissing, then, most likely was Henry James. In 1901 he had met Gissing when H. G. Wells brought him to Lamb House. Until Gissing's death in 1903, he enjoyed some contact with him, and Gissing's recent death would have made him a likely topic of conversation in 1904.

One reason that Wharton's novel about the need for money cannot compare with Gissing's *New Grub Street* in its savage strength is that she never experienced personally the one single condition necessary for the understanding of such a theme—poverty itself—either relative or absolute. She was born with a silver spoon and earned a golden one by her writing. *New Grub Street* was written during a very hard period for Gissing when he had to pawn his clothes and cut down on his lunches. *The House of Mirth* was written in luxury in one of the great houses in

Lenox, Massachusetts, and in a Park Avenue town house, facilitated by servants and surrounded by house guests like Henry James.

REFERENCES

1. C. S. Collinson, "'The Whirlpool' and 'The House of Mirth,'" *The Gissing Newsletter* 16, no. 4 (October 1980): 12–16.

2. George Gissing, *New Grub Street* (New York: Modern Library, 1926), p. 38. Future references are indicated by N plus page number.

3. Edith Wharton, *The House of Mirth* (New York: Scribner's, 1905), p. 77. Future references are indicated by H and page number.

4. Communication, Lord Clark, Saltwood, Hythe, Kent, November 6, 1979.

5. R. W. B. Lewis, *Edith Wharton: A Biography* (New York: Harper & Row, 1975), p. 151.

6. Henry James, *The American Scene,* introduction and notes by Leon Edel (Bloomington: Indiana University, 1969), p. 479.

7. Edith Wharton, *A Backward Glance* (New York: Appleton-Century, 1934), p. 208. Future references are indicated by BG plus page number.

8. Henry James, *Notes on Novelists* (New York: Scribner's, 1914), p. 438.

9. Collinson, "'The Whirlpool' and 'The House of Mirth,'" p. 12.

10. Henry James, *The American Scene,* pp. 479–80.

12

Edith Wharton and F. Marion Crawford

Edith Wharton had a curious and serious literary relationship with F. Marion Crawford, the American popular novelist who lived in Italy. Their relationship was largely facilitated through Edith's close friendship with Crawford's half-sister, Margaret (Daisy) Terry Chanler. As a child in Rome, Edith had played with her and her brother, Arthur Terry, and later on they met again and remained close friends until the end of their lives. On May 7, 1902, Edith Wharton wrote to William Dean Howells that she wanted to do an article on *The Three Francescas,* three plays based on the Paolo and Francesca legend. R. W. B. Lewis in his biography of Wharton claims that "At the request of William Dean Howells, she wrote a comparison of three versions of the *Francesca da Rimini* legend by F. Marion Crawford, Steven Phillips, and Gabriel D'Annunzio."[1] It seems, however, from the publication of the letters of Edith Wharton that she made the suggestion herself and that she asked Howells to then send her article on to Mr. Harvey of the *North American Review.* Since she was "not sure if he condescends to such frivolities as a dramatic criticism by a woman, I venture to approach him obliquely, by begging you to transmit my suggestion if you think such an article would be acceptable."[2] Apparently, her plan worked, for ten days later, she wrote to Margaret Chanler that she was actually writing it for the *North American Review.* She also wrote to Margaret Chanler that F. Crawford had sent her a copy in French of his *Francesca da Rimini.* "[It] seems to me a very strong and simple play, quite different in quality from anything he has ever written. I wonder if you agree with me? . . . I am so *emballée* about it that I am writing for the North American an article on the three Francescas. . . . if you haven't seen this [the French translation], I will send you my copy, as

I am sure Newport will not furnish one."[3] Edith probably did not need to send Daisy a copy because two copies are recorded in the Maggs's Wharton library list of those books owned by Wharton and stored by Sir Kenneth Clark. One is the French translation by Marcel Schwob of Crawford's *Francesca da Rimini* with presentation inscriptions from both author and translator, and there also is a copy in English published in New York in 1902. These are the only two volumes by F. Marion Crawford in this collection of Edith Wharton books.

Because of Edith's interest in Crawford's play and her article, which she evidently must have sent to him after it was published, it seems highly likely that he would send her the next volume he produced in the following year, *The Heart of Rome,* a novel, but there is no mention of it in any of Wharton's published correspondence. In the summer of 1903, Edith was probably working on *The House of Mirth.*

Presumably *The Heart of Rome* by Crawford, which had come out during 1903, probably was among the books she had been reading at the time. The reason one thinks so is that there are various elements in *The House of Mirth* that show a remarkable resemblance to some of those in *The Heart of Rome,* only with the appropriate sociological differences that would exist in a novel about New York society as contrasted to one about Roman society of the period.

Here is outlined the basic plot of *The Heart of Rome,* and readers of Wharton will see immediately its connection with *The House of Mirth.* The Conti family, once famous and wealthy in Rome, had been living for centuries in their ancient Roman palazzo but are now completely ruined financially because of the extravagance of Princess Conti, the fashionable widow of Prince Conti. One of her daughters is in a convent, but another daughter, Sabine, a minor, is at loose ends because her mother, originally an aristocrat from Poland, has fled back to her home country. The only place the abandoned daughter can be deposited is in the home of the Baron Volterra, a rich financier of clearly Semitic origins. (Volterra is a place name, which in Italy signifies that he is a Jew.) His wife, anxious for social advancement and a snob above all, wishes to court favor in Roman society and thus will benefit by giving young Sabine Conti a place in her home.

The ingredients of this plot are basically those of the international novel current at the *fin de siècle,* numerous examples of which can be found. They influenced even Henry James in his cosmopolitan novels around 1900, especially in *The Golden Bowl,* which had appeared in the fall of 1904. But that novel does not show the ingredients of *The Heart of Rome,* nor do any other of James's novels. However, Wharton's *The House of Mirth* does. Sabine is a young woman of good family and beauty, who, like Lily Bart, the heroine of *The House of Mirth,* is in need of money and, after the breakdown of the family fortunes has taken place, has been deposited as a guest in the house of people whom she does not like and whose family head had made his money originally in a pawnbroking establishment. That origin of his fortune is not what she dislikes. What she does dislike is snobbery and the obvious class differences that make their conversation and behavior incomprehensible to her. Sabine tells the baroness that she would prefer to be independent and not to live on their charity. Perhaps she could "learn to be a maid, to make hats or to feed babies with bottles," two activities which Lily Bart engages in, both actually or through her musings. But for Sabine, since she is the heroine of a Crawford fairy tale, no such ignominious end as Lily's is in sight. A young man of equally good blood, but who is also a distinguished archaeologist, takes rooms in her abandoned palazzo under the eye of the Baron Volterra (who, as the receiver for the house, wishes it to be sold at a profit) and finally rescues her.

Crawford's description of the baron as the Jewish financier gives Wharton a type which she imitates in Simon Rosedale, the Jewish financier who not only crosses Lily's path in *The House of Mirth* but also wants her as a possession for his own social advancement, just as the Baron Volterra wants Sabine. He desires it at least while Lily's reputation is untarnished. But as soon as she becomes a woman of dubious respectability, he retreats as a suitor. The Baron Volterra does not want Sabine for himself, since he is happily married, but for either one of his two sons. The hub of the plot depends in both cases on the ruination of the reputation of the young woman of good family who is financially without any support. Both girls are ruined because each one is suspected of having spent the night alone with a man—Sabine in her palazzo, which has become inundated by the "lost water" of Rome, and Lily on board the Dorsets' yacht.

The eighteen-year-old Sabine has a personality similar to Lily's, a compound of "innocence and simplicity, indifference and daring, gentleness, hardness and pride, all wonderfully amalgamated under a perfectly self-possessed manner all pervaded by the most undeniable charm."[4] Malipieri, the aristocratic archaeologist, and she are caught in the palazzo vault flooded by the "lost water" that still exists under certain old houses in Rome. The main point stressed in both novels is first the loss of money suffered by young girls brought up according to the highest standards of civilized living and second the loss of their reputations. The inheritance of good family is a necessary attribute of each heroine. Malipieri, equally well born, only from the Venetian, not Roman, aristocracy, does not propose to Sabine after the night they spend alone in the Conti palazzo, as would be expected in the respectable European society (even though they are in love with each other), because he is already married. He had taken this step in order to save the reputation of his dying best friend's unborn child. However, all turns out well. Before that final happy *dénouement,* when it does not seem possible for the two to get married, Sabine offers to live unmarried with her lover, which is a very independent and unusual move for a girl of good family to make in *fin-de-siècle* society in Europe.

This sacrifice is of course rejected by the noble suitor, but, since this is a fairy tale by Crawford, they become free to marry because his wife generously gives him the opportunity to divorce her. These fairy-tale elements surely have nothing to do with *The House of Mirth,* but the position of the young beauty disinherited from her natural background is also that of Lily Bart, and the financial ruin of both families has a similar cause in both novels—in *The Heart of Rome* the extravagance of the Princess Conti and in *The House of Mirth* that of Lily's mother, Mrs. Bart. What Lily does not share with Sabine is her will to survive and an independence of spirit, nor does Lawrence Selden, her ineffectual possible suitor, share any of the characteristics of Malipieri (although Selden too comes from a good family), which are those also of independence and the possession of a strong will. However, Wharton's reading of *The Heart of Rome,* which would have taken place just during the period she was writing *The House of Mirth,* would give her the initial situation, although her development of it would be influenced both by American society, as opposed to Roman society, and by the will to fail, a fault programmed into the characters of Selden and Lily.

Perhaps Wharton aimed at American readers more accustomed to the realist novel and readier to accept the truth about themselves. As Crawford himself admitted, he was only concerned in creating entertainment, not in pointing out certain basic faults in the society for which he wrote. What he has written, as he admits in the note at the end of his novel, is "a tale without a 'purpose' and without any particular 'moral' in the present appalling acceptation of those simple terms. If it has interested or pleased those who have read it, the writer is glad; if it has not, he can find some consolation in having made two young people unutterably blissful in his own imagination, whereas he manifestly had it in his power to bring them to awful grief; and when one cannot make living men and women happy in real life, it is a harmless satisfaction to do it in a novel. If this one shows anything worth learning about the world, it is that a gifted man of strong character and honorable life may do a foolish and generous thing, whereby he may become in a few days the helpless toy of fate."[5] However, Crawford does claim that he has based some things in his novel upon certain facts. One is the discovery by Malipieri of an actual colossal statue of gilt bronze that now stands in the rotunda in the Vatican museum. Another is the fact that many Romans were ruined by the financial crisis of 1888, yet he has not created the portrait of any persons he has known.

Another hint that Edith Wharton may have gotten from this book is that her opening chapter begins with a situation indicative of Lily Bart's character and behavior. It is a scene where she is discovered by Mr. Rosedale to have been visiting Selden in his bachelor flat. This corresponds to the initial chapter in *The Heart of Rome* where we are confronted with the *fait accompli* of the bankruptcy of the Princess Conti and with her depositing her daughter in the home of the Volterras.

The article, sent by Wharton in 1902 to the *North American Review*, where it appeared in July, is a comparative analysis of the three *Francesca da Rimini* plays by Phillips, D'Annunzio, and Crawford. She criticizes Phillips's version for reducing the necessary suspense of the drama, as well as being too skimpy in its use of local color.[6] Wharton thought that D'Annunzio, although good at creating characteristic Italian touches, had because of those touches arrested almost all the movement in the play, especially in the third act (3F, 25). Therefore, Wharton rated Crawford as having more successfully redone the legend of Francesca and Paolo than the other two writers. "He has preserved the simple outline which such a theme demands and his dramatic instinct has saved him from clogging it with unessential details" (3F, 26). Because it was written for Madame Sarah Bernhardt, Mr. Crawford has "used the simplest prose." She notes that "this nudity makes the structure of the tragedy more salient," and Crawford, "alone of the three authors, has turned to history for the chronology of his drama" (3F, 26). Wharton, who had just been deeply immersed in Italian history of the eighteenth century for her two-volume historical novel, *The Valley of Decision,* would admire Crawford's dependence on archival material, a procedure she had learned from Vernon Lee.

Crawford has made Francesca's young daughter "the innocent means of her mother's betrayal," and since now Paolo and Francesca, in Crawford's version, have had an adulterous relationship for many years' standing, while their own families were growing, Paolo's wife, Beatrice, finally comes to threaten them and then kills herself. This added the complication of Paolo's guilt about her death. "Francesca's jealousy has been lulled, but Giovanni's is awakened; and on Paolo's soul lies the weight of his wife's death. This psychological situation, brought about with masterly simplicity, serves to maintain the interest of the two remaining acts" (3F, 27–28).

Then Wharton admires Crawford's depiction of Francesca's husband and the change of Giovanni Malatesta into an experienced hypocrite who tries to awaken his wife's passion, which he cannot do, and the mature Francesca, meeting with Paolo again, relives her original experience with him where they had been reading a book together years ago and repeats with him their original embrace. Then Giovanni kills them. In "the long attachment of the lovers" and Giovanni's change "from a violent and outspoken man to a stealthy smiling assassin," Wharton finds that Crawford has realized how Italian lovers have histories of long attachments (3F, 29).

Because she thought that this play was superior to the two other versions of the Francesca legend, Wharton was probably very impatient to read Crawford's next work, for she felt, as she wrote to her friend Daisy Chanler, how his play, *Francesca da Rimini,* seemed to be superior to his previous works. What she made of *The Heart of Rome,* which was in its intentions only an entertainment rather than anything else, we can only find out by seeing those parts reflected in the novel she was working on at the time she read his book—*The House of Mirth*—parts she felt were most suitable to her picture of American life.

The heroine's name, Sabine, points to a woman of the Sabines, one of the earliest ancestors in Rome, which meant the girl was a true aristocrat. The gilt bronze statue now in the Vatican rotunda was found in a vault in the courtyard of the Palazzo Righetti when Crawford was a boy (HR, 395).

Lily Bart is someone who has nothing but her beauty, a highly decorative quality, and has to depend on the patronage of people she neither respects nor likes, such as the Dorsets, Trenors, possibly Gryce; she unfortunately puts herself in a position to ruin her reputation. And that is the situation we are faced with at the onset of *The Heart of Rome* by Crawford. Sabine is divested of her family money, which is her support, and must depend on the likes of the Baron and Baroness Volterra for her very existence until she rebels against it, at least verbally. Although she is saved by having a fine young man and equally nobly born Venetian aristocrat fall in love with her, her reputation has been ruined, just as Lily's reputation has been, because they both have spent the night alone with men through no fault of their own.

Sabine's mother is a parallel to Mrs. Bart, for they are both the same kind of fashion-ridden spendthrift, and Lily's aunt, Mrs. Peniston, is a fool. The story is made up of elements found in *The Heart of Rome,* which may have stimulated Wharton to make her turn on the same elements we find in Crawford's novel: the terms of marriage, the girl's threatened reputation and what it does for her future, her foolish mother and those people who have taken her in, for whom she has no respect. But this is not a fairy tale for Edith Wharton, and she shows how in real life New York Lily is doomed to failure and probable suicide. Wharton shows what really happens to the young women who cannot maintain the fictions of society and who are therefore ruined by the society they are trying to please. Their energy has been depleted by their financial predicaments, and they are unequipped to use their brains to challenge that society.

The importance of Edith Wharton's long, detailed, and analytic essay on Crawford's version of the legend of Paolo and Francesca for the argument of this chapter lies in the evidence it presents of the serious attention Wharton gave to Crawford's fictions.

REFERENCES

1. R. W. B. Lewis, *Edith Wharton: A Biography* (New York: Harper & Row, 1975), p. 108.

2. *The Letters of Edith Wharton,* ed. R. W. B. Lewis and Nancy Lewis (New York: Scribner's, 1988), p. 62.

3. Ibid., p. 63.

4. F. Marion Crawford, *The Heart of Rome: A Tale of the "Lost Water"* (New York:

Macmillan [1903], reprint, 1904), p. 100. Future references are indicated by HR and page number.

    5. Ibid.

    6. Edith Wharton, "The Three Francescas," *North American Review* 175 (July 1902): 22–23. Future references are indicated by 3F and page number.

13
Edith Wharton and Grace Aguilar

Mothers, Daughters, and Incest in the Late Novels
of Edith Wharton

The strained relationship between mothers and daughters is one of Edith Wharton's persistent themes in her late novels. Concealed within is the struggle for the father, a struggle that wounds their relationship. R. B. W. Lewis[1] and Cynthia Griffin Wolff[2] have pointed out in their studies of the life and work of Edith Wharton how the relations between parents and children contain the theme of incest that obsessed the American novelist in her later years. The existence of the pornographic fragment, "Beatrice Palmato," highlights Wharton's interest in introducing into her fiction an explicit account of the sexual act between father and daughter. This motif emerges in the fiction written in her sixties in a concentrated form in mother and daughter relations.

By this time Wharton had rejected the role of wife, had finished, as far as we know, her role as lover, and her yearning for biological children could now never be satisfied. Her progeny were her books; in letters to her friends she called her literary productions her "children." Her own deprivation as a mother encouraged her fantasies in this direction. During the war years her maternal feelings were directed to the orphans of the war and to a few young men, especially to one who lost his life early in the war and whom she memorialized in *A Son at the Front*.

The three novels, *The Old Maid, The Mother's Recompense,* and *Twilight Sleep,* published from 1924 until 1927, project this drama between mothers and daughters. The intensity of Wharton's feelings invested in these novels makes them very good indeed, and their excellence belies the gen-

Originally published as "Mother, Daughter, and Incest in the Late Novels of Edith Wharton," in *The Lost Tradition: Mothers and Daughters in Literature,* edited by Cathy N. Davidson and E. M. Broner (New York: Unger, 1980), 147–58.

erally accepted view that her late novels are her worst. These particular ones are compelling to read, and their plots are well organized. They leave us with tremendous respect for a woman who was trying to climb out of her class, out of the nineteenth century, and out of the box, that "convenient box, with nice glass sides, so that we can see out" from which Verena Tarrant implores men to release women in James's *The Bostonians.* In fact, it is the plot of James's short story, "The Chaperon,"[3] that we see behind the plot of *The Mother's Recompense.*

A Son at the Front (1923)[4] had begun Edith Wharton's parent-child dramas. It is concerned with a painter who, alienated from his son, allowed him to be raised by his wife's second husband because of his own selfish concern with his art. After the young man's death in the war, the father is left with the portrait he had made of his son and a commission for a monument in his memory. So he incorporates his son into the art for which he had rejected him. In this way Wharton masks her own persona and her own concentration on her work in the portrayal of John Campton, the father.

The next year *The Old Maid* (1924)[5] presents two mothers, neither of whom have a claim on Tina, the daughter—the real mother, Chatty Lovell, who has to conceal her true motherhood of the child conceived out of wedlock, and the adoptive mother, Delia Ralston, who takes care of the girl because she is the offspring of a man Delia loved. Delia's own biological offspring never means what this girl means to her, and the problem of the book is whether or not the real mother will divulge to the girl her true parentage.

The story is placed in the 1850s in New York when "dark destinies coiled under the safe surface of life" (OM, 120) and "the blind forces of life were groping and crying underfoot" (OM, 129). In it Wharton showed that a mother could have no relation to her illegitimate daughter in a society that knew of but would not accept such a relationship. In this way she denigrates the value of biological motherhood. Delia says to Chatty, "You . . . sacrifice her to your desire for mastery?" (OM, 155). It can do no good for Tina to know Chatty is her mother. Delia, her mother surrogate, satisfies the girl in relation to the society that determines her happiness. In fact, the point of view in the story is that of the adoptive mother, Delia, not of the real mother. Wharton, in addition to making plausible her own role as an adoptive mother, a role she played in regard to her friend's children late in her life, is also making a statement about families. Natural families are not the families of our choice, and children will turn to those who appeal to them through their personalities and satisfy certain needs, not to their biological parents. Wharton anticipated the point of view of our modern youth who have in so many cases surmounted the traditional guilt that children feel for their parents and have chosen other parent figures, although Tina was never given the choice, since she is unaware of who her real mother is. Wharton's ambivalent feelings for her own mother show how close to home this point of view was. When the question in *The Old Maid* is asked, "Which of us is the mother?" the answer is not readily available. Sometimes a child needs more than one mother, and here two mothers join in their love for Tina. In this novel Wharton has removed the mother role from its biological determinants.

Wharton's novelistic situations fleshed out after World War I pertained to the changing role of women. Having moved into the world as artists or war workers, women began to see that their roles as wives and lovers were breaking out of their nineteenth-century molds. Kate Clephane's difficulty in *The Mother's Recompense* (1925)[6] was going back to something she had really elevated herself out of, even though her flight from her family had been considered by her society twenty years before as a fall from grace. Wharton, of course, left her unhappy marriage for a life abroad as a writer. This parallels in some ways Kate Clephane's situation in the novel. Having abandoned her husband and infant daughter, Anne, for a life with another man abroad, Kate finds that the price she must pay for her restoration and rehabilitation in New York society is acceptance of the knowledge that Anne's fiancé is her own last, and much younger, former lover.

Kate Clephane's accomplishment was, Wharton seems to conclude, a breaking down of old containments that would never again be erected around this particular woman. She is conscious of her decision of twenty years before to give up the traditional roles of wife and mother and to take on the role as lover. Now having outgrown that role she has a new identity, the woman *without* a traditional role. She is faced with the task of finding a new one. At the end of *The Mother's Recompense,* Kate's recompense is knowledge about herself gained from hard experience. However, her notion of what her recompense should be has changed during the time of the book.

Wharton's *The Mother's Recompense* relates to the James story, "The Chaperon," in its initial situation, the return of the prodigal mother and her presentation by her daughter to her old role, only for Wharton the role is not Kate's resumption of her place in society; it is her role as mother, the center of the emotional life of a child deprived of her mother early in life, and the mother deprived of a full expression of her maternal feelings. Kate Clephane is brought back by her daughter Anne to a society that accepts her willingly enough and forgives her earlier betrayal of her family. All goes well until she discovers that her younger lover, who had appealed to her partly because there was an incestuous element in his extreme youth, is about to marry Anne. The agony of the story becomes Sophoclean, and the horror Kate faces is the realization that her role as mother and her role as lover can never be united in the same person.

The impossibility of her tolerating the situation gives the book a clear-cut dazzling intensity, although from the facts of the situation as presented this is clearly absurd. Why should a mother in 1925 living for the past two decades on the edge of the most sophisticated society in Europe regard her daughter's marrying her former lover as so horrifying? It can only be because Mrs. Clephane views the lover as a husband, and the coupling of her daughter and the man who represents the husband-figure becomes an incestuous act. The father, as it were, cohabits with his own child. Such a situation therefore can produce the kind of emotional pain and intense horror that Kate Clephane feels. Wharton has presented the same pattern of the discovery of incest and consequent horror shown by Oedipus.

In fact, it does not seem to me to be forcing the issue if we see the three novels, *The Old Maid, The Mother's Recompense,* and *Twilight Sleep* (1927),[7] as Wharton's Sophoclean trilogy. Given her preference for classical literature and Greek myths, it is not too hard to believe she may even have consciously modeled them on their classical predecessors. *The Mother's Recompense* is a novel reflecting the horror and the insupportability felt by a woman when she learns that her daughter is to marry the young man she herself has been in love with. But the horror is so incommensurate with her realistic situation that we realize it emerges, not from the situation in the book but from another situation that we know about from Edith Wharton's life, which operated both in her unconscious and her conscious fantasy. This situation has been revealed by the posthumous fragment, "Beatrice Palmato." Her horror really stems from the fact that her lover is having sexual relations with her daughter, as if the daughter were his own child. We see the horror of the situation in this novel, but we see the pleasure in the fragment. In the fragment, the daughter is enjoying the act of sexual intercourse with her father. In the novel, the mother experiences horror when she learns of the possible sexual intercourse of the "father" with her daughter. And the horror comes out with tremendous creative and artistic force. The placing of Guido's portrait of Beatrice Cenci in *The Mother's Recompense* gives us the clue, but what takes place in the novel is not really horrendous, especially since Edith Wharton had read Balzac's *Comédie Humaine,* where there are a number of situations in which mothers and daughters share the same lovers. Diane de Maufrigneuse, in "A Princess's Secrets," tells her lover that her marriage is unhappy because her mother married her to her own lover so she could go on having her relation with him. We know that *The American* by Henry James bases its dramatic core on the fact that Madame de Bellegarde had married off her daughter to her lover so she "could go on herself all the same," an actual quotation from the novel. This was a traditional pattern of behavior, at least in aristocratic French society. Why Kate Clephane could get into such a turmoil is that her anxiety is really based on another situation not in the novel, but back of the horror in Edith Wharton's mind. This explains why the ending is so factitious and so unreal. The key statement in *The Mother's Recompense* is the following quotation: "Jealous? Was she jealous of her daughter? Was she physically jealous? Was that the real secret of her repugnance, her instinctive revulsion? Was that why she had felt from the first as if some *incestuous horror* [my emphasis] hung between them? She did not know—it was impossible to analyze her anguish" (MR, 299).

Lewis thinks that *The Mother's Recompense* shows an attempt on the part of Wharton to reestablish some kind of contact with the American authors of the new generation and their new ways of doing things. He also tells us that it was around this time that she began a little diary in which she hoped to render a truer account of her inner nature than that attempted in reviews and comments about her. She

> commented to Berenson on a story by Moravia that in her view contained an inadequate treatment of the always interesting theme of incest. "Faulkner and Céline did it *first,*" she remarked, "and did it *nastier.*" She added that she herself had an "incest *donnée* up my sleeve that would make them all look like nursery rhymes," but that business was too poor and attitudes too prudish for her to risk trying to sell it. The *donnée* referred to, in all probability, was "Beatrice Palmato." (L, 524)

In Wharton's novel the mother's final recompense was that she gets back just what she had put in. She goes back to the life that she had made for herself, a life divorced from all aspects of her marriage, both the motherly aspects and the wifely aspects. Her recompense is that she is given back her own life, the one she had chosen to create when she left John Clephane and Anne. The definition of the word "recompense" is that we are given back something for that which has been taken away from us. But nothing had been taken away from her, for Mrs. Clephane had *thrown* it away.

The meaning of the book, then, suggested by its title, is that the recompense that the mother gets is her own identity in repudiating her husband and child. Once she has created it, she is committed to it. She has become an individual. Her recompense is the restitution of her own personality that confirms an existence beyond her relation to a husband or a child. In this sense Wharton is more like a woman of the second half of the twentieth century.

This brings us to the dedicatory paragraph with which Wharton prefaces her book: "My excuses are due to the decorous shade of Grace Aguilar, loved of our grandmothers, for deliberately appropriating, and applying to uses so different, the title of one of the most admired of her tales." Grace Aguilar wrote two novels about life with mother in 1847, which became the "how to do it" books for mothers with daughters and with the solutions to the problem of keeping them under their influence. The first, concerned with the raising of small children, was called *Home Influence.*[8] The second, and the more popular, was *The Mother's Recompense,* whose title Wharton appropriated for her own novel. In Aguilar's novel, getting the girls safely launched into society and finally married is accomplished through the "confidence" they have in their mother.

Grace Aguilar seems to have had a very satisfactory and comforting relationship with her own mother who survived her. The daughter of a Sephardic Jewish merchant who emigrated from Spain to England, Grace Aguilar wrote about a dozen books, among them explications of the Jewish faith: *The Perez Family, Women's Friendship,* and *The Vale of Cedars.* The books that were most popular were the didactic novels, advising mothers and daughters how to get along. A successful mother had to answer these questions: was her daughter properly introduced into society, did she behave herself well, and did she finally make the proper marriage? In Aguilar's *The Mother's Recompense,* the mother, Mrs. Hamilton, intervenes in her daughters' lives to the extent that she reads their mail and inserts advisory comments. Her second daughter, Caroline, has been influenced by a young girl with a poor relationship with her own sick and lazy mother who has lost control over her daughters. One of the girls takes on Mrs. Hamilton as a model foster mother and does well, but the other weans Caroline away from her mother and encourages her to flirt with a young earl in order to throw him over. Just as she is about to elope with a man with a bad reputation, she goes back to her mother, to whom her chaperon explains, "It was the recollection of your untiring care . . . that made her pause ere it was too late and she regains your confidence." The daughter concludes, "My mother was right." Mrs. Hamilton states her "recompense" very clearly as seeing "my children, as I do now around me, walking in that path which alone can lead to eternal life, and leading their offspring with them . . . and yet lavishing on me, as on their father, the love and duty of former years. . . . Is not this a precious recompense for all which for them I may have done or borne?" Mr. Hamilton ends the edifying book by saying, "long, long may you feel as you think on your mother, my beloved children, and teach your offspring to venerate her memory, that the path of the just is indeed as a shining light which shineth more and more unto the perfect day." The ending justifies working hard over raising children, for the mother will be remembered forever.[9]

This is the kind of advice that Edith's grandmother and other women of her generation in New York, as late as the 1870s, were given as to the proper attitude and the proper relationship between mothers and daughters. Daughters were to listen to their mothers and to respect them, especially when it came to making the big decision of their lives. Since Mrs. Hamilton devoted all her time and all her concern to the happiness of her children, she received her recompense. They all gave her blessings and were grateful that she had kept them from disorder and disaster.

Wharton apologized in her prefatory note to "the decorous shade of Grace Aguilar." However, she makes no apologies for nor even indicates her obligation in imitating very closely that same book in her next novel, *Twilight Sleep* (1927), for even though the customs of the New Yorkers of the 1920s she writes about bear no relation to those of the Hamiltons of the 1830s in England, there are striking similarities in both books.

It is astonishing how Mrs. Manford, the mother in *Twilight Sleep*, mimics Aguilar's Mrs. Hamilton in exerting the same kind of control over her children—daughter, son, daughter-in-law, and two husbands. We see in the same kind of family circle the mother who sets standards for her family, although the standards are handled ironically because they are all wrong. The name *Twilight Sleep* is taken from the name of the drugs that at this time were popular among the rich for painless childbirth. The elimination of pain is the aim of this upper-middle-class New York society. Anxiety must be avoided at all costs, and everything must be made easy; therefore, everyone in pain must be drugged.

Mrs. Pauline Manford, like Mrs. Hamilton in Aguilar's novel, had an "iron rule" in her home and conducted "the clockwork routine of . . . a perfect establishment." Nona, her daughter, is very affectionate to her mother, but they never talk to each other. Although Aguilar's book was based on the confidence one puts in one's mother and the restoration of that confidence, Nona and Mrs. Manford have no confidence in each other at all. Nona knows her mother covers everything over. Mrs. Manford has trained her butler to save the honor of the family by covering up an attempted murder by her first husband, who wishes to punish the couple involved in an incestuous affair. The family circle in this book certainly reminds one of Mrs. Hamilton's circle where the mother does everything she can to keep the *status quo,* but in Wharton's novel, much is hypocrisy.

Pauline Manford's activities include being the Chairman of the Mother's Day Association and a speaker at the Birth Control Banquet, and her daughter, Nona, is very amused to see that her mother can reconcile such contradictions. Like Mrs. Hamilton of the Aguilar novel she is the ideal mother, since she respects everybody's point of view, and, in this sense, she plays a role like Mrs. Hamilton's. "True, in Nona's case there had been Pauline's influence. Pauline, who, whatever her faults, was always good-humoured and usually wise with her children. The proof was that while they laughed at her, they adored her. They had to do her that justice." Here, as in Aguilar's book, there is a rich relationship between mother and daughter, as well as between the various people whom she brings into her circle, because she has energy and consequently strongly influences people around her.

In the Aguilar book one was expected to behave ethically, to marry, to produce children, and to increase the harmony in a family circle. So, too, in the Wharton book one is expected to live in harmony, to avoid pain, and to have life go on with the machinery unimpaired. But the ironical Wharton sees that this can be done only by self-delusion and the payment of a great price. The self-delusion must be continued from beginning to end.

Nona is a daughter who follows her mother's precepts and helps cover everything up, but marriage has been ruined for her. Wharton's book is like Aguilar's because the mother has lived in a certain way and has trained her family for their own good. The good is not religious as in the Aguilar novel, but it is moral. As in the Aguilar book, there had been one daughter for a while who rebelled. In Wharton's book even the rebellious characters follow the family necessity of hushing up everything. In Aguilar's story the family that greets life's problems with uncontrolled behavior comes to grief. Edith Wharton is showing in her book as Aguilar had shown before that an authoritative mother is the essential factor in a family's success. At the same time, the mother—like "twilight sleep"—represents the masking of pain, which, even when unfelt, remains. The attempted murder and the incest, even when covered up, do not entirely fade away. There are no real illnesses in this financially facilitated American world. Nervous tension is controlled by soothsayers, hypnotists, and psychic faddists.

Cynthia Wolff, in *A Feast of Words,* gives a very good explanation for the incestuous pattern in Edith Wharton's work, manifested in mother-daughter relations. Her emotional past had created a voracious need for affection, and as she grew older she carried it "into her attachment to her father and that crisis too was incompletely resolved." Wolff continues:

> However, one thing is worth recalling. A woman who has such a past can never completely eradicate its effects. Despite the resolute determination with which she attacked the impending remnants of her early failures, Edith Wharton would always carry certain emotional habits with her: an inevitable residuum from those early traumas remained to complicate the dilemmas of adult life. . . . Given that the implications of incest touched so many elements in Wharton's life, it is scarcely surprising to discover that the theme of incest was integrated into the apparatus of her fiction.[10]

Whether these psychological interpretations of Edith Wharton's early emotional life are correct in part or in whole, the point I have been trying to make in this chapter is that for Edith Wharton the struggle between mother and daughter projected so insistently in these late novels is the struggle for the father. Nor is it unworthy of comment that although she was a daughter but never a mother these novels are written from the point of view of the mother, not of the daughter. Thus she remains a lineal—if rebellious—descendant of Grace Aguilar, the very name of whose book she has made her own. Wharton's interest in Greek drama stemmed from her belief that the basic turmoil of life was best expressed for Western civilization in the Greek myths. For this reason, in her novels all the relationships within the family are archetypically expressed. Perhaps Edith Wharton wished to do the Sophoclean thing for the bewildering twentieth century, the period of her maturity, in which the form of the family itself reflected world changes. Since women's roles were most affected by these changes, she found in the relations between mothers and daughters the most dramatic, as well as the most personally touching representation of these changes.

References

1. R. W. B. Lewis, *Edith Wharton: A Biography* (New York: Harper & Row, 1975), pp. 524–26. Future references are indicated by L and page number.

2. Cynthia Griffin Wolff, *A Feast of Words* (New York: Oxford University Press, 1977), pp. 303–8, 379–80, 412–15.

3. Henry James, "The Chaperon," *The Complete Tales of Henry James,* vol. 8 (Philadelphia and New York: Lippincott, 1963), pp. 71–118.

4. Edith Wharton, *A Son at the Front* (New York: Scribner's, 1923).

5. Edith Wharton, *Old New York: The Old Maid (The Fifties)* (New York: D. Appleton, 1924). Future references are indicated by OM and the page number.

6. Edith Wharton, *The Mother's Recompense* (New York: D. Appleton, 1925). Future references are indicated by MR and page number.

7. Edith Wharton, *Twilight Sleep* (New York: D. Appleton, 1927).

8. Grace Aguilar, *Home Influence* (New York: D. Appleton, 1870).

9. Grace Aguilar, *The Mother's Recompense* (New York: D. Appleton, 1864), p. 499.

10. Wolff, *A Feast of Words,* p. 379.

14

Edith Wharton, Ernest Hemingway, and Vivienne de Watteville,
SPEAK TO THE EARTH

Edith Wharton's preface to Vivienne de Watteville's *Speak to the Earth: Wanderings and Reflections Among Elephants and Mountains* (1935)[1] has been curiously forgotten or ignored by her biographers, from Blake Nevius to R. W. B. Lewis to Cynthia Wolff, who, in an extended list of "Published Works of Edith Wharton" in *A Feast of Words,*[2] notes the three introductions to works other than Wharton's own but not the de Watteville preface. This is all the more astonishing because it has been known since 1968,[3] and in more detail in 1970,[4] that Ernest Hemingway in the original manuscript of "The Snows of Kilimanjaro" (1936) had planned to use a passage from *Speak to the Earth* as an additional epigraph but had decided, on the advice of Arnold Ginrich, *Esquire's* editor, to eliminate it and to use only the passage from Hans Meyer's *Across East African Glaciers.* The passage he eliminated reads as follows: "The difficulties, he said, were not in the actual climbing. It was a long grind, and success depended not on skill but on one's ability to withstand the high altitude. His parting words were that I must make the attempt soon, before there was any risk of the rains setting in" (129). On the manuscript next to the passage Hemingway's notation reads as follows: "Maybe better out, E. H."[5] The passage never appeared either in *Esquire* or in the book publication of stories that included "The Snows of Kilimanjaro."

Speak to the Earth, de Watteville's second book, was not about the hunting of wild beasts in East Africa as her first book, *Out in the Blue* (1927), had been but was about photographing them. Lewis and Westbrook be-

Originally published as "Wharton's Forgotten Preface to Vivienne de Watteville's *Speak to the Earth:* A Link with Hemingway's 'The Snows of Kilimanjaro,'" in *Notes on Modern American Literature* 8, no. 2 (Autumn 1984), Note 10.

lieve that the latter book also influenced Hemingway in his background material,[6] but the date of Hemingway's copy in Brasch and Sigman's *Hemingway's Library* is 1937.[7] If that is correct, then Lewis and Westbrook's belief that Harry's fictional death-bed scene was influenced by the real death-bed scene of Vivienne's father, the Swiss naturalist Bernard de Watteville (after his having been mauled by a lion), loses its credibility. We must assume that Hemingway read *Out in the Blue* in a later edition after having been impressed by *Speak to the Earth*.

How did Hemingway get to read that book, published as it was by a smaller press? Lewis and Westbrook suggest that since it had been "published with a preface by Edith Wharton, a first-rate American author and like Hemingway, also a Scribner's author, it is conceivable that Maxwell Perkins, Hemingway's editor at Scribner's who regularly obtained books of interest for his authors, had sent Hemingway volumes relative to work-in-progress."[8] Conceivable it may be, but not likely, since Edith Wharton had broken with Scribner's after 1911, the date of *Ethan Frome,* and Appleton-Century became her main publisher, although sporadically Scribner's published that work of hers that had appeared in their magazine.[9] It seems more likely that the book was sent to Hemingway by Edith Wharton herself, and the evidence for this comes from Vivienne de Watteville's record of her relationship to Wharton in connection with the circumstances surrounding not only Wharton's writing of the preface but also her close editorial supervision of the book. This material appears in Percy Lubbock's *Portrait of Edith Wharton* (1947), also an Appleton-Century book. Vivienne (also known as Mrs. Gerard Goschen) on a visit to the writer at her villa at Sainte-Claire heard her first book praised by Wharton ("But she's a born writer!") and from that moment gained enough confidence to work on her second book, *Speak to the Earth.* "For two years I was happy with the happiness of creative work, and when the proofs came in I wondered for the hundredth time whether I should dare ask Edith to write a preface. It must be she or no one, I thought jealously, for it was her book, she had called it forth. When she told me to send her the proofs, I begged that she would glance through them with a red pencil. . . . She had sent me a whole typed page of dry invaluable criticism, and granted me what every artist prays for, the opportunity to see the master at work, to be told not only 'this is bad,' but why it is bad and how to put it right." Edith had "gone through the whole proof page by page, penciling comments and suggestions, even correcting the punctuation. . . . She never condemned without suggesting an alternative." She concluded her letter to Lubbock with an illuminating sentence. "When the book, with her preface, subsequently appeared, she took endless trouble to send it to England and America for review, besides giving innumerable copies to her friends."[10] It is then that she may have sent Hemingway a copy. Evidence for Wharton's and Hemingway's mutual acquaintance resides in Carlos Baker's edition of *Hemingway: Selected Letters* (1981), for Hemingway in 1926 wrote to F. Scott Fitzgerald: "Haven't seen Bromfields, Edith Wharton, Conrad Bercovici . . . or any other of the little literary colony for some time."[11] Wharton, knowing that Hemingway's *Green Hills of Africa* had appeared in 1934 with its theme of East African safaris, may well have decided the book would interest him at the same time she would be promoting a book by a young writer she admired and with whom she had worked closely.

The preface to *Speak to the Earth* would undoubtedly have interested Hemingway, since the number of books by Wharton he owned indicated that he admired her. In the combined Finca–Key West library list we find *The House of Mirth* (1905), *Ethan Frome* (1911), *French Ways and Their Meanings* (1919), *The Age of Innocence* (1922), *A Backward Glance* (1934), and *The Best Short Stories of Edith Wharton* (1958).[12] Unlike Vivienne's first book, which had been an account of a hunting trip, *Speak to the Earth* was devoted to the peaceful photographing of animals and birds for which the author had a strong affection within a setting she loved. It was for this reason that Wharton wrote a preface, as she explains in the first lines of the 500-word introduction. As to her opinion of *Out in the Blue*, she remembered "exclaiming after I had read it: 'Oh, please write another book as enchanting as this one, but in which nobody wants to kill an animal, and they all live happily ever afterward!'"; she adds that it may have been rash of her to expect such a book, since she "feared there might be little more to say about big game untroubled by human violence than about countries similarly blessed." Her fears were "unfounded, and I ought to have known it," for "after all, I too have lived that life and stammered that language, though my mountain tent was only the library lamp-shade, my wilderness a garden, my wildebeest stealing down to drink two astute and arrogant Pekingese; and as one of the initiated I was aware that those who know how to talk to animals know also how to talk about them.

"And beautifully indeed you have proved it in these sunlit wind-swept pages. From the elephants romping with their friends, or twinkling at you ironically through the trees, to the least little bird hopping in at your

hut door, they all had so much to tell that they had evidently been awaiting such a confidant for ages; and you would never have been able to pack
all their yarns into one book if the Angel of Fire had not suddenly
driven you out of the Paradise where you and they had lain down so
happily around the Remington." This records the reason for the premature ending to the trip. Wharton longs for "the subsequent history of
creatures just glimpsed and lost again in your crowded pages. . . . You
had found . . . the exact language in which to tell us of these desert and
mountain friendships. . . . and then, just as you were drawing nearer to
the mysterious heart of your theme, as flower and bird and wildhoofed
creature were pressing about you to tell you their last secrets—just, in
short, as you were about to 'stroke the elephant's ear'—the crash came, the
sky grew black, and the golden gates clanged shut. . . .

"But luckily . . . not on us, your happy readers. For we are there again,
in your innocent Bestiary whenever we open your book; or even without
opening it, merely when we walk out and see through your eyes and hear
with your ears the tireless messages of Nature.

"Many will say this to you, many more will think it, and wish they
had the courage to tell you. I count myself privileged to have been the
first to walk with you in your wild places, and to have been asked to say
what I found there, and invite in others to share my delight."

It is probable that Wharton invited in Hemingway to share her and
Vivienne's sympathy with animals in Africa, for in "The Snows" his
Harry is shown photographing the beasts, not hunting them. In his tale
the message is the identity of Harry with the leopard in his quest for the
House of Heaven, that summit of Kilimanjaro of which Vivienne writes
as a place that she too never reached but that she viewed as heaven. After
reading her book one can understand how the direct, honest writing of
Vivienne de Watteville, the courageous traveler sensitive to the appeal of
nature and to animals of all kinds, affected Hemingway. It becomes clear
that her notion of Kilimanjaro as both "divine mountain and earthly
paradise" was closely followed as Lewis and Westbook have pointed out.
The epigraph to "The Snows" states that Kilimanjaro "is called . . . The
House of God."[13] One might add to their examples of sources in *Speak
to the Earth* for "The Snows" her final paragraph: "Life is the glorious
experiment, and Death the great adventure, when the mists shall at last
lift long enough for us to see clearly" (329). In Harry's dying fantasy, his
plane "seemed like flying through a waterfall, and then they were out
and . . . all he could see . . . great, high, and unbelievably white in the

sun, was the square top of Kilimanjaro. And then he knew that there was where he was going" (SN, 76). The intermediary between *Speak to the Earth* and "The Snows of Kilimanjaro" may well have been the perceptive and brilliant preface by Edith Wharton which, with the extraordinary adventures it prefaces, should emerge from its undeserved obscurity.

REFERENCES

1. Vivienne de Watteville, *Speak to the Earth: Wanderings and Reflections Among Elephants and Mountains* (New York: Harrison Smith and Robert Haas, 1935), Preface by Edith Wharton. Future references are indicated by page number. Wharton's preface is not paginated.

2. Cynthia Griffin Wolff, *A Feast of Words* (New York: Oxford University Press, 1977), p. 446.

3. Carlos Baker, *Ernest Hemingway: A Life Story* (New York: Avon Books, 1968; reprint 1980), p. 827.

4. Robert W. Lewis, Jr., and Max Westbrook, "Vivienne de Watteville, Hemingway's Companion on Kilimanjaro," *Texas Quarterly* 13 (1970): 75.

5. Ibid., p. 76.

6. Ibid., p. 77.

7. James D. Brasch and Joseph Sigman, *Hemingway's Library* (New York and London: Garland, 1981), no. 1756: *Out in the Blue* (London: Methuen, 1937); no. 1757, *Speak to the Earth,* Preface by Edith Wharton (New York: Smith & Haas, 1935).

8. Lewis and Westbrook, "Vivienne de Watteville," p. 75.

9. Wolff, *A Feast of Words,* p. 444.

10. Percy Lubbock, *Portrait of Edith Wharton* (New York and London: Appleton-Century, 1947), pp. 203–5.

11. Ernest Hemingway, *Selected Letters, 1917–1961,* ed. Carlos Baker (New York: Scribner's, 1981), p. 203.

12. Brasch and Sigman, *Hemingway's Library,* no. 7064 through no. 7069, p. 397.

13. *The Short Stories of Ernest Hemingway* (New York: Scribner's, 1996), p. 52. Future references are indicated by SN and page number.

15

Hugh Walpole's ALL SOULS' NIGHT and
Edith Wharton's "All Souls'"

Considering that Hugh Walpole and Edith Wharton were both independently so close to Henry James, it seems rather odd not only that they never met but also that their names never appeared in each other's essays or letters, except once, when Walpole tells us in his autobiographical *The Apple Trees* how he felt about Mrs. Wharton during those youthful years, especially when he was closest to James. As late as 1932, he wrote:

> I have never met Mrs. Wharton and I know that she is a delightful lady, but oh! how, in those young days, I learnt to loathe her very name!
>
> In general I have found in life that it is possible to keep up a real hatred of anyone only by never meeting them. Had I known Mrs. Wharton, I would in all probability have agreed that she was the wisest, the most radiant, most witty of all her sex. But I did not meet her. Only my *naivetés* were exposed naked to her sophisticated wisdom—all this in the kindliest fashion. But the kindliness only made me hate her image the more. Had it been a century or two earlier, I would have made a doll of wax, named it Wharton, stuck pins into it and roasted it over a slow fire.[1]

Walpole died in 1941, four years after Edith Wharton's death, but one wonders whether he ever had the satisfaction of knowing that, in all probability, her last tale, "All Souls'," published posthumously in 1937, seems to have depended rather heavily for its idea and atmosphere on one of his own tales, "The Silver Mask," published in a volume of collected tales called *All Souls' Night* (1933).

Wharton's tale was called "All Souls'," having almost the same title as the enveloping title of Walpole's collection of tales of ghostly ambiance. His epigraph for his book comes from W. B. Yeats's poem: "Midnight has come, and the Christ Church Bell / And many a lesser bell, sound through the room; / And it is All Souls' Night. . . . A ghost may come; / For it is a ghost's right. . . . " The heroine of "The Silver Mask" has nothing to do with ghosts, but she has to do with something much worse, that is, with her criminal servants, who trap her in her own house where she finally lies terminally ill in bed. For her there is no way out. Mrs. Wharton's tale, which takes place on All Souls' Night, October 31st, tells of a heroine equally entrapped in her own house with an injured ankle because all her servants have made a total exodus to attend, it appears, a coven of witches. Sara Clayburn, Wharton's heroine, is a widow of about fifty, the same age as that of Miss Sonia Herries of "The Silver Mask." Mrs. Clayburn goes for a walk on October 31st and meets a woman whom she does not know who says she is going to Whitegates, the Clayburn house in Connecticut where Mrs. Clayburn is living, to see "one of the girls."[2] On her way back, Mrs. Clayburn injures her ankle and has to be put to bed by one of her servants. It appears to be no real problem since she has a domestic staff to take care of her and a doctor to see her. Although it had begun to snow early this year, there is no reason for her to be much concerned. However, when she awakes at dawn after a bad night, it is to a cold house and no servants. After a difficult time maneuvering herself in great pain and making a fire, she goes to sleep to awake later on to a perfectly normal house, completely staffed once more with her servants, and she sounds like someone who has had a bad dream. She gets over the damage to her ankle, which has only been sprained, but a friend gets a call from her a year later. She tells her that she has met on October 31st the same woman whom she believes now is a "fetch," that is, a recruiting member of a witches' team, and knows now that there will again be the summoning of a coven as there had been on last year's All Souls' Night. She refuses ever to go back to her house again.

In relation to Walpole's story, Mrs. Clayburn at least regains her normal life. In "A Silver Mask," there are no ghosts and no witches, but there are evil servants, or people who act in the capacity of servants, who take over the life of Sonia Herries, a well-to-do, civilized, fifty-year-old spinster with a weakness for the personal beauty of the chief villain. She, too, meets a stranger on a cold night a few steps from her London house, just as Sara Clayburn had met the "fetch" a few steps from her own house on a cold day. Sonia is a bit drunk after a dinner party, and the young man who accosts her on the street appears so handsome that she lets him into the house and listens as he pleads a starving wife and infant. From then on, because of his charm, artistic knowledge, and appreciation for the things in her collection (especially a silver mask, which gives its name to the tale), she gradually allows him—his wife, child, and their friend—to infiltrate and dominate the house. Her own maid leaves. She herself has a heart condition, and, in the end, she is trapped in bed in an attic room forever.

The quality of the tale exists in the gradual specification of the way the criminal group takes over Sonia and her house, and the story corresponds to Wharton's itemized account of how Mrs. Clayburn had found the house and herself deserted the morning after the all-night coven in which her servants have participated. Although Sonia in Walpole's tale tries to get out of her bed to call a doctor, the criminal servants say it is not necessary and lock her up, they claim, for her own good. Meanwhile, Henry Abbott, the handsome young man in charge, has "sold her Utrillo," but he comes up to her room to hang on the wall the silver mask. " 'You'll want something to look at,' he went on, 'You're too ill, I'm afraid, ever to leave this room again. So it'll be nice for you. Something to look at.' He went out, gently closing the door behind him."[3] That is the end of the story and it is signed "October 21, 1930," just ten days away from All Souls' Night.

The scenario of each tale is more or less the same: the entrapment of a woman living alone, amid a certain amount of luxury, because of a conspiracy of her servants to control her. In Walpole's case, the woman is destroyed; in Wharton's case, the woman's home is destroyed for her as a place of security, although she herself is not harmed. They both, however, feel contact with evil.

Wharton never mentioned this story, nor did she ever, in any of her published letters, fiction or essays, mention Walpole or his work. However, there was in this collection of tales by Walpole one story called "Mr. Oddy," which someone must have called her attention to, for it contains a well-known portrait of Henry James. Walpole has put in his fictional Henry Galleon, an often reappearing writer in many of his novels, many recognizable traits of James. It seems highly likely that Wharton had handled the volume. A factor arguing for her having known the volume is that she called her tale "All Souls'," instead of "All Souls' Night." That may be because she knew that Walpole had used the latter as the title for *his* volume of collected tales, which deal mostly with ghosts or mysterious situations. She did not steal the tale; she emulated the atmosphere and selected the basic situation: the threat to the well-being of a single, middle-aged woman seemingly protected by wealth, taste, and servants. It is the servants who cannot be trusted. In both tales, they act in concert against the well-being of the unprotected woman. This situation probably reflected Mrs. Wharton's own fears as her loyal servants, who had been with her for years, were dying. Walpole, now a wealthy man, also a man living largely in the country and also dependent on loving servants, must have imagined such a situation as being possible.

So, beyond the interest that the question of "borrowings" or "parallels" may have for the reader of these two tales, there is the attraction of the underlying theme that unites them both: the threat of being abandoned by those who are paid to care for them, shared by all aging persons. The seventy-five-year-old Edith Wharton, with a degenerating heart condition, probably sensed the familiarity with such fears in the tale by the equally vulnerable bachelor, Walpole, who suffered from a serious and eventually fatal case of diabetes.

REFERENCES

1. Hugh Walpole, *The Apple Trees* (Waltham Saint Lawrence, Berkshire: Golden Cockerel Press, 1932), p. 54.

2. Edith Wharton, *The Collected Short Stories of Edith Wharton,* ed. R. W. B. Lewis, vol. 11 (New York: Scribner's, 1968), pp. 875–97.

3. Hugh Walpole, *All Souls' Night* (London: Macmillan, 1933), p. 40.

16

Consuelo Vanderbilt, John Esquemeling, and THE BUCCANEERS

R. W. B. Lewis has noted that Edith Wharton had been friends from early girlhood with a group of women who included Consuelo Yznaga (the Duchess of Manchester) and the Jerome sisters, "a cluster of comely trans-Atlantic invaders in the 1870s" to whom she "would devote her last and remarkable, though unfinished, novel, *The Buccaneers.*"[1] He also has noted that Conchita Santo-Dios of *The Buccaneers* "combines features of Minnie Stevens and of Edith's friend, the former Consuelo Yznaga" (L, 528). Actually, when one narrows down to a close reading of the novel, one can find a more specific source connected with these women, which creates the chief model for the novel.

The international marriage behind the marriages of the young American girls in Mrs. Wharton's novel, *The Buccaneers,* may well have been the marriage of Consuelo Vanderbilt, the American heiress of the Vanderbilt millions, to the ninth Duke of Marlborough, as well as the subsequent scandals connected with their separation. The summer before the marriage in 1895, Consuelo's mother, Alva Vanderbilt, had discovered that her daughter was in love with Winthrop Rutherford, the son of a professor of astronomy at Harvard and a distinguished photographer, a relationship she wished to break up because she had destined Consuelo, then an eighteen-year-old, for a brilliant, aristocratic, English marriage. Alva had met the Duke of Marlborough in England and invited him to Newport, and he accepted the invitation the following September. He spent two weeks there and was agreeable to the match. The wedding took place on November 6, 1895.

Originally published as "Consuelo Vanderbilt and *The Buccaneers,*" in *The Edith Wharton Review* 10, no. 2 (1993): 15–19.

William K. Vanderbilt had written in the marriage contract that he would deliver over to the Duke of Marlborough two million, five hundred thousand dollars, which, after the Duke's death, would revert to Consuelo. In 1920 the marriage was dissolved and finally annulled, just a few years before Edith Wharton began to write her novel in 1934 and at a time when the scandal was known throughout the world. Apparently, as early as 1907, the Duke and Duchess were at odds with each other.[2] Rather than divorce, they agreed to separate at the suggestion of King Edward VII, and they lived together only for a short time. In 1920, after their civil divorce on July 4, which was a virtual independence day for Consuelo, she married for love Colonel Louis-Jacques Balsan, a retired officer with the French army, wealthy enough to lead a gentleman's life. In 1926, because of Balsan's Catholic family, Consuelo applied for an annulment, which she obtained from the Vatican.

The whole problem had started when Consuelo, at seventeen, became secretly engaged to Winthrop Rutherford. At that point her mother took her to Europe. The documents in the annulment case of the divorce from the Duke, which were presented to the Rota, indicate in Consuelo's own words "that if I had succeeded in escaping, she [her mother] would shoot my sweetheart and she would therefore be imprisoned, and hanged, and I would be responsible" (Brough, 293). After she was married to the Duke of Marlborough, "the arrogance of the Duke's character . . . created in me a sentiment of hostility. He seemed to despise anything that was not British, and therefore my feelings were hurt" (Brough, 294). She related that she had broken down and wept, "she had nobody to whom she could turn" (Brough, 294). "Sarcastic comments on all things American"[3] were made by the Duke of Marlborough. His "archaic prejudices [were] inspired by a point of view opposed to my own" (GG, 40). She also stated in her autobiography that "Marlborough spoke of the link in the chain. He meant that there were certain standards that must be maintained" (GG, 70).

We are thus at that point in *The Buccaneers* where Laura Testvalley enters the novel. For Annabel St. George or Nan, Wharton's heroine, close in appearance to Consuelo, could only turn to her governess Laura when she found that her husband of an arranged marriage, the Duke of Tintagel, also despised anything that was not British. Alva Vanderbilt herself admitted to the Rota, "I forced her to marry the Duke. I have always had absolute power over my daughter, my children having been entrusted to me entirely after my divorce. . . . I therefore did not say, but ordered her to marry the Duke" (Brough, 295). Moreover, Miss Harper, Consuelo's own governess, played a role in these proceedings that may well be behind Laura Testvalley's role. Miss Harper was Consuelo's English governess, although she had both French and English governesses in her adolescence. When she said she wanted to marry her beau, her mother said that she would kill him if she ran away with him. "Even my governess, usually so calm, was harassed" (GG, 37). "How gratefully then I looked to Miss Harper for consolation and advice, how wisely she spoke of the future awaiting me in her country, of the opportunities for usefulness and social service I would find there, of the happiness a life lived for others can bring" (GG, 38). "And in such gentle appeals to my better nature, she slowly swung me from contemplations of a pure personal nature to a higher idealism" (GG, 38). "Marlborough proposed to me in the gothic room where the atmosphere was so propitious to sacrifice" (GG, 40).

Naturally, Mrs. Wharton does not follow all the specific details of this case. The St. Georges, her heroine's rich family, were not the outstanding millionaires in America as the W. K. Vanderbilts were, and the St. Georges were not divorced as the Vanderbilts had been. Nor was Mrs. St. George a replica of the tyrannical Alva Vanderbilt, but the situation is generally the same—that of the rich American mothers desperately wanting their daughters to marry into the English aristocracy and the daughters finding that life is not the romantic dream they thought it might be. The forced engagement of the young heiresses of American fortunes to British aristocrats seemed to create the same kind of problems. The classical example, *par excellence,* was that of Consuelo Vanderbilt married to the Duke of Marlborough. Her solution too was the solution that Edith Wharton described for Nan St. George, a second marriage with a more congenial man whom she loves. The trajectory of the lives of the fictive heroine and the real American heiress seems to be the same, and we may assume that the model from real life reinforced the authenticity of Wharton's fiction.

Of course, the character of Laura Testvalley is Wharton's own invention and is, in a way, her own personal solution of the problem. But Edith's own governess, Anna Bahlmann, who became her literary agent, also played a role in her own life. That same Anna Bahlmann had been a governess in the Rutherford family, and she became Edith's "fräulein" with a German background, which is inserted into the novel, for we read her frequent quotations from Clärchen's song from Goethe's *Egmont.*

Edith Wharton took on Anna Bahlmann in 1904 as her secretary and literary assistant while she was writing *The House of Mirth.* In 1909, she traveled with her to Germany, and Anna stayed with Edith in the 53 rue de Varenne apartment. She was there while Edith got her divorce in 1913, and she went with her on her trip to Algiers during the war. She continued to play an important part in Wharton's life until her death in 1916. In a similar fashion, Miss Harper, Consuelo's governess, played a focal part of her life and became one of the chief figures in the annulment proceedings, testifying to the forced marriage of Consuelo to "Sunny" Marlborough.

Why would Edith Wharton borrow the Marlborough case? It is probably because she herself in a way was closely involved with it. Winthrop Rutherford, whose love affair with Consuelo Vanderbilt Alva wanted to break up in order to make a more illustrious match, was not only a close neighbor when Edith was a young girl in Newport, but Edith herself was somewhat enamored of Winthrop. Wharton wrote in her autobiography that the boys of that family were extraordinarily handsome and "were the prototypes of my first novels."[4] She had also acquired from the Rutherfords the governess who was to become her close friend and literary executor. One of the Rutherford daughters was to become Mrs. Henry White, who became a close friend of Edith as the years went on and who also was close to Henry James.

In 1883, Edith Wharton was twenty-one and had already come out, and either she or her parents went to Mrs. Vanderbilt's spectacular costume ball of that year, since they were related to Mrs. Astor, the arbiter of New York society, who, after the ball, finally received the Vanderbilts. One of the outstanding features of this ball was the unusual dancing of the Virginia reel. As we read a description of that reel by one of the Vanderbilt descendants, we can recognize why Wharton must have used it as the source of her greatest scene for *The Buccaneers,* that of the Christmas ball at the Duke and Duchess of Tintagel's country house, Longlands. Here is the Vanderbilt ball as it ends: "A few of the older guests left after two o'clock that morning, but by six o'clock the party was still going strong. As Tuesday's sky paled above the city, Alva led a Virginia reel, her sign that the fancy dress ball had officially ended."[5]

Here is the scene Wharton modeled after it in *The Buccaneers:* Laura sits down at the piano and plays, "rattling off a noisy reel which she was said to have learned in the States and down the floor whirled the dancers."[6] Then there is a discussion about the origin of the reel, which the

English guests learn finally is as English as they are. Then the reel takes on a much more significant turn. It continues with the couples "forming a sort of giant caterpillar . . . spinning off . . . down the length of the Waterloo room . . . and the Raphael drawing room beyond" (BU, 281–82). The onlookers see "the wild train . . . sweeping ahead of them down the length of the Sculpture Gallery . . . and up the state staircase to the floor above. . . . Door after door was flung open, whirled through and passed out again, as the train pursued its turbulent way" (BU, 283). It is at this point that the young Duchess Nan and Guy Thwarte, who will become her love, drop out of the dance and go into her sitting room containing the Correggio *Earthly Paradise* paintings. Since Correggio never painted such a series (although he does have about seven unrelated mythological paintings, one of which once belonged to the Marquis of Londonderry and is in the British Museum, and the best-known one, *Jupiter and Antiope,* in the Louvre, Wharton must have known well), they are there to emphasize the sexual and sensual elements of love, which Nan does not enjoy with Ushant, the censorious Duke of Tintagel.

Other personalities revolving around the Vanderbilt circle and impinging also on Edith Wharton's world included the Belmonts. Alva married August Belmont's son after her divorce from William K. Vanderbilt, which took place a short time before the marriage of Consuelo to Sunny Marlborough. Belmont had appeared earlier in Wharton's work as Julius Beaufort in *The Age of Innocence.* The marriage of Consuelo and the Duke, as well as the successful introduction of the Vanderbilts into New York society, was engineered by Consuelo Yznaga, the Duchess of Manchester. She had been a good friend of Edith Wharton's in her girlhood and, in the early 1900s, again became very close and would naturally know of and keep Edith posted on the private details of the aristocratic marriage. It was she who, as Lady Mandeville, helped organize the 1883 Vanderbilt ball at which the Virginia reel was danced until dawn. That was the year when Edith Wharton was engaged to Harry Stevens, son of Mrs. Paran Stevens, who attended the ball as Queen Elizabeth. So Edith herself may have been there. She also was close to George Vanderbilt all through her life, and there are published letters in which she describes her visits to the huge American castle in Ashville built by him.

In general it is clear that the scandal of Consuelo's separation and final divorce had a long life, beginning with Consuelo's marriage in 1895 and ending around 1930 after her second happy marriage. Since she lived into the 1960s, she was always in the society news for as long as Edith

Wharton lived. After 1906 or 1907 and in her later years, Wharton frequented the aristocratic and exclusive drawing rooms of the British aristocracy, which included the Marlborough set.

The legal separation between Consuelo and the Duke took place in 1907, but the divorce, on the advice of Edward VII, was held off until 1920, long after the Monarch's death. Halfway between the two dates in 1913 Edith got her own divorce after she too had delayed as long as she could. Because of the similarity of the situations in the network of friends and acquaintances that united their social worlds, Consuelo's dramatic marriage and the circumstances accompanying it would interest Wharton. It seems to be a larger than life illustration of "The International Scene" begun by Henry James. James himself had made use of the fact that Consuelo's father, William K. Vanderbilt, had hired a corespondent to allow him to divorce Alva. James used this situation to create his tale, "The Special Type" (1900). It was time for Wharton to make her own invention based on the most notorious international marriage, as well as one of the most touching, of the twentieth century, but treated from a different angle from the international marriage she portrayed in *The Custom of the Country* (1913) in which the heroine or anti-heroine is hard-boiled and ambitious, exactly the opposite of both Consuelo Vanderbilt and Annabel Tintagel, her fictional *alter ego.*

For there are many aspects of Nan that tally with the personality of Consuelo Balsan (as she became after her divorce) revealed from biographies and her own autobiography. Consuelo did not elope romantically as Nan did. Although her governess helped her to get her annulment many years later, Miss Harper did not have, we are to believe from the unfinished novel, the necessary romantic and revolutionary character of Laura Testvalley to abet an elopement and to give up by that action chances for her own happiness as Laura had.

Let us review those elements in *The Buccaneers* that seem to reflect specifically the Vanderbilt-Marlborough scandal. We find a reflection of "Sunny" Marlborough's nickname in "Seedy," Lord Seadown, in the novel. "Sunny" was named so after one of his other titles, Lord Sunderland. Consuelo tells us that "The Earl of Sunderland had married the daughter of the first Duke of Marlborough" (GG, 82). The theme of the very rich girls without the sanction of New York society conquering the English aristocracy is very close to the Vanderbilt case for, although their extreme wealth and Alva's great aggressiveness could not finally keep them out, as *nouveaux riches* they were not considered equal to the original four hundred members of New York society. Although they finally got to Newport, their early years were spent at Saratoga, like the St. Georges in *The Buccaneers*. The fake title of "Colonel," which Mr. St. George assumed in the novel, corresponded to the fake title of "Commodore," which was that of the first Vanderbilt to make a fortune. R. W. B. Lewis says that Honourslove, the beautiful home of the Thwartes in England, is patterned on Lady Elcho's Stanway (L, 528). Wharton also became friendly with Harry Cust, who had courted and loved Consuelo Marlborough after her marriage and was a member of the society of the "Souls," a closed society mostly of the aristocracy among whom extramarital affairs were very common, although Consuelo appears not to have had any (Winston Churchill's mother, however, did). These connections would have reinforced Wharton's knowledge and interest in recreating a fictional equivalent of the Vanderbilt affair.

But even more convincing is the character in the novel of Concita Closson, who is the first of the American girls to marry into the British aristocracy. She is closely patterned on Consuelo Yznaga, as Lewis had noticed (L, 528). Consuelo Yznaga was partly Brazilian and partly American, just as Concita in the novel was partly Cuban and partly American. Consuelo Yznaga becomes first Lady Mandeville, then Lady Manchester, and arranges the marriage between Consuelo Vanderbilt and the Duke, just as Concita in the novel facilitates the introduction of her American friends to the peerage. Concita becomes Lady Marable (and the name Marable suggests Marlborough). It was Nan's "indifference to money and honours" that the young duke of Tintagel valued and that had also attracted Sunny who saw that Consuelo Vanderbilt did not appreciate the social value of marrying a duke.

In her synopsis of how the novel would end, Wharton states that the time she deals with is the 1870s, "the first time the social invasion had ever been tried in England on such a scale," and "admired in Saratoga, Longbranch and the White Sulphur Springs, they [the St. Georges] fail at Newport and at New York."

The Vanderbilts' acceptance into society, though reluctantly achieved, took place at the time of the ball in 1883; the occasion is not too far from the 1870s, and Edith Wharton herself was on the scene when Consuelo came out at the age of seventeen (as Edith had) in 1894. Consuelo "had no secretary and the job of writing and handling all the invitations was a burden in itself, but Sunny believed such wholesale entertaining was an essential part of her education as Duchess" (Brough, 112). Consuelo more generously tells us, "Since it was then considered ill-bred not to answer all letters oneself, I had no secretary" (GG, 81). In Chapter 19, Book 3 of *The Buccaneers,* Wharton shows us Nan, now the Duchess of Tintagel, laboriously also writing out invitations by herself with instructions on how to write and sign them according to protocol.

Consuelo, who visited the poor tenants on her estate and "read to the blind," at Christmas went "from house to house with toys for the children" (Brough, 125). She instructed Sunny's agent to offer work on the roads when there was hunger in the villages. This incurred Sunny's anger, but Consuelo said she could not tolerate such "striking contrast between their riches and other people's poverty" (Brough, 130). "When I announced my desire to provide work for the unemployed," Consuelo wrote, "it was labelled as sentimental socialism; but unable to reconcile our life of ease with the hardships of those who, . . . were yet our neighbours, I dispatched funds to institute relief work. Unfortunately the men . . . sent a letter to my husband, who, to his indignant surprise, discovered that the roads on his estate had been mended and his generosity exalted. It was only then that I discovered how greatly he resented such independent action and had I committed *lèse majesté* it could not have been more serious" (GG, 100).

Nan, in like manner, does the same kind of charitable work and also gets scolded by an irate Ushant Tintagel. Nan felt that "to help and befriend those dependent on him was a service she could render him" (*Buccaneers,* 251). But when she wants to have the drains fixed to wipe out typhoid fever, he disapproves and forbids her to go to the cottages while she is pregnant. She does and has a miscarriage. Like Consuelo, she is "fated to be a stranger among strangers" (Brough, 260). Sunny Marlborough "kept himself detached from humankind . . . denying himself the existence of emotion" (Brough, 201), just as Ushant did.

But Wharton of course does not follow the details of the Vanderbilt case, which involve the gradual separation and civil divorce in 1920 followed immediately by the marriage of Consuelo to Jacques Balsan. Wharton, through the introduction of the governess, Laura Testvalley, a member of the revolutionary and romantic family, which included Dante Gabriel Rossetti, acts as the *agente provocateuse* of an elopement. That produced the scandal for the novel. The scandal in the Vanderbilt-Marlborough marriage was the final divorce, as well as the separation, events not condoned by British society. The notoriety of the affair and the goodness and gentleness of the American heiress who suffered from the ambitions of her mother touched the newspapers and readers of the world, as well as giving them the glamour of a picture of aristocracy close to royalty. Since the Marlboroughs gave the name of their London house to the Marlborough Set, the circle dominated by Edward VII as Prince of Wales and later as king, everyone was interested in the story. Edith Wharton, who was so close to the main participants of this international drama, made profitable use of her knowledge in the general plot of her novel about how the "Invaders" of American society captured the British aristocracy.

What seems to have suggested the title and the leading concept behind this novel about the invasion into society of a band of gentle pirates is John Esquemeling's seventeenth-century book, *The Buccaneers of America* (1678), a twentieth-century reprint (circa 1925) of which Edith Wharton owned. There is no date on the volume reprinted by George Rutledge and Sons in London. It was among those books from Edith Wharton's library inherited by Lord Clark, stored at Saltwood Castle, England, and sold in 1984 by Maggs Brothers of London. It would therefore have been available to Edith Wharton a few years before she began her novel.

The Dutch author is very hard on the character of Captain Morgan, the most famous of the band of pirates known as the buccaneers, a member of which band was the author himself. The buccaneers were the chief marauders of the New World, the continent of America; their domination and cruelty had been equaled only by their extraordinary adventuresomeness. Andrew Lang, who introduced the first part of the volume, does not try to extricate the buccaneers from the imputations made by Esquemeling that the torture of their victims and their destruction of cities made them terrifying criminals in the eyes of the civilized world. It is the publisher who praises "the unparalleled courage of the buccaneers; the strangeness of their performances; the novelty of their exploits and with all, the glory and grandeur of valour which here is seen to be inherent to our English nation and is pregnant of great actions in the present as in the former ages."[7] The presence in Edith Wharton's library of this volume, which in essence exposes and yet exalts the exploits of these bandits, suggests that it may have contributed metaphorically to the exploits of the American adventuresses and their assault on English society. It is here a question of the biter bit. The young American beauties exact a revenge on the seventeenth-century buccaneers who invaded the Western hemisphere by repeating their conquests in reverse and invading England as their predecessors had invaded America.

REFERENCES

1. R. W. B. Lewis, *Edith Wharton: A Biography* (New York: Harper & Row, 1975), p. 41. Future references are indicated by L and page number.

2. James Brough, *Consuelo: Portrait of an American Heiress* (New York: Coward, McCann, and Gerghegan, 1979), p. 291. Future references are indicated by Brough and page number.

3. Consuelo Balsan, *The Glitter and the Gold* (London: Heinemann, 1953; later edition 1973), p. 40. Future references are indicated by GG and page number.

4. Edith Wharton, *A Backward Glance* (New York: Appleton-Century, 1934), p. 47. Future references are indicated by BG and page number.

5. Arthur T. Vanderbilt II, *The Fall of the House of Vanderbilt* (New York: Morrow, 1989), p. 120.

6. Edith Wharton, *The Buccaneers* (New York: Scribner's, 1938), p. 278. Future references are indicated by BU and page number.

7. John Esquemeling, *The Buccaneers of America* (1678; reprint, London: George Rutledge and Sons, 1925), p. 289.

PART THREE
Wharton's Uses of Art

17

FALSE DAWN *and the Irony of Taste Changes in Art*

Edith Wharton's taste has always been considered the top of good form because of her experience in interior decoration and because of her personal elegance in contemporary fashion. But little attention has been paid until recently,[1] especially in detail, to the role that art played in her fiction or in changing tastes in art in which she, as social historian, was interested. *False Dawn*, a novella, which is the first part of the quartet *Old New York* (1924), ironically treats the fate of an advanced artistic taste in the New York of the 1840s. Its hero, Lewis Raycie, is given five thousand dollars by his father to create "a gallery of Heirlooms," and is instructed to purchase in Europe pictures then highly esteemed in America. "Raphael, I fear, we can hardly aspire to top but a Domenichino, an Albano, a Carlo Dolci, a Guercino, a Carlo Maratta—" his father says, "one or two of Salvator Rosa's noble landscapes . . . you see my idea? There shall be a Raycie Gallery; and it shall be your mission to get together its nucleus."[2] In Venice, Lewis recognizes the beauty of his unappreciated fiancée in the Saint Ursula paintings by Carpaccio.

His enthusiasm for the painters previous to Raphael is encouraged by Ruskin (whom he meets in front of Mont Blanc), who takes a fancy to him, advises him, and introduces him to his English friends—Hunt, Morris, and Rossetti. Through them he learns to value and to buy paintings by the authentic pre-Raphael painters—Carpaccio, Piero della Francesca, Mantegna, Giotto, and Fra Angelico (rather than Angelica Kauffmann, whom his father would have preferred).

Edith Wharton did not invent out of the blue this tale of a man vic-

Originally published as "Changing Tastes in Art in Edith Wharton's *False Dawn,*" in *The Edith Wharton Newsletter* 1, no. 2 (Fall 1984): 1–8.

timized by society for having been too precocious in his artistic taste. She had before her two examples among American collectors who had suffered because of their advanced artistic purchases when she elaborated and perfected her short novel. Edith Wharton's hero who formed "one of the most beautiful collections of Italian primitives in the world" reminds us of James Jackson Jarves (1818–1888), fascinating New England traveler, art historian, and born collector. His assemblage of Italian primitives ridiculed by contemporary critics was based on the inheritance of "a little fortune most of which he spent in collecting pictures"[3] and which found a home in Yale, after Charles Eliot Norton had tried unsuccessfully to place it in New York or Boston. It was Jarves himself who had given Norton a letter of introduction to Ruskin.[4] Interestingly enough, R. W. B. Lewis writes that it was Norton who told Mrs. Wharton "about his meeting in Switzerland with John Ruskin,"[5] which is repeated in the crucial meeting between Lewis Raycie and Ruskin in *False Dawn*.

But an even lesser known and earlier collector, Thomas Jefferson Bryan (1802–1870) was the first to bring "primitives" to this country, but he did not have the support of Ruskin nor of Charles Norton, who helped get the Jarves Collection into the Yale University Museum. The son of the wealthy partner of John Jacob Astor, Bryan went to Europe in 1823 and returned in 1853 with 229 "masterpieces" including 30 examples of early Italian "primitives." In New York Bryan exhibited the collection at 30th Street and Broadway in what he called "Bryan's Gallery of Christian Art" with a catalogue of the entire collection and a larger "Companion" by R. G. White, who freed Bryan from the responsibility of "opinion upon the authenticity of many pictures."[6] If Edith Wharton and her family were not familiar with these publications and with the gallery, by 1924 she would have learned about them through James's recollections.

Among those who walked up two flights at 839 Broadway and paid a small admission fee was Henry James. He recorded it in *A Small Boy and Others* sixty years later: "It cast a chill, this collection of worm-eaten diptychs and triptychs . . . of black Madonnas and obscure Bambinos, of such marked and approved 'primitives' as had never yet been shipped to our shores," and it so affected his relationship to "a real Primitive" that he had "to take off the grey mantle of that night" when in later years he saw such a picture.[7] He continued his adverse response in *A Portrait of a Lady* (1881) when the inhuman Osmond collects "those primitive specimens of pictorial art in frames pedantically rusty"[8] and in *What Maisie*

Knew (1897). There a little girl responds negatively to "primitive" paintings when in the National Gallery she sat "staring" at pictures "with patches of gold and cataracts of purple, with stiff saints and angular angels, with ugly Madonnas and uglier babies."[9]

It may have been James who told Wharton about Bryan's Gallery, for in *False Dawn,* her young hero spends his father's money on a purchase of "primitives" that reflect the tastes of Ruskin and the Pre-Raphaelite Brotherhood. He exhibits them in a "Gallery of Christian Art," where he too charges admission. Wharton selected paintings from the non-primitives in Bryan's catalogue to indicate the accepted tastes of the 1840s, for old Raycie orders from his son paintings by Domenichino, Dolci, Guercino, Maratta, Salvator Rosa, etc., all painters in the Bryan collection. Lewis broke with tradition by buying Carpaccio, Piero della Francesca, and Fra Angelico, none of whom was represented in Bryan's Collection, which he gave to the New York Historical Society in 1867. Only Mantegnas and Giottos which Lewis buys appear in Bryan's collection. The fate of Lewis Raycie's Pieros and Carpaccios was to contribute to the ruin of his immediate family and to the unmerited fortune of his descendants who sold the masterpieces.

Wharton based her story of changing tastes on Bryan's abortive attempt to educate the uncultivated New Yorker. Even recently his "primitives" were on view for the general public.[10] Of the fourteen painters Lewis's father wanted him to purchase, none is listed in the index to Bryan's gallery. But the taste for Giotto, which in *False Dawn* is new to Lewis's father, is already accepted by Bryan, as is the taste for Mantegna. (It was perhaps only the Byzantine school paintings in this collection which Henry James had been unable to take as a ten-year-old). However, Richard Grant White, who wrote the handbook for the collection, called the Byzantine Panels "stiff, soulless, ill-colored works" that "became the mere mechanical filling up of set formulas." Included in the collection are a "Guido of Sienna" and a Cimabue, both of whom tried to free themselves from what they had learned. The Giotto, about whom little was known at this time, was then described as a pupil of Cimabue, whom he "soon surpassed in the blending of his tints, and the symmetry and correctness of his design."[11]

The Bryan Collection, then, had actual Italian primitives, truly devotional paintings. Among its 250 paintings at least two, Giotto and Mantegna, were new tastes for 1853. What Edith Wharton has done in her novel is to put into it what would become the advanced taste of the

1880s, not the 1840s, the period her book is devoted to. Out of the four-teen painters Halston Raycie wanted his son to collect, nine of them were included in Bryan's Collection, which means the prototype of Wharton's gallery was not advanced at all. But Edith Wharton uses the historical accuracy of there having been a Gallery of Christian Art to make vivid in her fictive account the destruction of a whole family, be-cause of a taste in art that was too early for the rest of New York, and to show that the "dawn" was "false." It was not until the 1920s that people began to collect Carpaccio and Piero, the two painters concentrated on as having been praised by Ruskin and his friends. She does refer to two pictures, the Piero *Girl* in the National Gallery in London and the Car-paccio *St. George* in California, that sound like real museum pieces, but there are no such paintings in those two places.

Mrs. Wharton's taste in art was the subject of a study in *Apollo* by Denys Sutton, although he unaccountably omits any mention of *False Dawn* in his catalogue. Her references in her travel books are to Bellini, Carpaccio, Botticelli, Botticini, Piero de Cosimo, Signorelli, and Roman-ino. She applauds the Carracci, an example of painters accepted by old man Raycie.[12] She appreciated Tiepolo, Longhi, and Guardi but said nothing in her various references to them in her nonfiction writings that others had not said about them. In 1904 she saw the great show of French primitives that led her to appreciate them on her motor trip through France in 1908. That enthusiasm is also put into Lewis Raycie's grand tour, which included the Near East.

Edith Wharton was not a collector, although Walter Berry gave her a Cézanne *(L'Allée du Jas de Bouffon)* and she owned two Odelon Redon flower pieces. In her novels the painters chosen by Lewis Raycie for his gallery appear occasionally about the time of *False Dawn's* publication. For instance, in *The Glimpses of the Moon* (1922) the young wife is af-fected by a Mantegna in the Louvre, whereas her husband likes Tiepolo. This written just before *False Dawn* shows the same taste change as in that later novel.

Sensitive to changes of taste, Wharton like most students of the fine arts admired the first-rate example of all schools of painting and archi-tecture. So, considering her familiarity with all schools of Italian art, which went into her *Italian Backgrounds* and *Italian Villas and Their Gar-dens,* we cannot be surprised as readers that the names of the artists whom Lewis is reacting against, and which his father wants him to purchase, appear more frequently and more prominently than the few who repre-

1. Vittore Carpaccio (1460–1526), *The Dream of Saint Ursula*. Accademia, Venice, Italy. Photograph from Alinari/Art Resource, N.Y.

sent the taste that is new to the 1840s. Carracci, Correggio, Albano, Domenichino, Carlo Dolci, Guercino, Carlo Maratta, and Salvador Rosa pop out of the pages of *False Dawn* with more than one mention each. The name of Carpaccio, newly discovered by Lewis, is found but neither his name nor the young saint he paints are named at first. Undoubtedly it was because Wharton wanted to surprise the reader, leading up to the naming of the artist through old Mr. Raycie's mispronunciation (Figure 1). The irony of this concealment of a name and a series of paintings so well known to the educated reader of the 1920s is that to the eye of the informed reader of the 1980s some of the painters considered *retardataire* at that time, such as Giulio Romano, now have been brought back from their downfall from grace during the years from 1920 to 1960 and now seem more interesting than Piero della Francesca and Carpaccio who were the most appreciated from 1900 through 1950. We are now reacting to the latter's universal popularity and are in turn rediscovering the values of the painters replaced in popularity by Piero della Francesca and Carpaccio.

Thus, by an irony that fits well into the mood of *False Dawn*, Edith Wharton's own avant-garde taste suffers from the inevitable reaction to the prevailing taste that each generation experiences. To most of the sophisticated museum haunters of the 1980s the name of Angelica Kauffman stimulates more interest than that of Fra Angelico.

The irony of the final destiny of the pictures in *False Dawn* may have had its source in Balzac's *Le Cousin Pons* where the treasures of an inspired collector end up in the possession of his vulgar relations. We know how Mrs. Wharton admired Balzac, especially in her later years. In *The Writing of Fiction,* published the year after *False Dawn,* she praises Balzac as "the first . . . to draw his dramatic action as much from the relation of his characters to their houses, streets, towns, . . . as from their fortuitous contacts with each other."[13] The particular point Wharton makes in her novella is that the New Yorkers at the turn of the century who inherit the collection of pictures prefer to turn masterpieces back into cash, for the precocious collector has failed in his mission to educate the taste of his society. This book allows Edith Wharton to sound the note of "frustration and waste that marks many of her books" as Denys Sutton asserts, especially since it here involves the resistance of Americans even of her own generation to alterations in taste.

References

1. See Helen Killoran, *Edith Wharton: Art and Allusion* (Tuscaloosa: University of Alabama Press, 1996), passim. (This reference was added in 1996.)

2. Edith Wharton, *False Dawn* (New York: D. Appleton, 1924), p. 53.

3. Van Wyck Brooks, *The Flowering of New England* (New York: Dutton, 1937), p. 470.

4. Ibid., p. 455.

5. R. W. B. Lewis, *Edith Wharton: A Biography* (New York: Harper & Row, 1975), p. 138.

6. Richard Grant White, *Companion to the Bryan Gallery of Christian Art,* with an introductory essay and an index (New York: Baker Godwin & Co.,

1853), p. 4. This was published in addition to the catalogue of the collection (*Catalogue of the Bryan Gallery of Christian Art*) from the earliest masters to the present time (New York: Snowden, 1953), pp. 1–11. In the *Metropolitan Museum Bulletin,* Summer 1982, devoted to "Fourteenth Century Italian Altarpieces" the director of the Museum, Philippe de Montebello wrote a prefatory note (p. 2) mentioning Edith Wharton's *False Dawn* in connection with the Bryan Gallery of Christian Art.

7. Henry James, *Autobiography* (New York: Criterion, 1956), pp. 152–53. Wharton may have reread the *Autobiography* at the time that she was helping Lubbock prepare the letters of Henry James for publication in 1920.

8. Henry James, *The Portrait of a Lady* (Boston: Houghton Mifflin, 1963), p. 193.

9. Henry James, *What Maisie Knew* (New York: Doubleday, 1954), p. 99.

10. Recently the New York Historical Society sold the Bryan Collection so that it can no longer be seen as a unit (note added in 1996).

11. White, *Companion to the Bryan Gallery of Christian Art,* p. 6.

12. Denys Sutton, "The Sharp Eye of Edith Wharton," *Apollo* 103, no. 167 (new series, January 1976): 7 and passim.

13. Edith Wharton, *The Writing of Fiction* (New York: Scribner's, 1925), p. 5.

18

Correggio and Rossetti in THE BUCCANEERS

Tradition and Revolution in the Patterns of Love

As we have seen, Edith Wharton was a social historian sensitive to the changing tastes in art, as *False Dawn* clearly shows her to be. In this short novel, the painters who were the sources of inspiration for the English Pre-Raphaelites had been touched on but not the mid-nineteenth-century painters whom they inspired, the Pre-Raphaelite Brotherhood. It is only in Wharton's last and incomplete novel, *The Buccaneers* (1938), that an actual painting by Dante Gabriel Rossetti, the *Bocca Baciata (The Kissed Mouth),* or at least a copy by Rossetti of the original oil painting, is placed in the collection of Sir Helmsley Thwarte. The old gentleman is seen in his shabby but beautiful ancestral home, Honourslove, "re-touching a delicately drawn water-colour copy of the little Rossetti Madonna above his desk."[1] He was a fine copyist, and "his water-colour glowed with the deep brilliance of the original picture" (BU, 270). He has promised this copy to Laura Testvalley, the original little governess. He tells his son, Guy, "She's Dante Gabriel's cousin. . . . Remarkable woman—one of the few relations the poet is always willing to see. She persuaded him to sell me a first study of the 'Bocca Baciata', and I was doing this as a way of thanking her" (BU, 270). We note that he is not making a copy of the *Bocca Baciata,* but of a Rossetti *Madonna,* which is a painting invented by Wharton, for Rossetti never seems to have painted a truly iconic madonna. But since the *Bocca Baciata* is mentioned by name, we are able to see that picture when we think of Laura Testvalley (Figure 2).

At the time of Wharton's novel, set in the 1870s, the famous Rossetti oil, *Bocca Baciata* (1859), was actually in the collection of G. P. Boyce, who

Originally published as "Pre-Raphaelite Painting and Poetry in Edith Wharton's 'The Buccaneers' (1938)," *Journal of Pre-Raphaelite Studies* 2, n.s. (Fall 1993): 16–19.

2. Gabriel Charles Dante Rossetti (1828–1882), *Bocca Baciata (Lips That Have Been Kissed)*. Gift of James Lawrence. Courtesy of Museum of Fine Arts, Boston.

had commissioned it, and it remained in his collection until July 1897. Wharton may have seen it close to the time of writing *The Buccaneers* (1934–37) when it appeared at the Sir James Murray sale at Christie's (April 29, 1927, Lot 84) or on March 5, 1935, at the Lord Lawrence of Kingsgate sale where it was bought by William Randolph Hearst. It is more likely, however, that Wharton saw the picture when it was exhibited at the Royal Academy in 1906.[2] It is a "first study" of this painting that Sir Helmsley buys.

    Why did Wharton choose this picture, a real one, although it is not the one that Sir Helmsley is copying, because the *Bocca Baciata* would be too intimate and sensual a gift for the "little brown governess"? It seems that she thought the mention of the *Bocca Baciata* with the image it raises in the reader's eyes would suggest the essential tie Sir Helmsley feels for the little woman. Virginia Surtees writes that the picture was "Condemned at the time by some as 'coarse' and 'sensual.'" It "represents a turning point in the career of the artist," foreshadowing as it does "his prolific output of studies of women . . . , sensual and voluptuous, mystical and inscrutable . . . until. In 1879 the apogee was reached with Mrs. William Morris as the *Donna della Finestra*" (*Surtees,* I, 68–69). She also tells us that "Arthurian and Dantesque subjects had begun to vanish from the easel; with the declining health of Elizabeth Siddal, the small angular figures . . . gradually disappeared, and in her place appears a new type of woman . . . in which the sweep of the neck, the curved lips, the indolent pose of the head . . . foreshadow his prolific output of studies of women" (*Surtees,* I, 69). Inscribed on the back of the painting is "'Bocca baciata non perda ventura, anzi rinova come fa la luna,'" from *Boccacio.* "'The mouth that has been kissed looses not its freshness; still it renews itself even as does the moon'" (*Surtees,* I, 68). The mention of this sensual portrait of a voluptuous model, combined with the gift of a copy of a madonna, is used by Wharton to indicate the promise of a fulfilled life of physical love and high privilege, which is presented to Laura Testvalley in the guise of the religious picture (the *Madonna*). It seems to suggest that Sir Helmsley is thinking of her in the terms of a very different kind of picture, which acts as an analogue to their relationship. The "little brown governess who wore violet poplin and heavy brooches of Roman mosaic" also "had eyes like torches, and masses of curly-edged dark hair which she was beginning to braid less tightly" (BU, 271). Although Laura had dressed herself in a sedate and virgin-like fashion, suggesting a madonna, she now, feeling her attraction for Sir Helmsley and his attraction for her, is wearing her hair loosely like the model in the *Bocca Baciata.* Nan, her former pupil and now the Duchess of Tintagel, also had begun to notice that her "hair's grown ever so much thicker; and you do it a new way" (BU, 335). Laura admits to "trying a new hair-lotion" and she "tried to flatten her upstanding ripples" (BU, 336). In these images, Wharton reveals that Laura's hair is meant to resemble Fanny Cornford's magnificent wavy hair when she posed for the *Bocca Baciata* and presented herself as the first of Rossetti's sensual women.

The authentic Rossetti painting contrasts sharply with the other imaginary paintings in the novel, the "famous Correggios," the *Earthly Paradise* series in the Duchess's private boudoir in the next chapter of the novel while the Christmas party is going on at Longlands, the seat of the Tintagel family. There is actually no such sequence by Correggio; it has been invented by Wharton to create "their own native world of sylvan loves and revels" (BU, 284), the proper atmosphere for the burgeoning intimacy between these two potential young lovers, Nan and Guy Thwarte. Correggio, we know, had painted seven individual mythological paintings now scattered over European museums. Wharton may have seen the single pictures themselves from reproductions in order to be able to create an equivalent earthly paradise, a painted world of sensual happiness made up from the individual panels that she could have seen by Correggio. Now in the National Gallery in London and formerly in the collection of the Marquis of Londonderry is *The Education of Cupid,* with Mercury, Venus, and Cupid in a charming family group of two naked gods and a goddess. Wharton had undoubtedly seen often the famous *Jupiter and Antiope* in the Salon Carré in the Louvre, along with the other Correggios, *Virtu* and *Vice,* in the same museum. Five other such small groups exist in Berlin and the Borghese Museum in Rome, but there is no such marvelous connected series of pictures lighted by their own "sunset glow" (BU, 283), which decorate the boudoir in Longlands. It is Laura Testvalley who encouraged Nan and Guy to break away during the Virginia reel danced at the Christmas party and to sit among these pictures, which, by their sensuality, stir up the attraction between the two young people.

Even before we reach the scene where Sir Helmsley is copying the small Rossetti, Nan tells Laura how Sir Helmsley had "a perfectly beautiful picture by your cousin . . . and Mr. Thwarte showed it to me. And so we talked of his [her cousin's] poetry too" (BU, 164). Laura answers that Sir Helmsley Thwarte "is an old friend of my cousin's, and one of his best patrons." She goes on to say that "there are people who don't appreciate his poetry . . . and I'd rather you didn't proclaim in public that you've read it all" (BU, 165). Nan answers, "They'd be shocked . . . because it's all about love. But that's why I like it, you know" (BU, 165). The picture that Nan calls "perfectly beautiful" is clearly not the *Madonna,* but the *Bocca Baciata,* with a mouth that has been kissed, and which represents a desirable woman. In this way we see that Nan encourages Laura to connect with Sir Helmsley through the means of a painting, as well as through the real poetry of her cousin, Dante Gabriel Rossetti.

Earlier in the novel, Wharton had laid the groundwork for the dominant aura in this novel of the Pre-Raphaelite contribution in both poetry and painting to the radical art movement in England in the 1870s. Laura Testvalley, while governess to the teenager Nan St. George, reads to her from her cousin's, Dante Gabriel Rossetti's, "The Blessed Damozel," charming her young charge through the poet's words (BU, 88–90). The sensuality of the verses condemned for that quality in their own time is reinforced by the sensuality of such a painting as the *Bocca Baciata*. What Wharton also appreciated was Rossetti's poetry, and she uses it to thicken the Pre-Raphaelite mood of *The Buccaneers*. The poetical work by Dante Gabriel Rossetti in Wharton's library included *Ballads and Sonnets* (Tauchnitz, 1892) and *The Collected Works* (two volumes, London, 1890), the latter with her bookplate.[3]

But long before *The Buccaneers,* Wharton had invoked Rossetti's "The House of Life." In *The Age of Innocence* (1922), Newland Archer receives a package of books from London. He "had declined three dinner invitations in favour of this feast" of Herbert Spencer and *Middlemarch,* but "he did not know what he was reading, and one book after another dropped from his hand. Suddenly, among them, he lit on a small volume of verse which he had ordered because the name had attracted him: 'The House of Life.' He took it up, and found himself plunged in an atmosphere unlike any he had ever breathed in books; so warm, so rich, and yet so ineffably tender, that it gave a new and haunting beauty to the most elementary of human passions. All through the night he pursued through those enchanted pages the vision of a woman who had the face of Ellen Olenska."[4]

The House of Life sonnets were printed in 1870 during which time Rossetti cultivated a passion for Mrs. Jane Morris, whose face haunted him. Ellen Olenska can be seen here as haunting Newland Archer in the same way. So we see that Wharton, in 1920, is likewise under the influence of Rossetti's sonnets. In *The Buccaneers* this influence becomes intensified, for she pays tribute not only to Dante Gabriel Rossetti but also to his father, the political rebel in exile. Wharton extends the talented family to include the plucky and independent governess, Laura Testvalley.

But now William Morris enters. In R. W. B. Lewis's biography of Wharton, we are told that around 1908, when Edith's affair with Fullerton was breaking up, she put into her commonplace book certain quotations with which to console herself. She devoted many pages to William Morris's "Defence of Guenevere," a poem about how adultery led to the queen's downfall and about the queen's musing on the disaster it caused. Lewis has called our attention to the reasons for Wharton's quotations from Morris's poetry: "Typically, she sought to appraise her situation—and its components of passion, infidelity, suffering, and intellectual challenge—by juxtaposed quotations in her commonplace book from the writings that had seized her attention. She covered more than thirty pages with such borrowings in 1908, much the most of any year in which entries were made. From William Morris's 'Defence of Guenevere,' she took eleven lines of the queen's reflective account of the adulterous affair with Lancelot: 'So day by day it grew, as if one should / Slip slowly down some path.'"[5]

Significantly, William Morris's *The Earthly Paradise,* a poem in three volumes (Boston, 1970), was in Wharton's library, which gives us a clue to the source for the name of the invented series of Correggios in Nan's boudoir (LW, 36). The stories are those of the loves of the gods and goddesses, covering the same kind of material that Correggio paints on his isolated canvases, but in Morris's poem James wrote in a review in *The Nation* that "Fate reserves for the poor storm-tossed adventurers a sort of fantastic compromise between their actual misery and their ideal bliss."[6] At the feast to which the adventurers are summoned each month, a different story is told each time. The adventures of Danae, Perseus and Andromeda, Cupid and Psyche, are among them, as well as Alcestis and Atalanta. Connecting the term "earthly paradise" from Morris's poem with the Correggio series in *The Buccaneers* makes clear how the version by Morris acts as an iconic parallel of the love between Guy and Nan, which will come as a sequel to the misery Nan has experienced as the Duchess of Tintagel and as a sequel to the scandal and social disgrace that will accompany their elopement. As Laura Testvalley, the Rossetti family member, has put the two young people in the presence of a group of paintings called *The Earthly Paradise,* so Laura's future itself is adumbrated in the Morris arrangement of tales; only, in her case, where she might have come into a comfortable, secure, earthly paradise with Sir Helmsley she will instead be judged as an *intrigante* who encouraged the disgraceful elopement of her pupil and the son of her possible lover. A connection between *The Earthly Paradise* paintings on the boudoir walls of Longlands and Morris's legend about a compromise between the ideal and the real can illuminate the futures of both Nan and Laura, the two women in this novel who engage our chief interest.

James remarks in his *Nation* review of *The Earthly Paradise:* "Mr.

Morris is indubitably a sensuous poet, to his credit be it said; his senses are constantly proffering their testimony and crying out their delight. But while they take their freedom, they employ it in no degree to their own debasement. Just as there is modesty of temperament we conceive there is modesty of imagination, and Mr. Morris possesses the latter distinction" (LC, 1190). This is the background for the burgeoning love affair between Nan and Guy Thwarte, a sensuous but modest one, and it contrasts to the authoritarian, cold relation between the Duke and the Duchess of Tintagel.

In the 1930s, Wharton's interest in Rossetti was comparable to her character Lewis Raycie's interest in the Pre-Raphaelite, Pre-Renaissance painters in Italy, which he brings into *False Dawn.* Wharton demonstrated in both novels the remarkable operation of her acute art historical sense.

Thus, *The Buccaneers,* as it stands today in its fragmentary form, seems to be a nostalgic reconstruction of the romantic temperament of the 1870s, as demonstrated in both the poetry and the painting of the Pre-Raphaelites. Edith Wharton, sensitive to tastes in art, endowed with the qualities that make a good art historian, functioning also as a practicing poet (the author of passionate poems to Morton Fullerton, her lover, such as *Ogrin The Hermit* [1908], *Terminus* [1909], and others), created the nostalgia of the 1870s out of the poetry and painting of the Pre-Raphaelite Brotherhood for her historical novel of international marriages. In it she emphasized the dominance of sensual satisfaction throughout this artistic movement that combined political with aesthetic rebellion.

References

1. Edith Wharton, *The Buccaneers* (New York: Appleton-Century, 1938), p. 269. Future references are indicated by BU and page number. Edith Wharton apparently knew that there was at least one copy known to have been made by Rossetti of the *Bocca Baciata,* and her source would have been *Rossetti Papers: 1862–1870,* ed. W. M. Rossetti (London, 1903); *Masterpieces of Rossetti* (London and Glasgow, 1923); and *Surtees,* Catalogue number 114, vol. 1, p. 69, note 5. The oil itself was reproduced in *Masterpieces of Rossetti* (p. 13. *Surtees,* vol. 1, p. 69, note 1). The oil is illustrated in *Surtees,* vol. 2, plate 186.

2. Virginia Surtees, *Dante Gabriel Rossetti, 1828–1882. The Paintings and Drawings. A Catalogue Raisonné,* vol. 1, text, and vol. 2, plates (Oxford: Clarendon, 1971), 1:68–69. Future references are indicated by Surtees I and page number.

3. *The Library of Edith Wharton* (London: Maggs Brothers), compiled by Edward Maggs, October 29, 1983, privately distributed, Adeline Tintner's copy. Wharton owned also Rossetti's *Ballads and Sonnets,* Tauchnitz, 1882, and *Collected Works,* two volumes, the latter inscribed by Edith Wharton. Future references are indicated by LW.

4. Edith Wharton, *The Age of Innocence* (New York: D. Appleton, 1920), p. 138.

5. R. W. B. Lewis, *Edith Wharton: A Biography* (New York: Harper & Row, 1975), pp. 229–30.

6. Henry James, *Literary Criticism: Essays on Literature* (New York: The Library of America, 1984), p. 1188. Review of the *Earthly Paradise* by William Morris. Future references are indicated by LC and page number.

19

Tiepolo's Ceiling in the Church of the Scalzi and
THE GLIMPSES OF THE MOON

The Importance of Home

In *The Glimpses of the Moon,* Nick Lansing "wandered up the nave under the whirl of rose-and-lemon angels in Tiepolo's great vault." He sees Coral Hicks "applying her field-glass to the celestial vortex,"[1] but the reader is not told why Coral is using her "open manual" or what Nick is viewing. From the passage in the book, we do not know that the ceiling fresco by Tiepolo is a painting judged by art critics to be "perhaps Tiepolo's most stunning ecclesiastical decoration."[2] The fresco no longer exists, but I was alerted in a lecture on Tiepolo and Edith Wharton's appreciation of the eighteenth-century painter in her travel essays; Rosella Mamoli Zorzi, professor of American literature at the University of Venice,[3] projected a slide of the fresco later destroyed by an Austrian bomb in 1915. As I had just finished reading once more *The Glimpses of the Moon,* I was fascinated by seeing what that fresco was all about.

The subject of Tiepolo's fresco represents the legend of the Transportation of the Holy House of Mary from Palestine to Loreto (Figure 3). The Virgin's small house was carried away from Palestine by a flock of angels to protect it from Muslim armies during the Crusades. Carried through the air, the house was finally deposited at Loreto in Italy, where the Carmelites became custodians of Mary's shrine. On the Feast of the Transportation of the Holy Home in 1650, the Church of the Discalced Carmelites in Venice was founded, and from 1743 to 1745 Tiepelo worked on the fresco in the church. In the finished version, the "Virgin, shown against an immense silver moon—her most enduring apocalyptic

Originally published in *The Edith Wharton Review* 14, no. 1 (Spring 1997): 4–12.

3. Giambattista Tiepolo, detail from *The Transport of the Holy House*. S. Maria degli Scalzi/Venice/, Venice, Italy. Photograph from Alinari/Art Resource, N.Y.

attribute . . . sits on the roof of the house with the Christ Child on her shoulder." [4]

The passage from Wharton's *Italian Backgrounds* cited by Zorzi shows the American novelist's precocious enthusiasm for the great ceiling decorator who was, at the time of her book, 1905, not yet appreciated by English-speaking spectators. Edith Wharton's description reads as follows:

> On the soaring vault of the Scalzi, above an interior of almost Palladian elegance and severity, the great painter of atmosphere, the first of the *pleinairistes,* was required to depict the transportation of the Holy House from Palestine to Loreto. That Tiepolo, with his love of ethereal distances, and of cloud-like hues melting into thin air, should have accepted the task of representing a stone house borne through the sky by angels, shows a rare sense of mastery; that he achieved the feat without disaster justified the audacity of the attempt. . . . The result is that the angels, whirling along the Virgin's house with a vehemence which makes it seem a mere feather in the rush of their flight, appear to be sweeping through measureless heights of air above an unroofed building. [5]

But Wharton's use of the Scalzi fresco in her novel, *The Glimpses of the Moon* (1922), seems to be more important than these appreciative lines of her admiration of Tiepolo. In *The Glimpses of the Moon,* when Nick Lansing sees a young woman "applying her field-glass to the celestial vortex, from which she occasionally glanced down at an open manual," it is Coral Hicks who emulates Edith Wharton herself looking at the fresco. The scene is important because Coral, here, in her conversation with Nick, makes it quite clear that "I *am* in love" and that it is Nick himself with whom she is in love (GM, 92–91).

We know how important certain scenes are for Wharton when the main characters meet in front of art in a museum or a church. In *The Age of Innocence* when Ellen Olenska and Newland Archer meet in the Cesnola collection of antiquities in the Metropolitan Museum of Art in New York City, we know how the idea of "change" will have a symbolic effect in the novel. The everyday appurtenances for living shown in the museum correspond to the table settings and utensils that have been set out when the Archers give a dinner for Ellen Olenska.

Encounters in the novels of Edith Wharton among people in front of works of art in museums, private houses, or churches are symbolically and iconographically important to the meaning Wharton wishes to attach to her novel. However, the use of the Scalzi ceiling raises certain questions. In the first place, when Wharton published her *Italian Backgrounds* in 1905, the fresco was in place, but in 1922 when *The Glimpses of the Moon* appeared in print, the fresco had been destroyed. Nevertheless, Nick and Coral are characters who, some time before 1914 and the outbreak of war, are looking at a fresco that was still there. Why does not Wharton explain the subject, the rescue of the Holy House by angels, for the reader? Does she think the reader knows it even though the fresco, by 1922, no longer existed, or that the reader would remember the description from her *Italian Backgrounds,* simply assuming that? Since the fresco itself is considered one of the most famous of Tiepolo's ceiling paintings, Wharton may have thought the reader was familiar with the subject. Only an informed student of Edith Wharton today would be likely to remember that she had described the subject in her essay.

Does the knowledge of the subject of the fresco make any difference to how one reads this book? The subject of the book throughout is the "honey-moon" of the young couple, Nick and Susy Lansing, who had made a bargain that, although penniless, they would risk their marriage by taking advantage of their rich friends' offers of rent-free occupancy of various houses. After a year, if either one feels she or he could do better, they will give each other their freedom to make comfortable marriages with wealthy mates. This pre–World War I new social set has hardboiled values, but the reader soon finds out that neither one of the young persons involved really believes in those values. Throughout the book one notices that the rich members of the fast, international set who own more than one house rarely stay in their houses and can be considered peripatetic, homeless persons. The absence of the young couple's own home is an ever-present subject. Even the Fulmers, the more admirable impecunious couple in the set, he a painter and she a talented violinist, with their five children, are rarely at their inadequate house in Passy. Nevertheless, it is the closest to a home because the Fulmer family has not been broken by divorce as the other families in the novel have been.

We must try to account for the scene's importance to the meaning of the novel. The subject of the Tiepolo fresco, the rescue of Mary's house by angelic support with Mary herself presiding, stresses the importance of the house as a permanent place, as a home. In the fresco, the Virgin is shown against a very large silver moon, "her most enduring and apocalyptic attribute,"[6] and we see the connection as another source for the title of the novel, in addition to the lines from *Hamlet*.[7] The scenes in which Nick and Susy meet under a sky where we, as readers, see the glimpses of the moon, repeat that element in Tiepolo's fresco where the Virgin is backed by a silver moon. Only glimpses of this moon are given to the young couple, until they finally realize how their love for each other has to throw off their social parasitism. When Nick Lansing sees the Scalzi fresco, he has been living in the borrowed Vanderlyn Palace in Venice owned by Nelson and Ellie Vanderlyn, for he and Susy are social parasites and have to sing for their supper in a manner that has become increasingly irksome for Nick. He sees that Coral Hicks, the plain daughter of an American millionaire, appreciates Tiepolo as much as he does. Both Nick and Coral would like a real home of their own, but both have no such homes. Nick and his wife, Susy, have only houses, not homes, which are lent to them for limited periods of time for certain services rendered. Their "home" depends on the caprices of the rich people who lend them houses when traveling back and forth to their other houses. The only person with a real home is Strefford, who, on becoming Lord Altringham, finally returns to his ancestral castle. The other places, even the Fulmers' place in Passy where they can park their children, are not basically homes. Their lack of the concept of home is an affliction of this social set.

This flaw in the life of the Lansing couple is made clear by having the legend of the rescue of Mary's poor little home in Nazareth dropped into the story's plot. Mary's house, so holy and cherished, although humble, transported by angels as if it were as light as air itself, is the unexpressed ideal of a home: lowly but loved. When Susy realizes that she cannot keep her bargain with Nick, that each will opt for freedom in a better marriage with someone else, she learns that life with the Fulmers' children constitutes a home because it has a family in it.

The critics of the novel have not grasped its prime message of the importance of having a home of their own for a newly married couple. Cynthia Wolff, in 1977, thought that Edith Wharton had not been able to "re-create the psychological complexity of human nature."[8] She criticized Nick's reaction to seeing at the end of the novel his wife, Susy, appearing " 'with a red-cheeked child against her shoulder through the veil of the winter night,' " when he saw her as " 'the eternal image of the wife and child' " (GM, 319). "Why these worldlings," writes Wolff, "should be moved by *this* experience escapes us" (FW, 347), and she concludes that Edith Wharton's "increasing interest in families" allows "this saccharine conclusion to stand" (FW, 347). When Cynthia Wolff writes that the sight of Susy appearing to Nick as "a thing apart, an uncondi-tioned vision" (GM, 319), "the eternal vision of the woman and child," which bears no relationship to anything in the novel that has preceded it, she thought so because apparently she did not know what the Scalzi fresco was about. It seems plausible that Wolff would too have noted that Nick's seeing Susy in a position like that of the Virgin and Child makes the ending of the book less a "saccharine conclusion" and more a sym-bolic one that gives the book an added dimension.

It is interesting that Helen Killoran, who has so much to say about Edith Wharton's uses of art and allusion, has so little to say about the role of the miracle of the Holy House in the Scalzi fresco. She never tells us what the subject of the picture is and, since the fresco has been destroyed, did not consult Edith Wharton's own description of the fresco in *Italian Backgrounds*.[8] Therefore she does not know that the rescue of the Virgin's home with its stress on the importance of a "home" has symbolically much to do with the plot of *The Glimpses of the Moon*.

By 1922, Edith Wharton had her own two "homes," first, St. Brîce-sous-le-Forêt, where she moved in 1919. It was just before she wrote *The Glimpses of the Moon* that she settled in by the Christmas of 1920 at Ste. Claire, Hyères, but it was at St. Brîce, during the summer of 1921, that Edith Wharton was busy with *The Glimpses of the Moon*.[9] For the first time since the sale of The Mount in 1911, Edith Wharton had her own home, split into her winter and her summer houses. So, as she wrote her novel, we can assume that she was aware of the importance of a home and for eight or nine years had considered herself homeless. Even before, the war with its refugees had made Wharton very much aware of the hoards of homeless people and led to her editing *The Book of the Home-less,* which contained contributions from celebrated authors and artists published by Scribner's in 1916, the same year she began *The Glimpses of the Moon*. Her work with the refugees of Belgium and other war-torn places affected her entire attitude to the notion of a home and to those dispossessed of their homes. The war and its activities occupied her until the Armistice, and then she began to look for a home for herself. Given her working habits and her social responsibilities, she needed such a sup-port; in fact, she needed two homes because of the climate in France, and they had to be in Europe. Knowing the presence of the idea of a home and the emotional insecurity that comes with homelessness, we can understand how the fresco of the Virgin regaining her home through angelic intervention brings an important parallel to the homeless young Lansings. Since it graphically illustrates the idea of homelessness with its corrupting influence on society, we are shown that this novel is not a frivolous attempt on Wharton's part to write a bestseller with a mechanically achieved happy ending for the young couple. Nick and Susy are shown as the innocent victims of society without a sense of "home," a base which the two young people must regain in order to save their marriage.

The Glimpses of the Moon, when seen in the light of the subject of the Tiepolo fresco, certainly seems to be built around the idea of the need to have a home. Nick and Susy only knew homes by "living . . . in the frame of other people's wealth" (GM, 193). When Susy contemplates marrying Strefford, now Lord Altringham, she realizes that instead of his castle she would have preferred "a little house on the Thames" (GM, 208). The Hicks family, having left their home in America, now live in luxurious Palace Hotels, and Coral's suitor, the Prince of Teutoburger-Waldhain, and his mother enjoy being guests at such hotels. Violet Melrose's "little place in Versailles" is not a home. It is simply a house she owns.

The house in the Tiepolo fresco is holy. The houses that Nick and Susy have borrowed are unholy. In fact, the silver moon behind the Virgin's little house, whose roof's overhang can be seen extending over its walls, acts as a halo for the house itself. That house becomes less of a thing and more of a presence because of the halo. The Holy House with its divinity places the Virgin, Child, and House in an original trinity. Joseph has not been included in that trinity, for we see him outside the circle of the moon on the right, praying to God the Father. It is a complex and beautiful pictorial invention of a theme rarely treated in painting.

Once one is alerted to what the fresco in the Church of the Scalzi is about, one has to reread the novel and see how the subject of this unusual fresco can determine the mechanics or the idea behind the plot. The two striking icons, which are both announced on the first page of the novel and which stem from the Tiepolo fresco, are that of the moon and of the house. The very first page shows us the young couple on their honeymoon in the evening under the moonlight on Lake Como in their first house borrowed from Strefford.

Susy and Nick discuss how many houses, which Susy numbers as five, have been offered to them to lengthen their honeymoon and to save their wedding cheques. "Houses were being showered on them" (GM, 24). Houses, as such, belonging to other people, and either rented or owned by these people, are only temporary and seasonal residences of the rich. They so dominate the book that they might even be called presences or characters in their own right. The second house in Nick and Susy's life is the Nelson and Ellie Vanderlyn palazzo in Venice, which again is only one of the Vanderlyns' places, elaborate as it is, for Nelson's big house on Fifth Avenue has been exchanged for an equally sumptuous house in Mayfair (GM, 87). The third house is one on the moor "let for the season" (GM, 189) to Fred Gillow, and the price for the young couple's living there is the same as it had been for living in the Venetian palazzo—to cover for Ursula Gillow's affairs as they had for Ellie Vanderlyn's. The fourth house offered to them is Violet Melrose's "little place at Versailles" (GM, 141), "an artless ingenuous little house," where Susy arrives after Nick leaves Venice, since Violet is supposed to be in China. However, Susy finds her there with Nat Fulmer, the painter, whose wife, Grace, the violinist, and their children are now in a Paris pension. The fifth house was one in the Adirondacks, which they do not visit, but the fifth house they do occupy is more like a home than the others. It is at Passy where Grace and Nat Fulmer have parked their five children. The other type of house is rented by the Hicks family, the rich Americans from Apex City. First they are antiquated old palaces because the Hicks family is interested in archaeology, and then they advance to modern Palace Hotels, where they can put up their titled friends.

In regard to this group of characters, Edith Wharton even uses proliferating architectural similes. The Princess's "eyes are perched as high as attic windows under . . . a pediment of uncleaned diamonds" (GM, 238), and Coral Hicks resembles "an old monument in a street of Palace Hotels" (GM, 238). The similes continue with house images: "Like a man whose house has been wrecked by an earthquake" (GM, 243). The making of character "was as slow and arduous as the building of the Pyramids" (GM, 243); it was "the Pyramid instinct" that "caused these fugitive joys to linger like fading frescoes on imperishable walls" (GM, 244).

In Part 3 of the book, Susy stays with the Fulmer children because she has a feeling that the small house at Passy "was beginning to greet her with the eyes of home," uncomfortable as it was (GM, 302), and the architectural figures of speech continue: "One watchtower of hope after another, feverish edifices demolished or rebuilt" (GM, 304); "her flag continued to fly from the quaking structures." Then there is Nick's "domicile" for the divorce (GM, 314), "a Home and a House desecrated by his own act! The Home to which he and Susy had reared their precarious bliss, and seen it crumble" (GM, 314). But the whole idea of having to rent such a place for the conditions of getting a divorce disgusts Nick. He goes out to Passy and, without being seen, sees Susy at the door "transfigured by the new attitude in which he beheld her . . . the eternal image of the woman and child" (GM, 319). It is here in this final scene in the book that, as we think back to Tiepolo's fresco, we see a reproduction of its iconography. Susy here shares her posture with the Virgin Mary and the Christ Child. Although, at this point, Nick thinks she is about to marry a rich, English aristocrat, he says to himself, "But she looks *poor!*" (GM, 320). The moon, which had disappeared from the book after the first part, now returns; the young couple feels "as on the night of their moon over Como" (GM, 353).

After it becomes clear that both Nick and Susy do not want their so-called fiancés, but they want each other and decide to have a second honeymoon in Fontainebleau, the "little house became the centre of a whirlwind" (GM, 354); the resemblance to the fresco now shows itself in similar details. The five Fulmer kids in their activity resemble the angels supporting the Virgin's house in the fresco. Young Nat Fulmer and his motor horn, which is referred to a number of times, resembles the angels on the right of the fresco with their horns. Susy's hair has "a ruddy halo" behind it (GM, 361). As the novel ends, as they are on their second honeymoon at the hotel, they look out at the night and watch "the moon," which had "cast her troubled glory on them, and was again hidden." Like their moon, their happiness comes and goes, but the moon behind the Scalzi Virgin is always a full moon, exposed and untroubled. Their's is not.

When the little house became "the centre of a whirlwind" (GM, 354), we are sent back to Nick in front of the Scalzi fresco (GM, 91). We also are sent back to Edith Wharton's travel essay in *Italian Backgrounds,* where she describes "the angels, *whirling* along the Virgin's house with a vehemence which makes it seem a mere feather in the rush of their flight" (IB, 194) (my italics).

The other icon that appears on the first page of the book is the moon and, of course, it establishes itself in the title, placed as the "tutelary orb"

(GM, 1) of the young, newly married couple. The entire opening scene takes place in the moonlight at Lake Como. We are reminded of it on practically every page of Chapter 1. "Look . . . there, against that splash of moonlight on the water. Apples of silver in a network of gold" (GM, 3). "The moon was turning from gold to white" (GM, 4). "She saw bits of moon-flooded sky encrusted like silver" (GM, 5). There is a break in the moon references as the young couple remembers how they met and what their courtship consisted of. The first chapter is bathed in moonlight and the happy thoughts about how they will be able to stretch out their honeymoon by taking advantage of their free use of various houses of their rich friends. Again, they have "long golden days and the nights of silver fire" (GM, 60).

After they leave Como, the moon disappears. Yet they look forward in Venice to being "alone with the great orange moons—still theirs!—above the bell-tower of San Giorgio" (GM, 97). And on the night when Nick leaves Susy because of her acceptance of the amoral conditions for their living at the Venetian palazzo, "There was no moon—thank heaven there was no moon!—" (GM, 116). With that, the moon disappears from the book not to reappear again until the last page. Nick has left Venice for Genoa, and the marriage seems to be over. The moon does not return until page 353 when Susy appears as the Virgin with a small child on her shoulder; Nick finally embraces her, "and the currents flowed between them warm and full as on the night of their moon over Como" (GM, 353). The moon reappears as they embark on their second "honeymoon," the spelling Wharton uses all through the novel.

There are more echoes of the Scalzi elements. "The celestial vortex" (GM, 92) referred to as Nick and Coral look at the Scalzi fresco, is another description of the feeling of a "whirlwind" (GM, 356). If we are to accept Helen Killoran's concept of primary allusions, secondary allusions, and autoallusions to literature and art as a conscious endeavor on the part of Edith Wharton, we cannot ignore these parallels between the Transport of the Holy House fresco and what goes on in this novel. But for the accident of my seeing this fresco as part of Professor Zorzi's lecture on Tiepolo, I too would never have realized what it looked like. But the sight of this fresco made from the Alinari photograph taken before its destruction alerted me to the part it seemed to have played in Wharton's novel, for, throughout the novel, there seems to be a subtext from the narrative in this fresco. Like the Virgin's domicile, the houses the couple borrow are small, although they are not precious to the couple because they do not belong to them. The Virgin's house, though humble, was her own. And it seems as if Wharton wished to keep the Tiepolo image before our minds because there are at least two places later in the novel where Nick remembers seeing it (GM, 185 and 188).

Yet, again we must wonder why Wharton does not tell us the subject of the fresco. Is it simply an autoallusion that refers the reader back to the description in her travel essay? Is it a subtext because the reader knows the fresco so well, which, at the time of Wharton's beginning to write *The Glimpses of the Moon,* had been destroyed recently and probably was known as a great disaster to the rest of the world? From reading it as a subtext, does the lack of explanation seem to indicate that it was less important than I have stated? The reason no scholar has commented on the subject of the picture is probably because no one has seen it or reproductions of it. There is only one other reference to museum art when Susy looks at Mantegna's *Crucifixion* in the Louvre, but where Nick regards other pictures that are more cheerful. But this seems to be just a random introduction, made merely to suggest Susy's sensitivity to tragedy. It appears to have no echo in the rest of the novel.

Susy's activity at the end of the novel, when she nurtures and acts as a surrogate mother to the five Fulmer children, gives her a finer sense of ethical behavior, which now matches her husband Nick's, and prepares her to be ready for a real home and family.

References

1. Edith Wharton, *The Glimpses of the Moon* (New York: Appleton, 1922), pp. 91–92. Future references are indicated by GM and page number.

2. Giovanni Battista Tiepolo, *Giambattista Tiepolo, 1696–1996* (Milano: Skira; New York: Metropolitan Museum of Art, 1996), p. 295.

3. Rosella Mamoli-Zorzi, "Tiepolo, Henry James, and Edith Wharton," lecture, March 16, 1997, Metropolitan Museum, Grace Rainey Rogers Auditorium, published in *Metropolitan Musuem Journal* 33 (1998): 211–29.

4. *Giambattista Tiepolo, 1969–1996,* pp. 300–301.

5. Edith Wharton, *Italian Backgrounds* (New York: Scribner's, 1905), pp. 193–94.

6. *Giambattista Tiepolo, 1696–1996,* p. 301.

7. Helen Killoran, *Edith Wharton: Art and Allusion* (Tuscaloosa: University

of Alabama Press, 1996), p. 70. Future references are indicated by AA and page number.

8. Cynthia Griffin Wolff, *A Feast of Words* (New York: Oxford, 1977), p. 347. Future references are indicated by FW and page number.

9. R. W. B. Lewis, *Edith Wharton: A Biography* (New York: Harper & Row, 1975), pp. 436, 439.

PART FOUR
Literary Lives of Wharton

20

A Poet's Version of Edith Wharton

Richard Howard's *The Lesson of the Master*

The Lesson of the Master is a dramatic poem in a volume called *Two-Part Inventions* (1974) by Richard Howard—poet, translator, and critic—in which we see a portrait of Edith Wharton with her very name kept. The description is based on Howard's knowledge and information about her gleaned from various books. The first source seems to be her volume of memoirs, *A Backward Glance,* and the second, Percy Lubbock's *Portrait of Edith Wharton* (1947). The others are Leon Edel's fifth volume of the life of *Henry James* (1972) and Louis Auchincloss's biography of Edith Wharton (1971).[1] In the early 1970s, before the 1975 revelations in R. W. B. Lewis's *Edith Wharton: A Biography* of Wharton's concealed love affair with Morton Fullerton, the object of her affections was assumed to be Walter Berry, a man whom she revered and honored all her life and near whose grave she wanted to be, and actually was, buried herself. Berry had died in 1927, and the basis of this dramatic dialogue by Howard is an imagined automobile trip that Wharton makes from Paris to Versailles to bury Walter Berry's ashes, but at a time, 1912, which is not true to the date of his death. She is accompanied by Mr. Roseman, a friend of the dead man, Gerald Mackenzie, in the poem.

The epigraph sets the mood for the poem: "Edith Wharton was here, an angel of devastation in her wondrous, cushioned, *general* car," a line from a letter written by Henry James. The title, *The Lesson of the Master,* gives us the main theme of the plot of this poem, which is one among a group of dialogues, including Oscar Wilde's visit to Walt Whitman in Camden, which center around homoerotic feelings.

Originally published as "The Figure of Edith Wharton in Richard Howard's Poem *The Lesson of the Master,*" in *The Edith Wharton Review* 9, no. 2 (Fall 1992): 11–14.

It appears from the poem that Henry James chose the companion for the automobile trip, a Gerald Roseman (an invented name and character), as an answer to Wharton's suggestion that he recommend someone whom she did not know. The lesson James wished her to learn was that her beloved friend, Gerald Mackenzie, whose ashes she is on her way to bury, was a homosexual and therefore could not love her in the way she wanted to be loved. This is the poem's message.

The dialogue between the two characters draws on Wharton's powers of "devastation," on her obsessive sense of order and her quirk of ordering others to create this order. It involves Howard's knowledge of her excessive smoking of special brands of cigarettes, her behavior with her omnipresent dogs, and her imperiousness in general. Through her companion, Edith Wharton will learn "the lesson of the master," which is that the man whom she had such strong feelings about, has been the lover of the man accompanying her. In this poem, we are to infer that Henry James thought that she needed to know what the true picture of Mackenzie's emotions was.

What is interesting about the delineation of Edith Wharton's character is that, from a position of arrogance and contemptuous attitude toward the Jewish young man who is accompanying her, she changes her behavior after she realizes from the tears the young man sheds that he is right about Gerald's feelings and that she did not share them the way this young man had. Here Wharton's rationality and intelligence are stressed. Richard Howard is an extremely skillful poet whose subject matter has often been taken from literature as well as art. His skill is demonstrated in this poetic dialogue by the gradual presentation of details of Wharton's character according to the sources then published, which are distributed as to make perfectly plausible the change in her behavior to her companion as the automobile ride comes to an end.

The very first lines show her drive or obsession to be neat and to control her environment, for she tells her companion not to litter the car with the ashes from his cigarette nor to throw them out of the window and litter the Bois de Boulogne. The cigarette ashes have been introduced to contrast them to the ashes of Gerald Mackenzie, the mutual friend, which she is conveying to a cemetery in Versailles. This is part of the correct information about where Walter Berry was buried in the Cimetière des Gonards in Versailles.[2]

Roseman reminds her that they have already met at Howard Overing's in London, a reference perhaps to Howard Sturgis's home, where

Roseman reminds her of the many "gold-tipped Egyptian" cigarettes she had smoked on the occasion in London when he met her. But she is completely insulting and arrogant in her attitude to Roseman because she claims that she had told James that she wanted someone who was "no one in particular," so that "one may say anything" to him. This reminds us of a letter in which James had written that Wharton "may be difficult" and here she surely is that. Although she believes at this moment that James has made a mistake in suggesting the young man, we realize at the end of the poem that James did no such thing, that he purposely sent this man who was a lover of Gerald Mackenzie to make clear to Edith Wharton the kind of men they all were. Howard assumes here that James wanted to tell Edith Wharton the fact that his whole group was a homoerotic one and that they had feelings about each other that she could not understand. This does not quite jibe with certain facts, such as the tale by Wharton, "The Eyes," in which she depicts a circle of homoerotic men of which the center is a man like Henry James. This circle resembles the Qu'acre group based in Howard Sturgis's home in Windsor close to London and composed of a group of friends dominated by Henry James. In "The Eyes," published in 1910, two years before this fictional trip in 1912, Wharton shows she knew the tastes of her men friends.

Roseman quotes Gerald Mackenzie as saying that "Edith Wharton is a self-made man." Edith Wharton next says that "Gerald found me when my mind was starved, and he fed me 'til our last hour together." This echoes the comment she makes about Walter Berry in *A Backward Glance:* "He found me when my mind was starved and my soul was hungry and thirsty and he fed them 'til our last hour together."[3] At which point Roseman remarks, "So you were not entirely self-made." As she gets more expansive, she tells Roseman that she "made something" of herself to give to Gerald as a person. She asks, "What were you, the two of you?" Roseman answers it was "why I was suggested for the job. . . . We were what you failed to be. . . . You and Gerald: one" (LM, 49). This is a great shock to her, and she stops the car and says, "I will not hear this." She resists the truth in her imperious fashion and asks her driver, whom Howard calls Georges (whereas her real driver was called Cook), to stop the car. Roseman continues relentlessly and says that she will not hear it because "you know 'this' already, Mrs. Wharton." There were "Eight years, during which you waited for Gerald Mackenzie to marry you."

During those years, he told her, his and Gerald's lives "overlapped"

(LM, 50). He quotes Gerald as having said that "women are for men who fail" and that a woman was "an abyss which might suddenly swallow you both." She asks him how would "*you* know anything at all about being a woman?" and he answers, "I *am* a woman for the same reason you are a man." He continues, "What did you make of Gerald's friends you met at Howard's. . . . what do you make of Mr. James? Surely you know what we are and what we do. You did know that, Mrs. Wharton, didn't you?" She answers, "I know what *you* are, Mr. Roseman, you tell me enough to know that, nor am I tempted to put you and Gerald and Mr. James in the same basket of crabs because you do—or say you did—the same things" (LM, 51). He has to tell her this in order to "spare you the needless expense of . . . what has already been expended." She answers by saying, "You are a Jew, Mr. Roseman, are you not?" He answers that his father was a banker, and she answers in her nasty way, "Each of us gets, Gerald always used to say, though doubtless not to you, the Jew he deserves" (LM, 52). This seems to reflect Edith Wharton's generally unsympathetic attitude to Jews, which Richard Howard gleaned from her letters and from other reports.

She tells Roseman that he takes from her "the Gerald I knew, the Gerald who invented me—for whom I invented myself . . . you take Gerald from me and replace him with a preposterous caricature who behaves as people behave in the newspapers, *some* newspapers and Elizabethan plays," to which he answers, "I cannot take from you what you never had . . . what I am saying is that Gerald led another life." The relation, he implies, was "not living—it is pretending . . . you liked Gerald to pretend and he liked pretending" (LM, 53). She asks him how he dares to "speak of 'our' Gerald . . . as if you had the right" (LM, 53). Then he lets her have it. "Certainly we have not lost the same meaning from our lives." When he heard her talk, "I heard all the harshness of a dogmatist mingling somehow in every sentence with the weakness of an egoist and the pretentiousness of a snob" (LM, 53).

At this particular point, she seems to have gotten the message she was meant to get and has dropped her contemptuous, superior, critical attitude: "I have always been everyone's admiration and no one's choice. It is I who have done the choosing. . . . Gerald did not love me. No. Affection and desire—those apparently were his poles, and we divide them between us, you and I" (LM, 55). Roseman has noticed her change of verbal behavior and says, "You speak so differently, Mrs. Wharton, the moment you are released—relieved . . . from Gerald. You become a different woman; it is a strange mutation." She adds, "I do not want a sense of the past, as Mr. James keeps calling it, and the future is deaf. . . . I want a sense of the continuous life" (LM, 58), and she suddenly notices that Mr. Roseman is crying.

His tears touch her and she decides, so released is she finally from her wrong relation to Gerald, that she will let Roseman take the urn by himself into the cemetery while she waits for him in the car. "When you come back we shall decide what to say "to Mr. James. . . . He has made his experiment in fiction—he has turned his screw, as I suppose he would say." They both agree that they shall say nothing about their conversation to James. Roseman says, "Thank you, Edith, if I may"; when she says that she would call him by his first name if she knew it, he says, "It is Gerald." Hearing that he has the same name as the man she has loved, that, in other words, they are really one, she suddenly bursts out laughing, which is the first time "in a week" that she has done so. She answers, now a totally changed woman in her relation to this young man, as well as to the Gerald whom she wanted to love her, and says, "Your story, the one we shall spare Mr. James, is what the American public always wants: a tragedy with a happy ending."

This particular portrait of Edith Wharton is very different from other literary portraits of her. It is an attempt to give an accurate portrait, for Howard keeps her real name and her characteristics have been lifted from the autobiographical and biographical works available at that time. Howard also makes her, in addition to her imperiousness, her snobbishness, and her relentlessness, a woman of great intelligence who is capable of accepting the truth when she understands it. In her ride from Paris to Versailles, she has learned a number of heart-rending revelations, the chief one being that Gerald was a homosexual or homoerotic, part of a circle of men of the same tastes. This is an imagined dialogue, but Edith's character is not placed under the disguise of a Mrs. Grace Elliot or a Mrs. Alice Gray, as in the cases of Louis Auchincloss's or Paul Bourget's "fictioning" of Mrs. Wharton but in the character of Mrs. Wharton herself. What is a fantasy is this drive from Paris to Versailles to bury the ashes of, presumably, Walter Berry. What is also imagined is the fact that the Walter Berry character is presented as homoerotic. We know from other sources that Walter Berry was a womanizer, as well as a playboy, and there is no evidence that he loved men. But since he is not called Walter Berry, but is a fictive character called Gerald Mackenzie, we have here a combination of real writers and fictional characters. In this poem, Henry

James and Edith Wharton live in a world inhabited by fictive characters in much the same way that we find real authors rubbing shoulders with fictive characters in some novels of the 1990s. There is Rebecca Goldstein's *The Dark Sister.* There William James, the actual American philosopher, and Dr. Austin Sloper, a fictive character from Henry James's *Washington Square,* together inhabit the world of the novel. There is Carol DeChellis Hill's *Henry James's Midnight Song* in which Edith Wharton, Henry James, and a host of others occupy the center of attention. We may say that Richard Howard was one of the earliest practitioners of this game of blending fact and fiction now reaching a high level of popularity.

In choosing as the title for his poem *The Lesson of the Master,* the title of a well-known story by Henry James, Howard is doing two things. First, he is telling us by the title itself what the message of that poem is: Henry James has picked out Gerald Roseman to tell Mrs. Wharton the truth about Gerald Mackenzie's erotic disposition with the revelation that he could never have had with her the relation she wanted. But at the same time he seems to be contradicting this because we recall that the meaning of the James tale is thought to be uncertain. Do we see Henry St. George, the "master" of the James story, as a villain who has manipulated Paul Overt, the "overt," innocent young man, to think that marriage will interfere with his writing and in that way steals the young woman St. George loves himself? Or do we see a man who knows he is a second-rate writer and who honestly believes he is saving Paul from a mediocre career by advising him to resist marriage and give up all for art? This ambiguity is also built into the meaning of Howard's poem. Has James really picked out this young man, Gerald Roseman, to be the messenger of the hurtful truth about Mrs. Wharton's would-be lover's true erotic deviation, or has the young man simply taken upon himself to tell her, using James as the inventor of the manoeuvre? We are left, I believe, with the same built-in ambiguity as in the James tale. Otherwise, we must assume that Howard has taken upon himself to use this rather crude, as well as cruel, device on the part of James to reveal his own sexual deviation, something I find hard to believe James would do, for it was of James that Walpole wrote in 1934 in *The Apple Trees,* "There was no crudity of which he was unaware but he did not wish that crudity to be named."[4] It was not only that James would not name that crudity, but he did not want anybody else to name it, if we are to believe Walpole, and so it would not be plausible that he would send Gerald Roseman on a mission to name it to Edith Wharton. Also, it is not consistent with what we know of James's character that he would deliberately hurt Edith Wharton, for whom he had a deep affection.

But aside from the possible interpretations of Howard's intentions in this "two-part invention," the character of Edith Wharton emerges with a rather striking validity and authenticity. All her positions are taken within what we know of her intelligence, character, and emotional depth. She is a convincing Edith, in spite of the genesis of the situation in which she finds herself. She is there with her asperity and her prejudices, but finally her intelligence and understanding make her triumph over her own class-conscious, imperious failings.[5]

REFERENCES

1. Richard Howard, *The Lesson of the Master, Two-Part Inventions* (New York: Atheneum, 1974), pp. 40–60. Future references are indicated by LM and page number. (These sources were the only places in 1974 where Howard could have found the biographical details necessary for his poem.)

2. R. W. B. Lewis, *Edith Wharton: A Biography* (New York: Harper & Row, 1975), p. 532.

3. Edith Wharton, *A Backward Glance* (New York: Appleton-Century, 1934), p. 119.

4. Hugh Walpole, *The Apple Trees* (Waltham St. Laurence: Golden Cockerel Press, 1932), p. 53.

5. The late James Gargano brought my attention to this poem and challenged me to interpret it. I dedicate this chapter to his memory.

21

Louis Auchincloss Deconstructs the Biography of Edith Wharton: From Invented Ediths to Her Real Self

Justice to Teddy Wharton in "The Arbiter"

If Judith Funston[1] would like to see someone's comment on Louis Auchincloss's explanation of the Wharton divorce ("Teddy Wharton, soon to be shed for having bored his brilliant spouse," a quotation from the *New York Times Book Review* of *Henry James's Letters IV* by Auchincloss), here it is. I speak only as a reader of Auchincloss, not for the author himself, since I doubt whether he would ever claim that "The Arbiter" gave *the* explanation of the divorce between Teddy and Edith Wharton. It is *an* explanation and one that no one who has read all the biographical material, in addition to the recently published letters, can possibly deny that it is plausible. In fact, Auchincloss refers to that aspect of Teddy once more in his review of *The Lewis' Edition of Wharton's Letters* in *The New Criterion* (May 1988), when he discusses the love affair with Fullerton when Edith was "forty-six, and her marriage to the boring and neurotic 'Teddy' Wharton was foundering."[2] That need to shed a spouse usually occurs the other way around, when a husband, becoming famous, finds his wife no longer adequate to his position and divorces her, to marry what we used to call "the sports-car-model wife" and now call "the trophy wife." That, of course, is not justifiable, but it is understandable. In the Whartons' case, the shoe was on the other foot, and it was Edith who grew. Teddy, who stayed in his groove, broke down under the pressure. But Edith always felt a responsibility to him and was aware of the social amenities of marriage in her circle, and Auchincloss has given that his full acknowledgment in his admirable life of Wharton written in 1971, four years before the Lewis biography appeared. In that book Auchincloss

Originally published as "Justice to Teddy Wharton in Louis Auchincloss's 'The Arbiter,'" *The Edith Wharton Review* 7, no. 2 (Winter 1990): 17–20.

makes it quite clear there is something to be said on both sides and tries to be fair.

> Here is how I should sum up the story of her marriage: she and Teddy were married at a time when she had no reason to believe that she would not always be satisfied with the social life of a New York society matron whose spouse Teddy seemed perfectly qualified to be. This life rapidly bored her, and Teddy, a neurasthenic, lacked the ability either to dominate her or to interest her. She took up travelling, decorating, and finally writing to compensate for the frustrations of her married life, and in doing so she discovered that she was made for a totally different existence. Teddy's near-lunatic temper and their childlessness made a bad situation impossible. In the end the only thing she could do was to cut loose and start afresh, in a new country, without a spouse. Who in 1971 can cast the first stone at her?[3]

Auchincloss, the biographer, is trying to be fair to both Edith and Teddy, but handling the facts in a strict biography is one thing and making a case for someone like Teddy in a fictional account of the crucial years of Edith's marriage is another. Auchincloss, the writer, actually has written the early married life of Edith Wharton twice: once in his factual account and once in a fictional account, a privilege to which he is entitled as an inventor of stories. He himself justifies this transmutation of literal facts into fictional form when he considers Edith's use of a friend for the figure of Mr. Culwin in "The Eyes."[4] He allows that a writer can make a figure of horror from someone for whom he has the greatest feeling of admiration and sincere love, since "such a characterization is perfectly consistent with the deepest friendship that a novelist can feel. Edith herself, in *Hudson River Bracketed,* would create a wholly sympathetic novelist's character who deliberately uses every emotional experience, however personal, however intimate, as grist for his fictional mill. She knew that thus novels are made."[5]

Thus short stories are also made, and Auchincloss's "The Arbiter" is an example of this process. It is one of a collection of tales called *The Winthrop Covenant* joined together as specific illustrations of the Puritan conscience, each of which is independent of the others. "The Arbiter" is a fine story and a successful illustration of his use of what Auchincloss knew about Edith, her marriage, her husband, and her circle (it was published in 1976, the year after Lewis's *Edith Wharton*) to invent a tale with these basic biographical ingredients, but with an alteration of some facts, a bias permissible to a writer of fiction.

In the tale, Teddy appears as Bob Guest and is the person with whom Adam Winthrop, the main character, the author, and the reader are most sympathetic. The main character of this story is a member and descendant of the Winthrop family, for the collection of stories is united by the fact that the Winthrops had originally received a covenant from God, who would protect them in their Pilgrim colony if they did not sin. The persistence of this collective conscience of members of the family through three hundred years, from the time of their arrival on the New England Coast, is the common element of the nine tales. The story devoted to the Teddy-Edith relationship is connected to the Winthrops through the main character in the tale, Adam Winthrop. Anyone knowing *A Backward Glance* will see that Adam is a revival of Egerton Winthrop, who was the Winthrop Edith knew as a young woman and who, according to her autobiography, meant so much to her as a mentor and friend in the years during which she was learning her craft. Edith describes Egerton as "an old friend of my family. A widower with grown children, he lived in 'a charming house'" and "was a discriminating collector of works of art, especially of the 18th century."[6] Although the real Egerton Winthrop was fixed on social life, Edith "saw only the lover of books and pictures, the accomplished linguist and eager reader whose ever-youthful curiosities first taught my mind to analyze and my eyes to see." Although a generation older, he "directed and systematized my reading, and filled some of the worst gaps in my education" (BG, 94). He was part of the group who "were active in administering the new museums, libraries and charities of New York. . . . In our little group Egerton Winthrop's was by far the most sensitive intelligence, and it transformed my life to find my vague enthusiasms canalized . . . he was full of wisdom in serious matters. Sternly exacting to himself, he was humorously indulgent towards others. . . . I found him, in difficult moments, the surest of counsellors" (BG, 96).

R. W. B. Lewis has seen Egerton Winthrop as the model for Sillerton Jackson, the gossip-loving New Yorker in *The Age of Innocence,* and Edith herself noted in her autobiography that "the more I ponder over our long friendship the more I despair of portraying him; for never . . . have an intelligence so distinguished and a character so admirable been combined with interests for the most part so trivial" (BG, 92). It may be this sentence in *A Backward Glance* that acted as a germ for Auchincloss to decide to take the admirable part of Winthrop and to portray him with certain changes. He emphasizes in his reconstruction of Egerton his other more commendable qualities—his taste as a collector, especially of eighteenth-century paintings, and his role as an "arbiter elegantiarum." "Everything you need for your art, Ada, is right inside of you."[7] He tells her that her "bluebird, like Maeterlinck's, was at home" (WC, 150). (In this passage, Auchincloss has introduced some elements from Henry James, who advised Edith to stick to her own "backyard.") Adam Winthrop remains in his story as her adviser and mentor, not as a gossip-monger. Another bit of material about Egerton from Lewis's biography was the image of life as having "its characteristic setting a prison cell."[8] Auchincloss seems to refer to this when Adam's wife Violet accuses him of having made her a prisoner in his museum-like house. " 'You've walled out life, Adam' " (WC, 136).

Bob Guest, Ada's husband, like Teddy, is usually broke, though, unlike Teddy, he was always a heavy drinker. He enters the tale by trying to get, as was his custom, a loan from Adam Winthrop who is about to pay one of his regular visits to Ada, the talented writer who helps support herself and her spendthrift husband by publishing her poetry and fiction. But the Bob we see seems to be the result of a decision on the part of the author to create a figure like Teddy, but one who presents his case with an articulate perception that Teddy did not have and who knows he will be an unhappy man if he goes to Paris with Ada, who wants her own circle away from an arid New York, as Edith had done at the turn of the century. "But the real truth is that she was a genius and I was already a drunk." He admired her for not leaving him and for writing and bringing in "most of the money on which we lived" (WC, 153).

The next scene is three years later when, after their move to Paris, Bob returns to talk to Winthrop at their club, The Patroons', and, although there have been stories of his drinking in Paris and his philandering, Bob now orders lemonade. He tells Adam he has decided to give Ada a divorce and explains how Ada has developed a salon of "expatriates with artistic leanings." Although Bob did what was expected of him, "she found what she called my Philistinism unbearable," but what finally broke him down was "the condescending kindness of her new friends."

Here he describes to Adam quite accurately the behavior of the group, including "an old bachelor Percy Hunt" (shades of Percy Lubbock), which did condescend to Teddy. "I began to be maddened by my gentle treatment as Ada's illiterate husband" (WC, 159). He adds, "I was made to feel a brute, a cad. When I came into the parlor they all stared at me as if I were a mad dog. I took up with other women, whores mostly. . . . And do you know what I began to understand, Adam? Ada was putting it all on. She was deliberately acting the martyred wife to her gallery of wizened dilettantes. She was determined to get rid of me, to drive me out and to be the wronged spouse to boot. Oh, yes, however wronged, she had to be right!" (WC, 160). Bob decides, therefore, to give Ada the divorce so that she can write. He wants her to achieve a great place in literature for, if she doesn't, "where are you and I? . . . What have we been but early chapters—or maybe footnotes—in the great biography?" (WC, 161). This reflects authorial prescience on the part of Auchincloss for what these characters have been, with changes and distortions—really footnotes in the pages of Lewis's autobiography, published a year before this story. Yet, at the end of the tale, Winthrop does not have the same high opinion of Ada's gifts as Bob does, and he considers her capable of "meanness." He calls her "vulgar" and tells Bob that she has "treated you in the worst possible taste."

This tale, of course, is an invention in which Auchincloss has postulated a scenario where Teddy is the victim of Edith, one who voluntarily gives in to the pressure of her genius that compels her to live her life according to her needs and not her husband's. It is a possible Teddy angle, if Teddy could talk the way Bob Guest does, if Teddy could think in such subtle and self-negating terms, and if Teddy could sacrifice himself to her superiority. Bob obliges Ada because he thinks she is better than he is and, in spite of Adam Winthrop, who has a Puritan conscience to satisfy because of the terms of his presence in this book, the reader has to agree with him.

The most striking fictional distortion lies in the behavior of Ada as presented by the otherwise intellectually improved Bob. Her pretending to be acting the martyred wife for her friends in order to "drive me out and to be the wrong spouse to boot" has been invented by Auchincloss for his fictive Edith and is not to be considered factual. For that, we must go to his biography of Edith, in spite of the fact that this Ada surely has many recognizable traits of Edith's character, and the events in Ada's life are close to the events in Edith's life. Ada's trio of New York friends resembles the circle that Edith describes in *A Backward Glance*. Her small house on Park Avenue, which in her autobiography she calls "the smallest of small houses" (BG, 93), is reflected in Auchincloss's story when Adam visits her in a "tiny brown-stone." Ada begins by writing historical novels, one about St. Luke composing his gospel, instead of one about eighteenth-century Italy.

This is not the real Teddy, but the way Teddy might or could have been, just as Ada is not the real Edith, but the way a rather "vulgar" Edith might have been. Adam Winthrop ends the tale by saying to Bob, "Yes, she's very vulgar. The way she has treated you is in the worst possible taste" (WC, 161). And Adam, when asked by Bob whether he would ever change places with Ada, the now successful novelist, answers, "Never!" (WC, 161). We are quite sure the real Egerton Winthrop probably would have, for he continued to be Edith's close friend, although he was a generation older than she was. This is a tale of a gifted woman married to a handsome, indolent, drinking, constantly broke man, which is what Teddy finally became, although his susceptibility to mental illness has been omitted. By manipulating facts for a story based on Edith and Teddy's life, especially at the time when Edith went to Paris in 1907, Auchincloss justifies Teddy's plight, married to a woman way beyond him in intellect and talent, capable of handling her life and needing to free herself from bondage to a boring, frustrating husband. Today this marriage would have been ended shortly after it had been made. But Edith had her inherited feelings about divorce and a sense of responsibility to her husband, herself, and society. Actually, only after she fell in love with Fullerton did her marriage became unbearable. No real blame can be attached to either partner, though one can also feel for the rejected male as one would have felt for the rejected female, if the case had been the conventional one. The role models were here reversed.

As a balance to Edmund Wilson's essay, "Justice to Edith Wharton," Auchincloss has allowed himself a fantasy of "Justice to Teddy Wharton," *if* Teddy had not been the utter bore he really was. Bob Guest, the Teddy figure, is therefore not a clone, for he is much superior, and thus he dominates the tale and wins our respect. It is a vote against Ada Guest, but then Ada is *not* the true Edith, although perilously close. It is implied that Ada might not be the genius her husband thinks she is, and the Winthrop of this tale rejects Bob's interpretation of their role in relation to each other. But, although the tale is not a true report, and undoubtedly Auchincloss never meant it to be considered so, it is a very good story. Created as an analogue of the real triangular relationship, the fictive and imagined one makes an especially effective reading. In its sheer ingenuity and great narrative, the story reminds one of Henry James's tale about the W. K. Vanderbilt divorce case, where certain facts are dramatized and exaggerated to create "The Special Type." In this sense, the story by Auchincloss continues the James–Wharton tradition of social comment.

References

1. "Correspondence," *Edith Wharton Review* 7, no. 1 (Spring 1990): 12.

2. Louis Auchincloss, "The Novelist in Letters," *The New Criterion,* May 1988, p. 69.

3. Louis Auchincloss, *Edith Wharton: A Woman in Her Time* (New York: Viking, 1971), pp. 97–98.

4. Culwin is assumed by me throughout the story to be Henry James.

5. Auchincloss, *Edith Wharton,* p. 67.

6. Edith Wharton, *A Backward Glance* (New York: Appleton-Century, 1934), p. 92. Future references are indicated by BG and page number.

7. Louis Auchincloss, *The Winthrop Covenant* (Boston: Houghton Mifflin, 1976), p. 142. Future references are indicated by WC and page number.

8. R. W. B. Lewis, *Edith Wharton: A Biography* (New York: Harper & Row, 1975), p. 87.

22

The Punishment of Morton Fullerton in
"The 'Fulfillment' of Grace Eliot"

A second Edith story by Auchincloss, like "The Arbiter" in *The Winthrop Covenant,* was probably also occasioned by a major find in Wharton scholarship. As "The Arbiter" in 1976 followed the revelations made in R. W. B. Lewis's 1975 biography about Wharton's lover, as well as the Edith-Fullerton affair,[1] so "The 'Fulfillment' of Grace Eliot," one of the collection of short stories called *Skinny Island* (1987), followed the equally revealing publication of Edith's letters to Morton Fullerton in *The Library Chronicle of the University of Texas* at Austin in 1985.[2] The exposure of Edith's emotional suffering at the hands of Fullerton, a man unworthy of her love, appears to have triggered this tale.

As Bob Guest (Teddy in an adapted form) in "The Arbiter" assumes Teddy's character, so Leonard Esher, who has had the affair with Grace Eliot in this tale and who finds that affair a bore, takes on the characteristics of both Walter Berry, especially in the latter's physical type, and Morton Fullerton in his fictive realization. Grace Eliot (the Edith Wharton character) is a figure of a lesser dimension than her real-life model, as Ada Guest had been in "The Arbiter." The format of a trio of two men and a woman appears again, only this time it is Leonard Esher and Bertie, Grace's literary agent and executor (who acts as the outside admirer of Grace and her work and who is shocked by her loving a bounder); the two men are related by their feelings about Grace. This, in form, is a repetition of the relationship of Bob Guest (Teddy) and Adam Winthrop (Egerton) in "The Arbiter."

The first-person narrator, Bertie, echoes the effect of the publication

Originally published as "Punishing Morton Fullerton in 'The "Fulfillment" of Grace Eliot,'" *Twentieth Century Literature* 38, no. 1 (Spring 1992): 45–54.

of the letters that Edith wrote to Fullerton from *The Library Chronicle* of 1985 in the very first sentence of the tale: "[T]he quiet, even roll of my retirement days . . . has been rudely shattered by my discovery of Grace Eliot's love letters," just as the discovery of the real Wharton letters had been a shock to Wharton's readers in 1985.[3] Even though the "name of the late great novelist has long been linked with that of Leonard Esher" (the fictive Fullerton who here more resembles Walter Berry), before that discovery "no one but myself could have proved that Grace and he had been lovers." But Grace's agent, "disciple and worshipper," had been "silent" about this affair because he thought that Grace had soon recovered "from a momentary lapse of taste and judgment" and had forgotten about this episode (SI, 181). The passionate letters, five of which are discovered by Bertie in a package of photos of pet dogs ("kenneled with curs"), prove otherwise.

Nevertheless, when Auchincloss reconstructs one of Edith's love letters and quotes from it, he deviates from a literal version of the letters that Edith wrote, although his parody does connect this particular letter with Edith's bad poetry. It begins, "O love of my life, imagine Brunhild . . . awakening to the silver clarion of Siegfried's horn only to discover that she is . . . old!" (SI, 183). Edith actually wrote to Fullerton: "If I had been younger and prettier, everything might have been different" (LC, 31). Among the transformations from the historical affair is a change in time, for now it is 1946 and the site is New York City. The stature of Grace is unlike Edith's. Grace is "forty, tall, fair . . . willowy," although, like Edith, she has rich, golden hair. Her lover (unlike Fullerton, who was three years her junior), is assimilated more closely to Walter Berry, who was three years her elder and who (before 1975 and Lewis's biography) had always been suspected of being Edith's lover—one who fits better into the picture of Leonard Esher. Here he is "at least ten years older" than Grace, and the image of Esher is close to the image of Berry from familiar photographs: "Grey hair and cold grey-blue eyes, so nattily dressed as to seem almost a parody of himself," a "thin figure" like Berry on whom "the shallow 'villains' of her fiction were modeled." Like Berry, he was a "constant, cool presence . . . judging everything and everybody" (SI, 184). Again, as in "The Arbiter," the narrator sees how "academics, scholars, critics . . . will snatch at any lubricious bits of sexuality to bring the supreme artists down to their own pawing, clutching level" (SI, 194). Various examples are predicted from imagined future scholarship. One of them is " 'Grace emerged from the love affair a completed woman and a greater artist.' "

Then Bertie recounts how the affair happened. It began at a party in the Eliots' "big double brownstone on Forty-eighth Street" (SI, 185), a conversion and reversal of the little double brownstone on Eighty-fourth Street and Park Avenue where Edith Wharton actually lived. At the party, Andy Eliot, Grace's husband, a more muscular version of Teddy and a prouder and more complacent one, acts as host, while Bertie is told by Grace that she "has discovered something in her own heart that means more to her than any book she's ever written" (SI, 187). She tells Bertie, who does not believe this, "Oh, the densities of incomprehension— the densities!" (SI, 187), words taken by Auchincloss from a letter from Wharton to her friend, Margaret Chanler (the letter was once in Auchincloss's possession and now is at Yale). The letter is a reply to Mrs. Chanler's response to Wharton's novel, *A Mother's Recompense*. Edith thanked her for having told her *why* she liked it: "to know why is a subtle consolation for densities of incomprehension."[4]

At Grace Eliot's party, Bertie is approached by "the tall, elegant figure of Leonard Esher like a peer in a Sargent portrait. At least he always struck me as having just changed from a scarlet huntsman's jacket" (SI, 188). Here Auchincloss invokes the well-known John Singer Sargent portrait of Lord Ribblesdale in the Tate Gallery in his hunting clothes (Figure 4). Esher, a snob and usually inattentive to the lower-born agent, is quite ingratiating, since he wants a favor from him, that is, the loan of his flat for the affair Esher is about to conduct with Grace. Before this, Grace is shown trying "perhaps to emulate a Mucha poster of Sarah Bernhardt as Hamlet" with her hand up to her breast (SI, 187) (Figure 5). The two art images give life to the participants in this love affair.

Bertie is insulted by this request for his flat and its implication that it is safe to conduct an affair in his apartment because "people think me such a eunuch" (SI, 189), an element that summons up shades of Henry James, whose sexuality was ambiguous even to his friends. The fact that he was present at the clandestine meeting between Mrs. Wharton and Fullerton at the Charing Cross Hotel seems to be the real-life antecedent for this part of the tale's plot.

After a few weeks, Esher tells Bertie that the affair is over and gives him back his keys. Esher cautions him, "Never get involved with a middle-aged virgin. They have too much to make up for. . . . My God,

4. John S. Sargent, *Lord Ribblesdale* (1902). Photograph from National Gallery Publications Limited, London.

5. Alphonse Mucha, *Sarah Bernhardt as Hamlet* (1899). Poster for the Théatre Sarah Bernhardt: "Tragique Histoire d'Hamlet, Prince de Danemark." Reprinted from *The Graphic Work of Alphonse Mucha.* Ed. Jiri Mucha. New York: St. Martin's, 1973. Figure 88, p. 63.

was I ever tossed about! There were moments when I actually considered setting off your fire alarm!" (SI, 192). At this caddish remark, Bertie finally erupts in anger. "You great clown, don't you know you have no existence except what Grace has given you?" (SI, 192). The story winds down with a quotation from another letter by Grace to Esher, parts of which have been taken from Edith's letter Number Two in the *Library Chronicle* (LC, 22). Here first is the fictive letter: "Oh, my lover, however little I may have given you, be assured that it was all I had. Had I been wiser I might have hoarded it and doled it out in smaller portions, but I could not do so. I opened my vault, my doors, my cupboards, my windows; I flung every gold piece and copper piece that I had at your feet. . . . Imprudent maybe but I care not. I shall be forever grateful" (SI, 192).

The actual letter from Edith to Fullerton is as follows: "And I'm so afraid that the treasures I long to unpack for you, that have come to me in magic ships from enchanted islands, are only, to you, the old familiar red calico & beads of the clever trader, who has had dealings of every latitude, & now knows just what to carry in the hold to please the simple native—I'm so afraid of this, that often I stuff my shining treasures back into their box, lest I should see you smiling at them!" (LC, 22). Although the exaggerated triviality of Grace's letter is in great contrast to the labored but colorful and poetic image Edith used in her letter, one can see what fun Auchincloss has had in producing very amusing and clever samples of Edith-type love letters. This pessimism of "the real thing" is in contrast to the optimism of Grace's letter, which ends: "When you look with the kindly patience of an uncle whose little niece still believes in Santa Claus, I'll murmur under my breath 'Bless you for not telling me he's a fable. Bless you for letting me pretend a little longer.'" Bertie's response to this is, "'Grace! Really! And I must read that in the *Hamilton Review* and the *Dartington Quarterly?*'" And he must, because these letters have to "be entered into the record" and have become part of the public exposure of Edith's intimate love life.

As in "The Arbiter," Wharton's dimensions have been reduced for the purposes of fiction. As the prize over which the two men are fighting, one who reverences her and the other who belittles her, the fictive character has a personality that has been somewhat vulgarized in the present story. We are meant to concentrate on the lack of response by Fullerton-cum-Berry to Edith's passion, rather than on Grace's true correspondence to Edith. Actually, the five letters had been sent back to

Grace Eliot by Esher in a more gentlemanly act than Fullerton was capable of, for he never sent back her letters, even though Edith made many requests for him to do so and, in the end, they were sold and became public property. Grace Eliot herself is thus not an accurate portrait of Edith, nor is she meant to be. There is just enough of her yet transposed to the present to make her recognizable, especially in her relationship with her husband and lover. The words Auchincloss puts into Esher's mouth have no basis in reality, but their tenor has, for the fact is we know them inferentially from the letters of Edith Wharton.

The narrator's vision of how the letters will be used by scholars in learned journals ("Could I not already imagine the phrases in the literary journals"; "'Grace emerges from the love affair a completed woman and a greater artist'") (SI, 184) corresponds to a similar situation in "The Arbiter." It also tallies with the published accounts of Auchincloss's feelings about the matter, for he thought that Edith Wharton's fiction should not be read in the light of her love affair, which must be separated from her professional work. It is Bertie's fear that like "Emily Dickinson's [being] bedded with a minister and poor old Henry James doing the unmentionable with a young sculptor," academics will surely see the fiction as reflecting the love affair. Auchincloss parodies their comments: "'After that year a warm roseate streak makes its unmistakable appearance in the once cool marble of her perfect prose.'" We here see a reflection of Auchincloss's own beliefs in the quotation he gives us from these imagined critical reactions, and, in time, his predictions have turned out to be true.

We may also speculate about the two portraits brought into the tale as pictorial equivalents of Grace Eliot and her lover. One is the well-known Sargent. The narrator sees "the tall, elegant figure of Leonard Esher, [as] a peer in a Sargent portrait. At least he always struck me as having just changed from a scarlet huntsman's jacket" (SI, 188). He wrote recently in a review, "I should enjoy seeing an edition of James's work illustrated with Sargent's portraits," and then he goes on to select the Sargents he would use for specific works of James's fiction, among them "Lord Ribblesdale for Lady Barberina's father, Lord Canterville," an aristocrat heavily addicted to blood sports.[5] Here is where Walter Berry as material for his Leonard Esher comes through the Sargent portrait, for Berry was a long, lean man like Ribblesdale and was actually a friend of the peer and his wife. Surely the Sargent portrait summons up Berry rather than James's Lord Canterville, and Auchincloss's witty eye saw immediately the astonishing resemblance with the known photographs of Berry. (Lady Ribblesdale had contributed to the opinion Auchincloss quotes concerning the character of Walter Berry in Auchincloss's biography of Edith Wharton.[6]) Fullerton, we know, was a short man and, from his pictures, of an entirely different type. Berry, therefore, comes in for his share of chastisement for his cold and standoffish attitude to Edith, although he was a friend interested in her activities.

The Mucha poster of Sarah Bernhardt as Hamlet has been selected as an appropriate artistic analogue for Grace-Edith. "Now she put her hand to her breast with a deep sigh, trying perhaps to emulate a Mucha poster of Sarah Bernhardt as Hamlet" (SI, 187). The poster also satisfies the hair color of the real Edith, which was red-gold like Sarah's, and Sarah's gesture of hands crossed on her breast resembles the gesture, somewhat theatrical, which Grace Eliot (if not Edith) makes in this tale.

Like Ada Guest in "The Arbiter," the character of Edith is fictionalized, so she appears as a kind of caricature of herself, and her moving letters to Fullerton are travestied to fit the kind of writing we see only in Wharton's poetry, that is, in what seems now to be her poorest work and her work most apt for parody. However, the kind of burlesque of Edith's prose in the first of the two letters Auchincloss has invented for his Grace Eliot, the one in which she imagines herself Brunhild and her lover Siegfried, is very reminiscent of Henry James's parody of Wharton's *The Fruit of the Tree* in his tale, "The Velvet Glove."[7] The precedent had already been created by James, who, although one of Edith's best friends and sincerest admirers, was also one of her harshest critics.[8] But Auchincloss, as a creative writer thoroughly grounded in James and Wharton scholarship, clearly enjoyed getting in line with James as a parodist of Wharton.

"The 'Fulfillment' of Grace Eliot" serves as a pendant to Auchincloss's earlier Edith Wharton story and exists as a comment on the latest revelatory publication of the discoveries of Edith's personal life. Again, it illuminates how the imaginative processes of a gifted writer like Auchincloss—the biographer of Wharton, a collector of Wharton materials, an inheritor of anecdotes from members of her own set and admirer of her extraordinary gifts—apply themselves. Naturally, as fiction, there is elimination, as well as exaggeration. There is a fusing of Berry and Fullerton, and the ironic suggestion of Percy Lubbock, even of Auchincloss himself (both brilliant critics of E.W.) in the character of the first-person narrator. Grace, with her quotations from *Hamlet* (SI,

187) and her theatrical gestures, is said to feel her love affair meant more to her "than any book she's ever written." It is not likely that either Auchincloss or a reader would believe that of Edith, although we suspend our disbelief when we read this tale in which choosing love before writing is given as a characteristic of Grace Eliot. As before in "The Arbiter," we are here treated to a triangle of two men and a woman, a format in which there is one man who acts as the admiring champion Edith seems to have missed in real life, at least during the time she was involved with Fullerton. In this tale there is enough of the real Edith to create a justification for her deep feelings in her affair with Fullerton. We are invited to roast the two men who caused her great suffering, Fullerton especially, but also, in certain overtones, Walter Berry. This time, the story is about justice to Edith Wharton and serves as a condemnation of the sexual adventurer Morton Fullerton seems to have been. The quotation marks around "Fulfillment" in the title are also a comment on those critics who view the affair as such.

Auchincloss has made his "Edith" heroine less like Edith herself than are the women in the other tales in *Skinny Island,* women whose biographies do not repeat Edith's but whose characters resemble hers in their strengths, their imperiousness, and their interest in ideas or art, chafing under marital restraints, enfranchised by widowhood, and seen as either basically unattached to their children or passionately attached, as the case may be. Auchincloss is the Balzac of Edith's world more than her own fiction is.

The "Edith" tale also is determined by its place in this collection of stories. "The 'Fulfillment' of Grace Eliot" is the tenth tale in a collection of a dozen, which, like those in *The Winthrop Covenant,* advance in years, here from 1875 to the present day (1987). Story after story shows how New Yorkers of the WASP world, rich and powerful figures, react to the changes in their society that three wars, the Civil War, World War I, and World War II, bring to them. We see how they handle and mishandle the problems created by the changes in their society. They reflect the concerns of people like Edith Wharton and her heirs in many of her attitudes and prejudices. Her demanding personality and her charm are equally expressed in the women characters whose strong natures inhabit these pages.

One such male character, Adam Peltz, who keeps "A Diary of Old New York" in 1875 and whose grandfather had been a friend of John Hay and Alexander Hamilton, initiates, in the first story, a tradition. The last story ends with Lucian Day, an effete descendant who, with his ex-wife in the 1980s, attempts without success to control Peter Chisholm, a genius whose ethnic background is ambiguous, "the avenging angel" of the corporate takeover. He is the conqueror of the residue of the older social culture of New York, a man of "shadowy" social and ethnic origins, but one who has gained control of the city's financial machinery. He collects art and, in contrast to Peltz, who more than a hundred years ago lived on Washington Square and owned a "great Sully portrait of President Washington," he lives in a penthouse on Central Park West and is learning how to be an art collector because it is the "thing" to be now.

It is interesting that the eight stories in between these two have their own pictorial and artistic equivalents as well. Peter Chisholm in the last story has to be told what he should like in art: "Would Meyer Schapiro approve of Vigée-LeBrun?" (SI, 217). When he is confronted by a picture by Walter Gay, a painter of interiors, "one of those exquisite expatriates of Edith Wharton's world" (SI, 219), a close friend of Edith Wharton who painted her rooms and those of her friends, he does not know what to make of it. Lucian Day owns part of a gallery, and his ex-wife, Abbie, thinks what Chisholm should buy is some Scythian gold for his tomb where he "would be buried with his cattle and horses and wives all walled up alive with his jewel-decked corpse," the same situation in which Abbie finds herself. The ancient régime is now bested by the intruders into society, an accurate picture of the shift in social control within Manhattan, the "Skinny Island" in the last one hundred years, and reminiscent of *The Custom of the Country*.

There seems to be a uniformity about the narrative technique in this collection, since each tale contains its own illustrations, its gallery drawn from art, examples that exhibit the taste of the particular decade the story illuminates. In the story placed in 1900, "The Wedding Guest," the taste is for Nattier portraits. In the story that takes place around the years of the First World War, we meet a Greek Revival villa and in one of the 1930s a Palladian villa. In the 1940s tale, a character is likened to a Daumier and the women are Boldinis. The tale about two artists in the 1950s concentrates on abstract painting. In the tale placed in the 1960s, the painting of Martin Heade is now a new taste, a historically accurate fact. In "The Reckoning," the entire plot is devoted to a collector of painters like Arshile Gorky, Adolf Gottlieb, and others of that school. This allows us not to be surprised that in the next tale the Sargent portrait and the Mucha poster, analogues for Grace and for Esher, are those that were popular in the *fin de siècle,* the true period of Edith's love affair with Fullerton. Lord Ribblesdale by Sargent was painted in 1902 and Mucha's Bernhardt as Hamlet in 1899. These pictures do not represent the taste of the time during which the fictive love affair takes place, that of 1946, but of the period of the real affair between Edith and her lover, although Sargent and Mucha are now both again having their own revivals in the 1980s and 1990s.

This fiction of Louis Auchincloss should be part of the required reading of every Whartonian, for, with his keen "painter's eye" and his careful illustration of almost every aspect of the life of his own class and a particular sector of New York society, the author gives us a more accurate picture of the world from which Edith came than many of her novels or stories do. In order to understand her peculiarities, her prejudices, and her drives, we must see their equivalents in the women who resemble her moving in the society that nurtured her. It is not that Auchincloss's fiction can explain Wharton's fiction but that it can and does explain the society Edith Wharton moved in, as well as the same society that has changed since her lifetime.

References

1. Adeline R. Tintner, "Justice to Teddy Wharton: Louis Auchincloss's 'The Arbiter,'" *Edith Wharton Review* 7, no. 2 (Winter 1990): 17–19. See chapter 21.

2. Louis Auchincloss, *Skinny Island: More Tales of Manhattan* (New York: St. Martin's Press, 1987), pp. 181–93. Future references are indicated by SI and page number. Mr. Auchincloss drew my attention to this second "Edith" story.

3. *The Library Chronicle of the University of Texas at Austin,* new series no. 31, 1985. Passim. Future references are indicated by LC and page number.

4. Louis Auchincloss, *Love Without Wings* (Boston: Houghton Mifflin, 1991), p. 58.

5. Louis Auchincloss, a review of *The Museum World of Henry James* by Adeline R. Tintner, *New York Review of Books,* April 9, 1987, p. 29.

6. Louis Auchincloss, *Edith Wharton: A Woman in Her Time* (New York: Viking, 1971), p. 158.

7. *The Complete Tales of Henry James,* ed. Leon Edel, vol. 12 (Philadelphia: Lippincott, 1964), pp. 249–50.

8. See Chapter 2 on "The Velvet Glove."

23

Morton Fullerton's View of the Affair
in "They That Have Power to Hurt"

In a collection of tales by Louis Auchincloss, *Tales of Yesteryear* (1994), we recognize on the first page of the third tale, "They That Have Power to Hurt," a fictional portrait of Morton Fullerton in the character of Martin Babcock, the first-person narrator. Now aged seventy-five and living in Paris, "a small antique American gentleman . . . nattily attired," he sits thinking of his "undistinguished but amusing past." In that description we see a replica of a well-known photograph of Fullerton. That past seems to be like that of the journalist Morton Fullerton, for he too is distinguished for "a little record of my encounters with some of the major artists and writers of my time."[1] His name here, Martin Babcock, seems to be the only variant on "Morton" that has been left over since Henry James called his hero "Merton" in *The Wings of the Dove.* He speaks about how academic scholars have reacted to the "uncovering of Arlina's letters" (the "Edith figure," is Arlina Randolph). Academia reveled in Arlina's "sexual fulfillment at the ripe age of forty-three in an adulterous affair. Great news!" Martin (and Auchincloss) condemn the belief of scholars that Edith's affair with Fullerton made her art better, something both the character in and the author of this tale believe is not at all true. Auchincloss believes her first novel, *The House of Mirth,* is her best, published two years before she met Fullerton.

Like Bertie, Grace Eliot's agent, Martin in old age recapitulates his affair with Arlina. We also are told on the first page that one of Martin's distinguishing characteristics had been "an easily detected minor char-

Originally published as "Louis Auchincloss's Four 'Edith' Tales: Some Rearrangements and Reinventions of Her Life," *Edith Wharton Review* 13, no. 2 (Spring 1996).

acter in a couple of important American novels" and surely Fullerton as Merton Densher is one of these. Martin is annoyed because he has not been given "any credit for my share in Arlina's renaissance" (TY, 67), and he is angry with "that grand old ham Hiram Scudder" (recognizable as Henry James in many of his peculiarities) who points out that Martin's "soul, like his personal stature, was small; he was a busy little animal who played below the belt with both sexes and had no real concept of what went on in their minds or hearts" (TY, 58). Martin responds, "certainly not beneath *your* belt, horrid old man, embracing young men in homo-erotic hugs" (TY, 58). Henry James was known for his hugs. Therefore, Martin tells us that he will "provide my own lens in the form of this memorandum which may one day be found among *my* papers . . . by a graduate student" (TY, 58). So here we find Auchincloss's attempt to do justice to Morton Fullerton just as in 1976 he had rendered justice to Teddy Wharton and in 1987 had given Berry's unpleasant and insulting view of the affair in "The 'Fulfillment' of Grace Eliot."

So far the facts about Fullerton's life were only known through R. W. B. Lewis's *Edith Wharton: A Biography* and scattered through Leon Edel's *Henry James: The Master.*[2] For instance, Auchincloss here takes from Lewis's review of Fullerton's life the fact that he was very promising when an undergraduate at Harvard where he was on the editorial board of the *Harvard Monthly* with Santayana and Berenson,[3] and that James called him "a cluster of promises."

When Arlina says to Martin, "Youth, youth . . . you are so cruel" (TY, 70), she is echoing, although not quoting exactly, the line (Edel tells us in his *Treacherous Years*) that James underlined in his copy of the English translation of the novel *First Love* by Turgenev.[4] Actually, James marked the line in the margin with a vertical line beside those words. It was in one of Constance Garnett's translations in the Gilvary collection of James material that went up for sale in 1987, the kind of thing that Auchincloss would most likely have looked at.

The publication of Edith Wharton's letters to Fullerton obviously gave Auchincloss further material for his story. Lubbock quotes Edith Wharton as saying that there is nothing worse than illicit love, and we find that reflected in this tale (TY, 71) when Arlina speaks of "the 'tragedy' of illicit love" in *Tristan and Isolde* (we know from her letters to Fullerton that she read the life of Wagner).

As Arlina says, "It would have been better for me if we'd never met"

(TY, 82), so Edith Wharton had written to Fullerton, "My life was better before I knew you,"[5] although she takes that back (*Letters,* 54) a year later.

Auchincloss has also gone to Fullerton's *Diary* and his correspondence with Margaret Brooke, the Ranee of Sarawak (both quoted by Lewis), and makes use of the few letters from the correspondence between Fullerton and Margaret Brooke for their classical allusions. In courting Arlina in Auchincloss's story, Martin Babcock tells her that he has "been as pure as Hippolytus since the day we met" (TY, 76). She became before the affair "the warmest of friends, the kind of sisterly mentor to a man rejected by his own mother" (TY, 73). According to Lewis, Morton was not rejected but adored by his mother, so Auchincloss varies his facts. Fullerton had compared Margaret Brooke to "a figure of Hellas" and he abounds in biblical and classical allusions (RL, 188–90). Babcock describes Arlina in the same terms Fullerton described his ideal figure to Margaret Brooke: "Her tall full firm figure . . . her alabaster skin and large pensive dark eyes gave her the look of a priestess of classic times, a Norma erect before an altar" (TY, 66). He also in his candid manner in this story attributes his attraction to Arlina because of "the itching yen of a small randy male for a fine large female figure, the lust of a Niebelung to pollute a Rhine maiden," which is added to complete the Wagnerian motif in the tale. In a letter from Edith to Morton she remembers when she heard an opera with him where the hero kisses the heroine "*and then she can't let him go*" (*Letters,* 31), and she adds she felt this too when Morton kissed her. Fullerton seems to have written to her "that's something you don't know anything about" (1908). Auchincloss uses this when he has Martin kiss Arlina to find out whether she would respond. "Her response was all I could have wished" (TY, 77). Then the love affair begins. It is great at first, but then Arlina began to be "too anxious to possess every aspect of my nature." She wanted "to question me about the exact quality of my feeling for her" (TY, 78).

Martin, like Fullerton, in the letters Lewis quotes written to Margaret Brooke, thinks of their love in terms of classical metaphors: He "enhanced his lust with images of a proud Roman dame submitting helplessly to the rape of a barbarian, her aroused appetite whetted by humiliation and shame" (TY, 78). His "inner style" was not like Arlina's whose style was more like that of Tristan and Isolde whereas his was dependent on classical images as Fullerton's had been. While Arlina is on a book tour, she demands daily letters from him during her absence, but he fails to write. When the old famous homosexual painter, Dan Carmichael, gets

Martin to pose, he also makes love to him physically. Hiram Scudder in a jealous mood walks in on the episode. When he reports it immediately to Arlina, she breaks off her relations with Martin.

What is new in this third portrait of Edith is that Auchincloss abandons for the most part Edith's letters and shows Arlina in personal and direct confrontation with Martin, although some of the lines that she speaks recall Edith's letters to Fullerton, for we have no other evidence of the real relationship outside those letters. Martin thinks that the passion he stirred in the painter, Dan Carmichael, and in Arlina, had nothing to do with him. "Passion in great artists is as much the product of their imagination as it is of their hearts" (TY, 83). He bemoans the fact that "academic researchers" give their sympathy to her "disprized love" (TY, 84), which "only is further grist for their busy mills" (TY, 84), while, for "the poor partner of this love, well, out upon him!" (TY, 84). Auchincloss sees Wharton scholarship as merely biographical and does not have much respect for it.

The story ends with the octet from the Shakespearean sonnet number 94, whose first line is the title of the tale. We now add to the title, "and will do none," and "who moving others are themselves as stone." But Martin adds that the sextet reminds the reader that those "lords and owners of their faces" are also lilies that when festering "smell far worse than weeds!" His last word in the story is about the last word of the artist: "Trust the artist to have the last word," and Auchincloss as the artist of this tale in a way has the last word too in creating this invented version of the love affair. The moral of the story is that, although treated badly by Martin, Edith the artist is remembered and her lover is not.

In this version Edith Wharton's relation to the men around her differs from that in the other two versions because the point of view is that of Morton Fullerton. It is not so much that he defends himself but that he explains his position in the light of his needs and his personality, which were not geared to the needs and demands of Edith Wharton. A love affair for Martin as well as for Morton was a cosmopolitan sexual exercise, perhaps more surrounded by illusions than such things are today. The affair was clearly limited to the natural life span of such exercises. Yet for Edith Wharton it appears to have been a deeply felt love affair and, although she finally accepted the inevitable end of it, it took her time. We have remarked on the significance of art references in the other two "Edith" stories. However, the art references in this third story are technically used in a very interesting manner, for the tone of this story is very different from the other two. The mood here reflects the second half of the twentieth century, although the action takes place in the 1940s and Martin was born in 1912. Martin candidly shows his character to be weak-willed, pleasure-loving, amoral, and interested in any kind of sexual experience, as Morton Fullerton was. The artist in "They Who Have Power to Hurt and Do Not," Dan Carmichael, is described "as the youngest member of the Ashcan School. He was a big, bony, black-haired hirsute oleaginous man whose angry canvases of Coney Island bathers, drunken sailors and crowded urban streets on hot summer nights had been considered appropriately powerful and radical in the Depression years" (TY, 63). Martin, who is an art critic, writes a review of Dan's show, which so pleases Dan that he introduces him to Arlina Randolph and takes him to one of her evening parties. In his description of Dan, according to Auchincloss, the author had no particular Ashcan painter in mind, but the sexy sailors were taken, he wrote me, from Reginald Marsh.[6] The artist in this story is described as exactly the opposite of Reginald Marsh, who, although obsessed with the roiling overpopulated masses of proletarians on Coney Island and in crowded urban streets on hot summer nights, was a man who came from the same social stratum, actually, as both Edith Wharton and Auchincloss, although not originally a New Yorker. His parents were very well-to-do and he went to Yale, something he kept hidden. However, I have not been able to find a drunken sailor or a sexy sailor in illustrations of his work as there is in the art of Paul Cadmus, a contemporary. But there are Coney Island bathers in Marsh's work, and there is something, as everyone has noted in monographs on him, very Michelangelistic about his figures to the extent that his prostitutes, his streetwalkers, and his supposedly sexy girls look like men in drag, which makes it possible to see Reginald Marsh, although he had two wives, as either a repressed homosexual or perhaps a homosexual known only to his own group. The introduction of such scenes as the Coney Island bathers brings out the realism that Auchincloss wishes to underline in this story. It is realism and openness and bisexuality and heterosexuality itself brought up even to the present day in tone. Actually, when Martin makes the great mistake of posing in the nude for Dan and at the same time is agreeable to having sexual congress with him, we are reminded more of such a figure first by Reginald Marsh but more recently of such figures as nudes painted by Lucien Freud. Freud had a large exhibition at the Metropolitan Museum in New York City during the time that Auchincloss was writing the story; because so many of these recollections are something he himself cannot put his finger on, such a figure as Freud's nude self-portrait would reconstitute the scene of discovery of Martin's homosexuality in the tale in terms of 1994. There is a kind of postmodern bitter taste in the extreme realism in this story, and the character of Martin as Fullerton does have a kind of acrid flavor. Martin assures the reader that "If I have had affairs with beautiful and elegant women, ever ready to smile on a pleasant unattached young man with a literary flavor, I have always ended them, I hope, with tact and kindness. I have entertained an odd little faith in my own ability . . . to augment the well-being of every person with whom I found myself in any serious relationship" (TY, 62–63). This sentence could have come out of Fullerton's mouth, yet it seems to express a certain breakdown of moral standards, even in Edith's generation, and certainly would fit into the world that Martin Babcock is describing, a world that today is out of the closet. Then there is also the mention of three Whistler Venetian scenes that Arlina had given Martin. Nobody knows whether Edith Wharton ever collected Whistler etchings or etchings of Venice, but her stand-in here gives three of them to Martin. We know that Henry James was given a Whistler etching (whether or not it was Venice nobody knows) by Whistler himself because there is a letter of 1897 thanking him for it, but neither James nor Wharton was a collector in any real sense. Auchincloss writes that he himself owns a Whistler Venetian canal scene that "creeps" into his fiction. There is a still-life by Odilon Redon at Dumbarton Oaks, which Edith left to the Tylers. Piranese prints, in a certain stage in her career and in her life, when she was at Land's End, were appropriate as decoration for her library. She may have given these to James when he decorated Lamb House, but as her houses became more and more aristocratic and royal in The Mount and in the two country-houses, we do not see etchings. We see, as usual with her, walls covered with fabric of some kind in the French manner. Works of art create their own worlds, which often are at variance with the world the interior decorator has established. But it is interesting to see that there is an underlying analogue of art objects in all three tales in the fashion that Henry James used art objects and in the way Edith Wharton often did, art that furthers the themes of the stories and that enriches each one.

One thing Auchincloss does harp on and mentions in the last two of these stories is his annoyance with the academics who believe that the discovery of this passionate love affair with Morton Fullerton affected Edith's fiction. He even mentions academic repossession of Edith's life in the first story, where he has Bob Guest and Adam Winthrop speak about their being only footnotes in some later scholarly attention to Edith's life.

In the third tale, "They Who Have Power to Hurt," Martin himself wants to be written about in some scholarly work: "I can provide my own lens in the form of this memorandum which may one day be found among *my* papers in some university library that accepts *any* bequest . . . by a graduate student looking desperately for a novel aspect in the sex life of an American writer" (TY, 58). Yet he deplores what will happen: "the great Arlinas" will be "receiving the lachrymose sympathy of academic researchers for every supposed pang of 'disprized love' they may incur. . . . while as for the poor partner of this 'love',. . . . Who was he to play gross tunes upon the harpstrings of genius?" (TY, 84).

The moods of the three stories range from the first, which is a moral and rational analysis by Adam Winthrop of Ada's selfish victimization (supported by the art of the eighteenth century) of Bob, to the second story with Grace Eliot's rough treatment by an imperious kind of unsympathetic lover, which now exposes the love affair buttressed by imitations of Edith's passionate letters. But it is a different mood we find in the third story where the sexual aspects are now fully discussed and described but where Arlina is shown to be a noble and yet an over-romantic gifted novelist surrounded by a group of homosexuals and homoerotics, seduced for the only time in her life by the undependable young man (like Fullerton, only younger) by whom the story is told.

Whether consciously or not, Auchincloss also seems to have felt there was a similar rhythm in each "Edith" tale. We detect it as we read them, one after the other. In "The Arbiter" there is the clash between eighteenth-century Rationalism shown in the art and the demands of Ada's intransigent Romantic genius. In "The 'Fulfillment' of Grace Eliot," there is the conflict between the cold-blooded Walter Berry figure and the *fin de siècle* histrionic Grace (or Edith) as a passionate lover represented by the late-nineteenth-century portraits of an arrogant peer and of a melodramatic French tragedienne, by Sargent and Mucha. In the third tale there is the opposition between the upright yet sentimentally passionate Arlina and the ambidextrous sexual athlete Martin Babcock, who is more at home with the realist twentieth-century images of Reginald Marsh and even Lucien Freud than Arlina is, yet she, supported by the motif of Shakespeare's sonnet, has "the last word," because she is "the artist" (TY, 84). Either instinctively or as part of a plan Auchincloss has arranged that each "Edith" tale follow a repetitive template: that of Edith functioning in a complex relationship with two men in a kind of power triangle. In each she is shown in conflict with one man, and that relation is judged by a man from outside that conflict. There are Bob and Ada Guest, judged by Adam Winthrop; there are Grace Eliot and Leonard Esher, judged by her adoring agent Bertie. And then there are Martin and Arlina, brought together and then sundered by Hiram Scudder.

References

1. Louis Auchincloss, *Tales of Yesteryear* (Boston and New York: Houghton Mifflin, 1994), p. 56. Future references are indicated by TY and page number.

2. Leon Edel, *Henry James: The Master* (Philadelphia: Lippincott, 1972), pp. 412–21.

3. R. W. B. Lewis, *Edith Wharton: A Biography* (New York: Harper & Row, 1975), p. 185. Future references are indicated by RL and page number.

4. Leon Edel, *Henry James: The Treacherous Years* (Philadelphia: Lippincott, 1968), p. 348.

5. Alan Gribben, "'The Heart Is Insatiable': A Selection from Edith Wharton's Letters to Morton Fullerton, 1907–1915," *The Library Chronicle of the University of Texas at Austin,* new series no. 31, The Harry Ramson Humanities Research Center, University of Texas at Austin, 1985, p. 55. Future references are indicated by *Letters* and page number.

6. Louis Auchincloss's letter to me, March 20, 1995, is the source of the information he gave me in reference to the questions I raised.

24

The "Real" Mrs. Wharton in THE EDUCATION OF
OSCAR FAIRFAX

Auchincloss found that he was not finished with his Edith figure after his three tales. Only a year after the last, he brings her in again in a chapter of a short novel, but this time she is undisguised, under her own name as Mrs. Wharton and at the height of her career. She appears in *The Education of Oscar Fairfax* (1995) in one of three cameos, which include Walter Berry and the Abbé Mugnier, part of her Paris circle,[1] although they have more space devoted to them.

In presenting the real Edith in two-and-a-half pages, Auchincloss manages to include her severity to the *femmes fatales* in the group and her pride in her garden. Both Berry and Mugnier were her close friends, and Auchincloss establishes the atmosphere of her circle in Paris in the 1920s. He has taken his material from Wharton's *A Backward Glance* and perhaps from a more recent article by Leon Edel on Walter Berry.[2]

The Education of Oscar Fairfax is loosely modeled on *The Education of Henry Adams.* The hero, a young New York lawyer who wishes to write a book on the golden *fin de siècle* in France, gets part of his education from interviews with friends of the great writers of that period. Edith in this novel is no longer totally reinvented by Auchincloss's imagination but is visible as herself, nor do we see a rearrangement of Edith's life as the other three stories exhibited it. Although in each one Edith was pictured as a gifted writer, she is always an imagined character placed in situations or in interrelations analogous to but not identical with those she enjoyed with her husband and her friends.

Originally published as "Louis Auchincloss's Four 'Edith' Tales: Some Rearrangements and Reinventions of Her Life," *The Edith Wharton Review* 13, no. 2 (Spring 1996): 12–14.

In this novel, Oscar Fairfax and his wife, Constance, are guests of Edith Wharton "at a Sunday lunch party at the Pavillon Colombe" (OF, 78) because of letters to her "from mutual friends," and because Oscar "had successfully handled a small legal matter" (OF, 79) for her. She is described as being "in her mid-sixties" as she truly was in 1927. She has "fine strong features, a straight back and a high clear voice that perfectly articulated her neatly constructed sentences" (OF, 79). In the conversation between Mrs. Wharton and Oscar, we are allowed to see two of her well-known animosities evidenced in the published material by her or concerning her. The first is her antagonism to women attractive to and successful with the men in her own circle, here an invented Princess Nelidoroff (perhaps modeled on Anna de Noailles), a sexually liberated poetess whom she calls a traitor and Mrs. Wharton refuses to have her as a subject of conversation: *"Parlant d'autre chose"* (OF, 79). Her next remarks indicate how her admiration for Proust is tempered by the "lapses in his moral sensibility," which "must deny him the very highest rank" (OF, 80). She then cites the passage where Marcel on a ladder watches Jupien and the Baron de Charlus "involved . . . in 'an unedifying scene,'" material extracted from Wharton's chapter on Proust in *The Writing of Fiction*.

The four people Oscar consults about the "belle epoque" finally let him down in the long run. His discussions with Walter Berry, which include a lunch and three visits to his flat, are a disappointment because Berry refuses to talk about his famous friends and is interested only in the "roaring twenties." The chapter in which these four friends appear has been named "The Novocaine of Illusion" because Oscar, through them, loses his illusions about these survivors of a golden past from whom he has expected to get interesting and illuminating anecdotes about the great writers of the period. What Oscar had thought was a golden age seems to have turned out to be "an age of tinsel" (OF, 78).

When we arrive at Mrs. Wharton's luncheon at the Pavillon Colombe, her discussion of Walter Berry seems promising at first for Oscar's book of memoirs until he mentions the Princess Nelidoroff. When it comes to her discussion of Proust, she reveals both her squeamishness and her prejudices. She admits to refusing to meet Proust because of "his social climbing" (OF, 80). Even Walter Berry, who had been a close friend of Proust's, does not have anything specific to say about him, when Oscar had told Berry that he was, in his book, trying to deal with "the last great sunset of unity," which to him meant "the last great explosion of *style*—

and isn't style the essence of civilization? And haven't we lost it?" (OF, 74). Berry is not forthcoming either about Proust's conversation or about the wit of Anatole France. The upshot of his interview with him makes Oscar think that basically Berry is jealous of "his friends' accomplishments" (OF, 76). Violet, the princess, tells Oscar stories that only show herself to be the star, and when it comes to their short affair, she proves herself to be merely a mechanical lover.

In this particular instance, Auchincloss again shows his use of art as an index of a person's character as he had demonstrated in the first three Edith stories; throughout the vignette the names of Boldini, a society portraitist of the period, of Walter Gay, who specialized in interiors, of Sargent, and of other American artists of the time continue to indicate his interest in thickening the *Zeitgeist* of whatever era he deals with by including its plastic artists. A Fragonard painting is brought in to show how the Abbé Mugnier is a sensualist, and instead of talking about the great writers he knew, he gives Oscar worldly advice about how to handle Constance's possible adultery. The upshot of Oscar's disillusionment with the people he meets is that he wakes up from his dose of the "novocaine of illusion," and "because of the worldliness of my chosen craftsmen," abandons his book (OF, 95). Berry, Wharton, Mugnier, and the princess have disillusioned him about their friends, as well as about themselves.

In this fourth Edith story, Auchincloss has brought the real woman on the scene, but in spite of her name and the biographical data utilized for her luncheon party, there is still a reinvention of her figure and a rearrangement of some of her comments from her book, *The Writing of Fiction*. Auchincloss has transposed her recorded reactions to a woman like Sybil Colfax, who married two of Edith's friends, to an invented foreign princess. Her breaking up of her luncheon party to avoid responding to the embarrassing turn Constance has given to the conversation is a fictive construction made by Auchincloss, but it is a reasonable one, based on Edith's known behavior patterns. Whether this is the end of Auchincloss's fun with the elements of Edith's life and those of her intimate friends remains to be seen.

The four tales tell us a lot about Auchincloss as an ingenious and inventive author, for although Edith is shown in all four cases as a great novelist, he knows enough about her to see her faults. The fact remains that the "real" Edith helps, along with her "real" friends, Walter Berry and the Abbé Mugnier, to disillusion Oscar Fairfax through her own prejudicial attitudes. When the discussion becomes argumentative at her luncheon party, she forces her guests, in a domineering fashion, to leave the table and admire her roses. Thus the "real" Edith joins the three previously invented Ediths and shares their similar faults. In spite of them, every one of these Ediths is presented as one of the great writers of our time.

REFERENCES

1. Louis Auchincloss, *The Education of Oscar Fairfax* (New York and Boston: Houghton Mifflin, 1995). Future references are indicated by OF and page number.

2. Leon Edel, "Walter Berry and the Novelists: Proust, James and Edith Wharton," *Nineteenth-Century Fiction* 38 (March 1984): 514–28.

25

Edith Wharton as Herself in Carol DeChellis Hill's HENRY JAMES'S MIDNIGHT SONG

From 1993 to 1995 Edith Wharton appears as herself in three novels: Carol Hill's *Henry James's Midnight Song,* Louis Auchincloss's *The Education of Oscar Fairfax,* and Cathleen Schine's *The Love Letter.* In the first of these three, *Henry James's Midnight Song* (1993), we are treated to a very knowledgeable history of the Viennese *fin-de-siècle* with its familiar stars, Carl Jung and Sigmund Freud, along with Martha, Freud's wife, and Minna, Freud's sister-in-law, and one of Jung's sweethearts.[1] Henry James and Edith Wharton also enter into this European psychoanalytical circle. Wharton, who has come to Vienna to meet clandestinely her lover, Morton Fullerton, and Henry James, who has come to consult Freud about his sister Alice, are all involved in a murder mystery in which a corpse is seen in Freud's study and thereupon vanishes. Presumably it is one of nine serial murders of women that seem to be taking place in Vienna at the turn of the century.

When Henry sees Freud about his sister's illness, the sharp-eyed Dr. Freud discovers Henry James's own guilt for having strangled a cat and for having been the cause of Fenimore Woolson's suicide. This disturbs James, but it disturbs Edith Wharton even more because she has taken upon herself the role of James's caretaker and is in charge of everything he does. After James refuses to attend a dinner with an invented American family, the Mains, also characters in the book, he still eats six heavy biscuits with jam, which Edith Wharton finds bizarre, and he settles down to read *The Trial of Madeleine Smith,* one of the Scottish murder trials sent to him by William Roughead. James is distinctly troubled by the fact that Freud saw his dyspepsia and his insomnia as signs of his repressed feelings and his neurotic relationships with his family.

Back in Paris, Wharton is again aware of James's disturbed condition, and since she is a woman of action in this novel, she drives her own Panhard car. She travels back to Vienna and breaks into Freud's study to eliminate any references that may implicate James or herself in the murder, by climbing through a window in spite of her elaborate and fashionable clothes. In the process she leaves her large ornamental hat behind her. But in her clandestine entry she manages to tear out of the visitors' book both James's name and her own, yet she leaves behind the letters "rton."

Hill has shifted the well-known meeting of Wharton and Fullerton from the Hotel Terminus in London to the Hotel Europa in Vienna. She also includes James's presence, as if conniving with the lovers' illicit rendezvous. However, by this time James has learned to like Freud, although Wharton still resists penetration into her own problems, for she is shocked by his investigations into the sexuality of children, presumably because it hits home with her. It was "totally shocking to me" (MS, 251). Throughout the book Wharton is seen not only as someone taking charge of James but also as a kind of know-it-all. On visits, for instance, to the museum in Vienna with the Mains and others, she gives them a lecture on every piece of art exhibited. In addition, Wharton is shown as having read Nietzsche's work. "Without God, especially, you must have art . . . and love." She also advises the investigative detective, Cuvée, on "how to do a crime." Fullerton is seen as the kind of man who secretly reads Wharton's papers among which he finds the Beatrice Palmetto fragment, Wharton's pornographic, unpublished piece, which here in this novel is reproduced in its entirety from Lewis's biography of Wharton (MS, 307–10). But Wharton finally reads Freud's *Studies in Hysteria* and realizes that he is "a born storyteller"; she ponders over Nietzsche's saying, "We have art in order not to die of the truth" (MS, 336).

Ostensibly presented as a novel in the form of a murder mystery solved by an astute detective, Carol Hill's *Henry James's Midnight Song* displays her well-researched account of the exciting literary and artistic environment of *fin-de-siècle* Vienna, including Klimt the painter, Schoenberg the composer, Karl Kraus the caustic journalist and writer, to say nothing of the allusions to Kafka and Wittgenstein and references to Otto Weininger's *Sex and Society*. Yet the novel at the same time allows the author to extrapolate from the known Edith Wharton to display the latter's character and especially the caring and protective attitude she always assumed in relation to Henry James, whom she loved dearly. Hill is fair to Edith Wharton in her just representation of the writer as both imperious and interfering, and yet at the same time she shows her as a highly intelligent woman who sees beyond her prejudices to recognize the worth of Freud's and Nietzsche's contributions to modern thought. Hill's novel allows her to extend James's visits to the Boston psychiatrist, Dr. Putnam, to his short psychotherapy session administered by Freud himself. Also, her account of Wharton's lover, Morton Fullerton, seems an accurate portrait of this curious sexual adventurer as one knows him from published sources. Hill has, in essence, brought the lives and behavior of Edith Wharton, Henry James, and Morton Fullerton into modern times.

REFERENCES

1. Carol DeChellis Hill, *Henry James's Midnight Song* (New York: Poseidon, 1993). Future references are indicated by MS and page number.

26

Cathleen Schine's THE LOVE LETTER

A short novel, *The Love Letter* (1995), by the literature-savvy young novelist, Cathleen Schine, depends in a subtle way on a few lines from one of the love letters Edith Wharton wrote to Morton Fullerton. Introduced fairly early in a book built on allusions to love letters, as well as letters written by authors to other authors, it enters the novel on the heels of a plot involving an anonymous love letter. The heroine, Helen MacFarquar, the owner of a small bookstore in a New England town, has been sent this letter by mistake. Its aura dominates the novel, and the reading of various collections of letters, in both the store and the local library, allow for the plausible quotation from Wharton's letter to Fullerton: "'There would have been the making of an accomplished flirt in me, because my lucidity shows me each move of the game—but that, in the same instant, a reaction of contempt, makes me sweep all the counters off the board & cry out—Take them all—I don't want to win—I want to lose everything to you!'"[1]

After this introductory quotation, Helen goes on to bring many changes on all kinds of love letters, both hysterical and personal, and letters significant for her theme of a love affair of her own, which will flower in this book. Helen's love affair is one between a forty-year-old woman with lots of sexual experience and Johnny, a young college student of twenty. The most significant and relevant letter reference is the citation of one from Freud to Fliess, in which the notion of the Oedipus complex (the mating of the mother, Jocasta, with her son Oedipus) corresponds to Helen's mating with Johnny, a generation removed from her (LL, 171). A few pages later, Helen writes: "I'll treat him as if he were my own son. The dear old Oedipus theory" (LL, 175). Johnny himself writes Helen a letter in which he includes a sentence from Freud's letter within his own courtship letter (LL, 195).

Although Helen feels guilty about taking on a young lover and is about to tell her mother, the latter tells her that she is in love herself with the sixty-year-old lady librarian of the town, a New England aristocrat. The embarrassment of such a relationship Helen finds much greater than the embarrassment of her own cradle-snatching. She therefore gives in to her love for the lovesick Johnny at the end of the book, and her justification is the Edith Wharton letter to Fullerton. Although Wharton was only a couple of years older than Fullerton, and not by a whole generation, as in Helen's case, yet her words, repeated once more from her letter to Fullerton, give Helen sanction for letting herself go in her complete final abandonment to her love for the college boy. On the last page of the novel, we read for the second time: "I don't want to win," Edith Wharton wrote, "I want to lose everything to you!" (LL, 257). So Helen, too, loses it all, but she finally admits her love for Johnny on a postcard to him, which she locks in her drawer along with the original love letter, which was not a letter at all but part of a mystery novel written by Constance Scattergood, Helen's mother's lover.

Beyond the other love letters, beyond the mention of Chérie and her young lover, beyond the quotation from Elizabeth Bishop's poetry, it is this letter of Wharton's that gives permission for a strong-minded woman to get into a passion, even though the object of it seems to be unsuitable, whatever the generational differences between the two participants. This treatment is a current example of how Edith Wharton's legacy, as represented by her love letters rather than by her fiction, plays a justifying role in the gradual acceptance of passionate love, however unconventional the surrounding circumstances might be.

References

1. Cathleen Schine, *The Love Letter* (New York and Boston: Houghton Mifflin, 1995), p. 120. Future references are indicated by LL and page reference.

PART FIVE

The Legacy of Wharton's Fiction: Three Rewritings

Louis Auchincloss Reinvents Edith Wharton's "After Holbein"

In addition to his use of Edith Wharton as the model for each of the three women writers in three of his stories, Louis Auchincloss, who has written a formal biography of her, also seems to have made at least one raid on her fiction. In *The Partners* (1973–74), a novel composed of individual tales about members of a New York City law firm, Shepard, Putney and Cox, there is an episode entitled "The Diner Out" in Chapter 5, in which the author appears to have adopted a section from Wharton's famous tale, "After Holbein," to flesh out his own highly inventive story.

In his tale Burrill Hume, a member of the law firm, reacts to a loss of faith in him by many of his old clients. He is consoled—or almost consoled—by the fact that these betraying clients, all shortly after leaving for another firm, die. However, it has been suggested by Cox, the senior member of the firm, that Hume retire, since he is now seventy-three years old. When Hume asks what he is to do with his time because his work at the law firm has been his life, Cox replies that he will always have his "dinner parties."[1] How seriously Hume takes his dinners can be seen when Cox asks him to dine that night with him. Hume tells Cox that he has already accepted a dinner engagement that he will not break, for to him these dinners are "sacred," once "you've accepted one!" (*Partners*, 89).

It is at this point in the story that it seems that Auchincloss has plundered that part of "After Holbein" that is the most interesting section of the somewhat labored, although artfully crafted and embroidered tale published in Wharton's 1930 collection of stories, *Certain People*. Almost

Originally published in *Studies in Short Fiction* 33, no. 2 (Spring 1996): 275–77.

fifty years after the publication of "After Holbein," Auchincloss seems to have rescued the story's best part to embellish his own tale. In Wharton's tale, Anson Warley, the sixty-three-year-old diner-out, who only wants the best dinners and the best society, has contempt for old Mrs. Jaspar, once New York's leading hostess, but now a pathetic has-been. As he prepares to go out to dinner at somebody else's house, the expression on his valet's face tells us that Warley does not look well. But, after a moment of vertigo, he seems to feel all right. Auchincloss reminds us of this scene from Wharton's tale when he has Burrill Hume's housekeeper tell him that "that pasty face of yours says you're not going out" (*Partners,* 90). Like Anson and his vertigo, Burrill has a short period of time when his "heart was pounding" (*Partners,* 91), but he feels fine after a short rest.

Whereas Mrs. Wharton's tale breaks in at this point with a lengthy and complicated scene in which Mrs. Jaspar has been gotten into her evening clothes by her servants for the charade of her nightly fiasco of pretended dinner parties, Auchincloss moves on to section four of Wharton's tale, in which Anson tells his valet, Filmore, who wants him to take a taxi, that he prefers to walk to his dinner party. Then he suddenly forgets where he is to dine tonight. "Where the dickens was he going to dine? And with whom was he going to dine?" (*Certain People,* 91). Auchincloss's Burrill also has a moment of forgetfulness when he asks himself "to dinner at—where was it? Mrs. Trane's?" (*Partners,* 90).

Wharton's Anson walks along Fifth Avenue in the cold air and seems to feel very good. Yet, although he was to be dining at someone else's house, he finds himself walking in front of Mrs. Jaspar's house, which is all illuminated for one of her parodied, pseudo dinner parties. Then "he remembered it quite clearly now—it was just here, it was with Mrs. Jaspar that he was dining. . . ."[2] It is at this point that Auchincloss changes the details in his own version but still depends on his aging hero's memory lapse. Burrill knows where he is dining out, but he has forgotten the correct address. Since, like Wharton's Anson, he is vain about his youthfulness in spite of his advanced years, he reads the address incorrectly and, unlike Anson, he takes a taxi, he drops off at 1065 Park Avenue, an address that his failing eyesight has incorrectly read. After many trials and exposure to "cold, stony Madison Avenue," he finds a telephone booth on East 86th Street and learns, by telephoning Mrs. Trane's apartment, that it is 1055, not 1065 Park Avenue where he is to dine.

Auchincloss is now on his own again. Arriving at the dinner party, which is a real one, Burrill sits next to his old client, Mrs. Fanny Bloxham. He learns from her that she, too, must leave his law firm as a client in order to go with her grandson's law firm, so he can, through her influence, become a partner. In revenge for this shock, he tells her how all the other clients who broke with him died shortly after their break. Since Mrs. Bloxham is over eighty years old, she is frightened by his statement. However, thinking it over and realizing that Mrs. Bloxham's daughter would make reprisals, this man with a weak heart himself decides that he should confess his strategy to his client. He tells her that, if he fires her, instead of the other way around, he will remove the jinx, especially since he must retire anyway. Since she herself has the problems of old age, she leaves the dinner party early and offers to take him with her.

Although Auchincloss has invented a fine and original ending of his own, it is clear that for certain details he turns once more to the ending of Wharton's "After Holbein." There, after Anson Warley has engaged in a grotesque parody of a feast with Mrs. Jaspar at an otherwise empty dinner table, he emerges once more into the cold night air. "He smiled again with satisfaction at the memory of the wine and the wit. Then he took a step forward, to where a moment before the pavement had been—and where now there was nothing." This ends the tale (*Certain People*, 101). It is clear he has dropped dead.

"The Diner Out" ends with only a premonition of the hero's death, not with its actuality. Burrill Hume senses, when Mrs. Bloxham offers him a ride home in her "chariot," that he as well as she are now "beyond the reach of the life-giving force of his firm." He sees the "big black glistening limousine" that belongs to Mrs. Bloxham and realizes that "it might have been a hearse!" Yet he sees that "The luxurious upholstered interior is brilliantly illuminated" (*Partners,* 100). "'Are you coming, Burrill?,' his friend asks, as she steps forward into the dark." Thus Auchincloss uses almost the same words for his ending as Wharton has in her tale, for the last line of "The Diner Out" mimics the last line of "After Holbein" quoted above. Auchincloss's story ends as a recognizable modification of Wharton's ending (*Partners,* 100). We know both characters are going to die, but not at this moment, although the symbol of the car as a hearse suggests it. In Wharton's tale, Anson's only life was his dining out. For Burrill Hume, it was the balancing of his law firm life *with* his dining out and of his need for both. Mrs. Bloxham, as she "stepped forward into the dark," anticipates Hume's also stepping forth into the dark and then stepping into the hearse-like limousine. This final line makes one think of Mrs. Wharton's final line, since it is clearly Auchincloss's variation of it.

Louis Auchincloss has thus apparently incorporated Edith Wharton's "After Holbein" into his own "danse macabre." Behind both tales are the Holbein illustrations of the presence of the skeleton or Death at every banquet, whether it be a royal feast or the meal of a commoner. In both Wharton's largely imagined dinner party and Auchincloss's real one, the shadow of Death hovers over feasts that are as close to royal occasions as American aristocrats can achieve.

REFERENCES

1. Louis Auchincloss, *The Partners* (Boston: Houghton Mifflin, 1973–74), p. 88. Future references are indicated by *Partners* and page number.

2. Edith Wharton, *Certain People* (New York: Appleton, 1930), p. 91. Future references are indicated by *Certain People* and page number.

28

Daniel Magida's THE RULES OF SEDUCTION *and* THE AGE OF INNOCENCE

We do not find that the rewriting of Edith Wharton's novels and tales has been done in the postmodern novel as often as the rewriting of Henry James's fiction. However, one novel, *The Rules of Seduction* (1992) by Daniel L. Magida, published in 1992, does include strong factors that point directly to Wharton's *The Age of Innocence* (1920) and that the reader of her work cannot ignore. Why should the main characters in Magida's novel be named Jack Newland, Kate Welland, and Ellen Archer? These names summon up immediately the slightly different ones of the recognizable characters of *The Age of Innocence* who are Newland Archer, May Welland, and Ellen Olenska. They correspond as well in their roles to those fictional personages original with Wharton. Newland Archer in Wharton's novel must make a choice between May Welland and Ellen Olenska, just as in Magida's novel Jack Newland must make a choice between Kate Welland and Ellen Archer. As in Wharton's novel, Ellen Olenska represents the unconventional intruder into the tightly knit family of Newland Archer, so Ellen Archer, now a lady physicist, is the unusual and exotic member of the Archer family in *The Rules of Seduction*.

In both novels, the hero's consciousness is the central consciousness of each book, although Jack Newland's consciousness is closer to a state of unconsciousness until he supposedly finally resolves the problem of his own responsibility for his drunken father's death. Jack, who is a heavy drinker himself, has a drunken memory of his father's statement that his boy is "my keeper. I don't have to worry as long as Johnny's looking after me" (RS, 420). One says "supposedly" because, on the final pages of the very long novel, it is difficult to see which woman Jack actually has chosen since his last words indicate that the woman who chooses him first will get him. In this sense, he also imitates Newland Archer in *The Age of Innocence,* who also has his life manipulated by May Welland in final collusion with Ellen Olenska. He too was unable to make his own choice.

The Rules of Seduction shows a picture of an adolescent who grows up to be a twenty-eight-year-old man bound from the beginning by the rules of his group and class. He actually is made immobile by this subordination to the desires of others. Particularly is he made inactive by the mysterious causes of his father's auto plunge over a cliff, carrying himself and his wife to certain death. The example of Wharton's Newland Archer in his tight bondage to the customs of his family is before Magida on every page of his novel, although he goes beyond *The Age of Innocence* often to respond to certain novels of Henry James that also underline *The Age of Innocence.* The locale of both Wharton's and Magida's novels is the New York City of the social register and the outlying water holes and resorts frequented by this class.

Jack Newland in *The Rules of Seduction,* who is a cultural columnist for a small magazine in New York City, simply because he has social connections, and who is also a volunteer for hospitalized AIDS cases, has become engaged to Kate Welland because his family expects it. His sister Elizabeth has been prodding him to announce it while Kate is in Europe with her father, and he is busy trying not to hurt the feelings of other people who find him attractive. He fully expects to marry her because of his general pattern of doing what people want of him, but he is in no rush about it, because he is hemmed in by the same rules of seduction, the rules of the game, as the other married couples in his family. A graduate of a Connecticut prep school and of Yale University, he is called more than once an "observer of the scene"[1] and is forced to enter Kate's cultural milieu. A shrewd woman friend of his tells Jack, "You seem like such a nice person, but scratch the surface and it's like there's nothing there" (RS, 211). Like the man without a shadow, he seems to be a victim of anomie. He finds himself falling in love with Ellen Archer, whose name also indicates that of James's Isabel Archer, whom she resembles in physical appearance with her black hair and blue eyes.

Timothy Archer, a roommate from his old prep school days, but not of a high enough social position to be accepted by Yale, had introduced him to his sister, Ellen, who breaks away from the women of Jack's class by becoming a working scientist. Jack's love for Ellen makes him want to leave "behind a woman" (Kate Welland) for "another woman who occupied by contrast very nearly the most central place in that life. He had broken all the rules," for "he was falling in love with a woman who had no place in the usual order of his life" (RS, 251).

This event follows the pattern of Newland Archer in *The Age of Innocence* when, after his engagement to May Welland, he meets and falls in love with Ellen Olenska, also with "no place in the usual order of his life." The chief difference in the Wharton novel is that May and Newland are married when his attraction to Ellen becomes intense. May's premature but false announcement to Ellen of her pregnancy prevents Newland's leaving his family because Ellen will not disrupt the pattern of their marriage, which now includes a child. She too follows the rules.

In *The Rules of Seduction* the resolution of Jack's guilt for his father's death seems, however, to be the result of his habit of letting others take command of his life. Magida has preempted the "code" and the social rules from *The Age of Innocence,* and they lead not to Newland's choice but to the choice made by the two women. Had not that been what took place to resolve the situation in *The Age of Innocence?* May has a meeting with Ellen and announces her "pregnancy" and thereby makes her rival refuse to elope with Newland. In *The Rules of Seduction* the two rivals also negotiate the future of Jack Newland's life: "Kate and Ellen would settle matters," since Kate had asked Ellen to come to her apartment; he would wait until one of them came to him. He follows "the rules of seduction" (RS, 420).

Holding out his mangled hand, the result of too much alcohol and a signal of his mangled life, he says in front of the two girls, "I'm here," at which point the book ends. Like Newland Archer who is kept from making his own choice, so Jack Newland cannot make his own choice either. The fate of both heroes has been decided by the collusion between the two women who are rivals for his affection.

The other thing Magida seems to be doing is showing how codes and rules influence even his rather formless society as long as the family has entry to the right schools and the right colleges, seeing to it that their children know also how to follow the rules, whatever they may happen to be. These rules of conduct now have become the rules also of seduction.

Although Wharton is never mentioned in this novel, Henry James is mentioned twice. The first time occurs when Jack quotes the famous statement by Henry James reported by Edith Wharton in *A Backward*

Glance that "summer afternoon" are the two most beautiful words in the English language, and when Jack is asked what he has been thinking about, he automatically answers "Henry James." The second time James is mentioned is when Jack is characterizing certain families as opposed to his own. "He knew there were such families, where a line of distinguished predecessors stretched back through the Social Register, the Jameses and the Lowells, in which each generation seemed to produce another giant of the cultural scene." Although not word for word, this material also comes from *A Backward Glance.* "His own family was from a different tradition, New York merchants, businessmen who moved ships and railroads the way Henry James moved commas" (RS, 154). The basic irony is the same in both Wharton's and Magida's novels. Newland Archer had told Ellen Olenska, "New York society is a very small world compared with the one you've lived in. And it's ruled, in spite of appearances, by a few people with—well, rather old-fashioned ideas."[2] When Ellen makes no answer, he adds, "Our legislation favours divorce—our social customs don't" (AI, 109). What Jack Newland repeats from *The Age of Innocence* is Newland Archer's statement to Ellen Olenska: "I'm the man who married one woman because another one told him to" (AI, 243). This society muffles the tragedy of the individual in "the warm shelter of habit" (AI, 325).

In *The Age of Innocence,* the code, and the rules are engineered by May and ritualized by the farewell dinner she gives for Ellen. "There were certain things that had to be done and, if done at all, done handsomely and thoroughly; and one of these, in the old New York code was the tribal rally around a kinswoman about to be eliminated from the tribe" (AI, 337). Ellen and Newland appreciate it because they too seem to say to each other, "'Oh, do let's see it through'" (AI, 339). In the end the social unit wins, for "The silent organization which held his little world together was determined to put itself on record as never for a moment having questioned the propriety of Madame Olenska's conduct, or the completeness of Archer's domestic felicity" (AI, 342). The following sentence, "The worst of doing one's duty was that it apparently unfitted one for doing anything else" (AI, 354), seems to have affected the basic character of Magida's interpretation of Newland Archer, for his Jack Newland can do nothing else except follow certain rules. His apathy replaces Archer's resigned but active role as husband and father.

In Newland Archer's refusal to see Ellen Olenska again years later after his love for her has ebbed, he shows his desire to keep his romantic vision of her intact. In some way Jack Newland's father's favorite song, "Isn't it Romantic?," fits into this pattern, perhaps ironically. Magida's novel is evidence again of the postmodernist novelist's need to attach himself to some classic example of literature to achieve his own form. If this novel were only a poor imitation of *The Age of Innocence,* Magida would not have given his characters names so similar to those of the characters in Wharton's novel. These echoes appear to be signals to the educated reader that he is making in his novel, written seventy years after *The Age of Innocence,* an updated version of it.

References

1. Daniel Magida, *The Rules of Seduction* (New York: Houghton Mifflin, 1992), pp. 28, 46. Future references are indicated by RS and page number.
2. Edith Wharton, *The Age of Innocence* (New York: D. Appleton, 1920), p. 109. Future references are indicated by AI and page number.

29

Lev Raphael's THE EDITH WHARTON MURDERS

Lev Raphael, in his second mystery, has made Edith Wharton the central figure of his plot, as she has been the focus of his university teaching in his academic career, recently abandoned for a full-time writing career. The author of a well-considered scholarly work on shame in Edith Wharton, he here makes his sleuth, Nick Hoffman, Wharton's bibliographer. Nick also teaches her fiction in a midwestern state university.[1]

The world here is what Raphael's world was until recently, that world of Edith Wharton's scholarship. Nick has been elected to put on an Edith Wharton conference in this university, since Wharton is a noncontroversial figure, appropriate for emphasizing women's issues. There are two Wharton societies, one traditional and the other radical, that are in conflict with one another. The novels themselves and an occasional short story by Edith Wharton are inserted to emphasize the points that arise in the attempt to solve the two murders that ensued from the heated and passionate relations among the conferees. Nick here is made the Wharton bibliographer of note, creating a tool necessary to Wharton scholars but existing beyond any controversy, so Nick can more or less stand aside and function, with his lover Stefan, as detective to solve the murders. What helps solve them also is the presence of paperbacks of Wharton's novels, *The House of Mirth, The Age of Innocence,* and *Ethan Frome,* found at the scenes of the crimes.

Wharton dominates this novel in another way. Each one of the three parts into which the novel is divided is decorated by appropriate quotations from her novels. Daniel Magida is quoted as well in the epigraph to the book, and Magida is a writer, as we have seen, who is one of the few who, in addition to Louis Auchincloss, makes use of Wharton references in his novel *Rules of Seduction*.

The occurrences of Wharton references have multiplied in the 1990s. Whereas in the 1970s there were only two such attempts, one by Richard Howard and the other by Louis Auchincloss, and in the 1980s only one by Auchincloss, in our present decade six novels have resorted to Wharton material. This surely is a sign of the times and the absorption into popular culture of Wharton's fiction, as well as of the legend behind her life. The films of *Ethan Frome* and *The Age of Innocence* and the completed novel *The Buccaneers* in a televised play have, during 1993, accelerated this process of Wharton adoption by popular culture, and one must expect to see further examples in the near future of Wharton-inspired fiction, dependent either on her biography or on the plots of her fiction. Henry James's penetration into the popular world of fiction and film has shown a similar course, culminating in the presence of eleven different terms of reference either to James's figure or to his fiction during the one year 1997.

This transplantation of literature to personal history, films, and plays is a pretext for theoretical argumentation and opinions that constitute academic literary discourse. Those pieces of literature that satisfy the current interest in sexual irregularities, as well as dysfunctional families, help stimulate popular interest. The authorial presence has been removed to the more popular forms of communication. In *The Edith Wharton Murders,* her works of fiction have been used as objects helping as clues and suggesting in their themes some aspects of the interpersonal hatreds bred in the more fanatical members of the Edith Wharton academic cults. The three novels, *Ethan Frome, The Age of Innocence,* and *The House of Mirth,* are those most popular of Wharton's novels that have become available through film to the average reader of mysteries. Although they are presented here for dramatic results as two warring Edith Wharton societies led by two belligerent presidents, one conservative and one radical, headed in the first instance by a distant cousin of Wharton's and in the second by a "bipolar, anoretic, lesbian leader," actually there is only one existing Wharton Society, yet one recognizes the fact that there are two different schools of Wharton criticism. As one character in the novel expresses it, "You read the articles and you come away thinking there are two different Edith Whartons. One's a powder puff and the other's a carnival side-show act! What the hell is going on here?" (EWM, 66). Grace-

Dawn Vaughan has written a passionate biography of Wharton as a passionate woman. The three novels invoked are explained in different circumstances by Nick: *The House of Mirth,* a novel that describes the possible suicide of Lily Bart, is summarized to the police officer on the case. The police officer thinks that Chloe DeVore, the first woman murdered, has a first name that is close to "chloral," the lethal medicine with which Lily Bart overdosed herself. Because the novel is found at the scene of the crime, it seems to function as a clue. Those academics who expound clichés on *The House of Mirth* at the conference are made fun of by Nick and his friend Stefan (EWM, 133). There are Wharton jokes inserted into the book, such as, "Well, since Edith Wharton was so bossy, if she had married Morton Fullerton, would he have been Morton Wharton?" (EWM, 136). Also, "Wharton scholars tend to know only their own field, and even there just a small part of it" (EWM, 134). There are also judgments made about the recent films based on Wharton novels. *The Age of Innocence* is shown at the conferences. "It brought the conference closer together, with almost everyone united in contempt and superiority" (EWM, 139). Jones, the president of the conservative Wharton Society, says about Scorcese, the director of the film: "He's been seduced by surfaces. He's gotten the book all wrong and made a showy, vulgar movie out of a witty and subtle novel" (EWM, 139). After the applause, the author joins in agreement, "since Jones was right" (EWM, 139). When Priscilla Davidoff, the second person, is murdered, she has near her in her car a copy of *Ethan Frome* in which there is also an attempted suicide. But Priscilla's is only a fake.

The detective story is a fine popular device to include many judgments, literary and otherwise, about Wharton, including quotations relative to the tale at hand and from the accumulated store of Whartoniana, which a teaching and scholarly career enjoyed and suffered by Lev Raphael alone makes possible. It seems that his talents and sense of fun are ideally suited to this popular form of resurrecting Wharton in a milieu that does justice to her work, her reputation, and her future as a literary icon.

REFERENCES

1. Lev Raphael, *The Edith Wharton Murders* (New York: St. Martin's Press, 1997), passim. Future references are indicated by EWM and page number.

Appendix
A Book and Four Friends

Henry James, Walter Berry, Edith Wharton, and W. Morton Fullerton

In a copy of Romain Rolland's *Vie de Tolstoi* (Paris: Hachette, 1911) from the library of Henry James, there is inscribed in pencil on one of the endpapers a five-line love poem in Edith Wharton's handwriting. No one of its previous owners seems to have read the book and, as far as I can determine, the poem has never been noticed, and of course, it has never been published. The book, a gift from Walter Berry to Henry James, offers an interesting puzzle related to its migrations.[1]

The book carries on the front flyleaf a penciled inscription in Walter Berry's handwriting, which reads "Recommended for marine use" (Figure 6). Underneath are the initials W. B. Below that inscription the novelist James has written "*Henry James* (from Walter Berry.)" On the back flyleaf of the book, at right angles to the page, there is to be found the lightly penciled, perfectly legible, five-line poem. It reads:

> You come between me & the night.
> Closer than sleep you lie with me.
> You are the air, you are the light,
> You are my hearing, you my sight,
> And you are all I hear & see . . . (Figure 7)

Various experts confirm that this poem is in Edith Wharton's handwriting.[2] The poem appears to be "of her own making."[3]

How did Walter Berry come to possess in 1911 a book with a love poem by Edith Wharton at a time when she was still in love with

Originally published as "An Unpublished Love Poem by Edith Wharton," *American Literature* 60, no. 1 (March 1988): 98–103.

6. Romain Rolland, *Vie de Tolstoy,* front flyleaf with inscription from Walter Berry to Henry James. Courtesy, collection of Bill Blumberg.

7. Romain Rolland, *Vie de Tolstoy,* back flyleaf with five-line poem written in the handwriting of Edith Wharton. Courtesy, collection of Bill Blumberg.

Morton Fullerton, as the recent publication of the letters from this period testifies?[4] Assuming that the poem was written not to Berry but to Fullerton, how did the book get from Fullerton to Berry? And why did Berry then give this book, bearing an intimate private message (apparently not to him but to Morton Fullerton), to their mutual friend Henry James? The answers must have something to do with the fact that the book has thus never been read, although its pages have been cut;[5] neither Berry nor James ever got to the end of the book where the faint lines of the poem were written. It is also possibile that the book may have passed through Morton Fullerton's hands; he may have received it (and the poem) from Edith Wharton as a gift and a message, but he too never read it through before he passed it on to his friend Berry. After all, how many readers of books look at the blank end pages?

Morton Fullerton would appear to be the most likely person to whom the lines were addressed. It seems "highly unlikely that she would have addressed such sentiments" to Berry in 1911.[6]

Edith Wharton's love affairs have been a matter of public interest ever since R. W. B. Lewis published his biography of the novelist in 1975. What he confirmed was that an American journalist named William Morton Fullerton, a friend of Henry James's, had become her lover in 1907 and that the attachment continued until 1910. What has been revealed in the publication (1985) of excerpts from her newly found letters to Fullerton, now in the Harry Ransom Humanities Research Center at Austin, Texas, is that the attachment lasted on her side until 1911 during which time she was addressing him as "cher," "dear" and "cher ami," terms of endearment which indicated that her feelings were still involved. (Until Fullerton was identified it had been thought that Walter Berry was the lover she addressed in her Day Book and that the poem "Terminus" printed by Lewis was devoted to Berry because of her life-long love and admiration for him and because she had herself buried near him in the Versailles cemetery.) One letter, dated Thursday evening, 1911, begins "Thank you, dear, for writing. I don't mean to bother you like that often. But send me a line now & then to tell me how things are in the normal world outside this house."[7] As late as May 15, 1911, she begins her letter by writing "Cher." In it she speaks of Walter Berry, and we might speculate that it could have been on one such occasion that Berry was given *Vie de Tolstoi,* which Edith Wharton may have sent originally to Fullerton. We may conclude this from the following sentence in the same letter: "I am glad you had a pleasant lunch with W. — you call him 'Happy Man' and he writes me he is sick to death of everything" (C, 59). The love poem would fit in with the fact that Wharton still at this time had strong feelings for Fullerton, which he no longer shared. Alan Gribben writes to me that "though her erotic 'Terminus' poem appears to date from 1909, it is entirely conceivable that she would be continuing her love lyrics even two years later."[8]

That these good friends exchanged and handled each other's books is well documented. "Wharton, James, Fullerton, and (sometimes) Berry frequently exchanged reading materials."[9] Leon Edel informs me that during a visit to the Pavillon Colombe in 1936 he asked Edith Wharton whether she had any books inscribed to her by Henry James. "She took me," he writes, "to a series of shelves at the rear of her library and showed me a shelf filled with Henry James novels. I remember looking at a copy of *The Wings of the Dove* and I think *The Sacred Fount.* Both were inscribed affectionately to William Morton Fullerton. I saw none inscribed to Edith Wharton. She smiled at me and said, 'Mr. Fullerton left these with me several years ago. Come to think of it, *my* inscribed James books are at Ste. Clair.' "[10] In the article that introduces the pertinent issue of the *Chronicle,* Gribben specifies that a copy of Henry James's *The Spoils of Poynton,* inscribed and presented by James to Fullerton, has Edith Wharton's bookplate pasted in and that Wharton made vertical pencil marks on pages 200 and 201 where "Owen finally embraces and kisses Fleda" along with a note, "The greatest kiss in fiction. E.W." (C, 11). In 1911 Wharton "had obligingly kept" in her apartment a number of boxes of books belonging to Fullerton (C, 11). On September 22, 1911, Wharton wrote to Fullerton, "*Please* don't talk of the books at 53 rue de Varennes as *mine.* They are the property of my dear friend Mr. F., to which I rejoice to give shelter until they find their way back to his shelves, as they will someday" (C, 63). She was to put a call in for Fullerton to collect these books in 1915 through her secretary, Anna Bahlmann, who wrote a note saying that "she is up to her eyes in work" and that she has asked "if you could conveniently send for your books, as she has to find room for a lot of furniture. Of course she has been delighted to keep the books for you, but now she is herself pressed for room. . . . They have been carefully packed in 25 or 30 boxes. Could you make it convenient to send for them on Wednesday morning?" (C, 71). Wharton's statement to Edel quoted above indicates that Fullerton never did so, so the *datum post quem* of 1915 seems to be irrelevant and to eliminate the idea that between the period of 1911 and 1915 *Vie de Tolstoi* must have done a certain amount of wandering. Indeed, it is in the recent publication of Henry James's Pocket Diaries that we find a good clue as to when the book may have been presented by Walter Berry to Henry James. For the July 30, 1911, James wrote just after he had departed from New York for Europe on the *Mauretania:* "on this Tuesday noon drove into Boston and took train to New York—Harry joining us at station. Went to H[otel] Belmont; beautiful cool rooms. Went after dinner to see Mrs. Smalley. . . . Walter Berry called when I got home—10 o'clk. Then a.m. Wednesday motored early (7.30) to Cunard Dock. . . . A departure easy and beautiful on big and not crowded Mauretania. . . . George Meyer—Sec. American Navy—offered me a place at his table etc."[11] It is tempting to think that Walter Berry, during this late ten o'clock visit the night before the novelist was to sail for Europe, presented James with Rolland's *Vie de Tolstoi,* with the inscription "Recommended for marine use." It is also tempting to think that Berry might have received this book directly from Edith Wharton, although the poem's sentiments seem to indicate Fullerton as the dedicatee.

Did Berry receive the book directly from Wharton, and was the poem she inscribed at the back written for *his* benefit? Did Wharton forget that she had intended to give the book to Fullerton with a poem inscribed only for his eyes and instead gave it to Walter Berry who then presented it to James? Did the book get directly to Fullerton who, bored with it, never read it to the end and consequently never saw the delicately in-scribed poem, and did he then give it to Walter Berry who also never read it, neither the Rolland nor the Wharton text? Although we have no precise answer to any of these questions, we may also assume from the almost mint condition of the book that Henry James never read either the book or the poem. What seems to give force to this speculation is that there are no further entries in the James diaries during the trip on the *Mauretania* until after he disembarked on August 7 and no mention at all of any of his activities during his marine journey (incidentally, the last of his life). However, he never gave away the book because it re-mained in his Lamb House library during his lifetime. It is highly un-likely that Wharton found the book in James's library and inscribed the verses to James because of their erotic content; but we cannot totally dismiss the lines as destined for Berry. However, the Texas revelations sug-gest that they were meant for Fullerton. All we can really say with cer-titude is that Wharton wrote the poem and that Berry gave the book to James.

It seems fairly certain that the poem Wharton wrote was her own. According to Gribben, "Wharton forgot that she had penned these lines in the book and that it then went to Berry and to James. She was in the habit of using odd pieces of paper for composing notes and poems, and she probably failed to remember jotting down this unsigned verse";[12] Among the uncataloged letters at the Harry Ransom Humanities Research Center at Austin are two "love" poems that date from 1910 (two pages and one page in length) and are of greater length than the five-line poem in *Vie de Tolstoi*. There are shorter notes, but they "consist of romantic quotations and messages." Since our five-line poem is not surrounded by quotation marks, one may assume Wharton composed them.[13]

We know from the 1984 catalog of Edith Wharton's library that Wharton had her own copy of Rolland's book.[14] It seems probable that she first bought that copy, liked it, and then bought another copy for Fullerton. After she obtained the second copy, it also seems probable that she put it among his books or in some place in her apartment near his books, expecting to return them to him at the time he would call for them. Perhaps she penciled the lines at the back as a kind of afterword for him when he would have finished the book. It is possible that she forgot this and gave the book to Walter Berry. The lines do not appear in her one volume of published verse, *Artemis to Actaeon* (1909).

Edith Wharton's concern with Rolland's life of Tolstoi deserves some comment beyond noting her general interest in the Russian novelist, which is clear from her letter to Sally Norton, February 26, 1912: "I sent you some weeks ago a life of M. Angelo by Romain Rolland, thinking it was the 'companion volume', so to speak of his wonderful Beethoven and Tolstoy. I have just discovered that he has, strangely enough, written *two* lives of M. A. . . . and of course I sent you the wrong one."[15] This letter also tells us that she was in the habit of sending copies of books she admired to her friends. We may speculate further that Chapter Nine, devoted to *Anna Karénine,* would be of a special personal interest to Wharton, since the story of Anna might suggest parallels to her own situation with her husband and her lover. One can understand how she could have identified herself and her passion for Fullerton with Anna's passion for Vronsky. Rolland wrote that "the fatality which broods over the romance is no longer as in *War and Peace* . . . the Destiny of empires, but the madness of love, 'Venus herself.' " It is she who "endows the innocent beauty of Anna . . . with an almost infernal seductiveness." "She it is who . . . installs herself in her heart, never to leave it until she has destroyed it. No one can approach Anna without feeling the attraction and the terror of this hidden daemon. . . . Anna herself is perfectly aware that she is no longer her own mistress. As the story develops the implacable passion consumes, little by little, the whole moral structure of this proud woman. All that is best in her, her sincere, courageous mind, crumbles and falls; she has no longer the strength to sacrifice her worldly vanity; her life has no other object than to please her lover; . . . jealousy tortures her; the sensual passion which enslaves her obliges her to lie with her gestures, her voice, her eyes."[16] As Anna recovers from her illness they (Anna, her lover, and her husband) are all three sensible of "the existence of another force, brutal but all powerful, which was directing their lives despite themselves, and which would not leave them in peace."[17] Wharton's moving love poem, appended to a book concerned with one of the great literary treatments of a woman's self-destructive love, passed through the hands of the three important men in Wharton's life and as far as we can determine was never read by any one of them. The subject of the poem, who is the whole world to the author, who is "all I hear and see," could be either Fullerton or even possibly Berry, whose possession of the book is proved by his initialled inscription and by Henry James's written note underneath. Ironically, it is the one member of the trio who actually ended up with the book—Henry James—who is the least likely to have inspired the poem.[18]

REFERENCES

1. After Henry James's library at Lamb House was dispersed, the book was in William James Jr.'s library at 95 Irving Street, Cambridge. I acquired the book, which also at one time belonged to Leon Edel, from Glenn Horowitz, the book dealer. The book had been given to Leon Edel by John James, a son of William James Jr.

2. R. W. B. Lewis: "The handwriting is unmistakably Edith Wharton's," personal communication, October 1, 1986. Alan Gribben: "the poetry is unquestionably written in Wharton's hand, in my opinion," personal communication, October 2, 1986. Cynthia Griffen Wolff: "The handwriting is, to my eye, unmistakably Wharton's," personal communication, October 28, 1986. Millicent Bell, Clare Colquitt, and C. Sammons, Acting Librarian, Wharton Collection, the Beinecke Library, Yale University, all experts in Wharton manuscripts, agree that the handwriting is that of Edith Wharton (personal communications, October and November, 1986).

3. R. W. B. Lewis: "I suspect that the poem is of her own making," personal communication, October 1, 1986. Alan Gribben assumes the lines are by Wharton: "she probably failed to remember jotting down this unsigned verse," personal communication, October 2, 1986.

4. Alan Gribben: "One would expect to find this sort of thing belonging to the years just before 1911. But I have seen no corroborating evidence that would suggest Berry as the recipient of (or inspiration for) these sentiments in 1911. Primarily, then, they seem to argue in favor of our viewing the Wharton-Fullerton affair as extending into that year," personal communication, October 2, 1986. It has also been suggested that the poem might refer to the book itself that Wharton is reading, except that lines four and five argue against that interpretation.

5. Except for the first few pages, the remaining pages have never been bent back.

6. Personal communication, Alan Gribben, October 2, 1986.

7. *The Library Chronicle of the University of Texas at Austin,* new series, no. 31,

1985, p. 53. Future references to this issue of the *Library Chronicle* will be indicated by C plus page number.

8. Personal communication, Alan Gribben, October 9, 1986.

9. Personal communication, Alan Gribben, October 2, 1986.

10. Personal communication, Leon Edel, December 16, 1986.

11. Leon Edel and Lyall H. Powers, *The Complete Notebooks of Henry James* (New York: Oxford University Press, 1987), p. 339.

12. Personal communication, Alan Gribben, October 2, 1986.

13. Personal communication, Cathy Henderson, November 12, 1986, Research Library, Harry Ransom Humanities Research Center, The University of Texas at Austin.

14. *The Library of Edith Wharton* (London: Maggs Brothers, 1984), p. 43: R. Rolland, *Vie de Tolstoi* (Paris, 1911).

15. Personal communication, R. W. B. Lewis, October 19, 1986.

16. Romain Rolland, *Tolstoy,* translated by Bernard Meall (New York: Dutton, 1911), pp. 122–23.

17. Ibid., p. 128.

18. The clearly defined fingerprints at the bottom of the page, which one can see on a Xerox copy of the poem seem to be those of Edith Wharton and those of her left hand. The prints have the same tone as the discolored-by-time edges of the page, and it is probable that she held the page down with her left fingers while she wrote the poem. We can eliminate the possible prints of the three men involved with the book so long ago because my argument is that they never saw the poem and consequently could not have left their prints on the page they never touched. Leon Edel never saw the poem, and any prints later than that would not have been discoloured by time.

Index

Hemingway, Ernest, 4, 133–38

Hemingway: Selected Letters (Hemingway), 136

Hemingway's Library (Brash and Sigman), 135

Henry James: The Master (Edel), 35, 38, 45, 46, 49, 50, 51, 52, 53, 211

Henry James: Treacherous Years (Edel), 211

Henry James's Midnight Song (Hill), 4, 222–24

"Hermit and the Wild Woman" (Wharton): Berry as Hermit in, 9–10; Edith Wharton as Wild Woman in, 12–13, 15; Henry James as Hermit in, 2, 9, 11–15, 61; James's possible reading of, 17, 18–19 (n. 10); and James's "Velvet Glove," 15, 17; "Ogrin the Hermit" as sequel to, 17; publication date of, 9, 17; William James as Saint of the Rock in, 11, 14

High Bid (James), 30

Hill, Carol de Chellis, 1, 4, 190, 222–24

home, importance of, 174–80

Home Influence (Aguilar), 129

homelessness, 175–76

Homer, 24

homoeroticism, 4, 53, 54, 61, 185, 187–88, 189, 190–91, 211, 212–13, 214–15, 216

Horowitz, Glenn, 248 (n. 1)

House of Life (D. G. Rossetti), 67

"House of Life" (D. G. Rossetti), 166

House of Mirth (Wharton): Auchincloss on, 210; and Bourget's *Cosmopolis,* 2–3, 96; and Bourget's *Idylle Tragique,* 2, 95–96; classical literary references in, 111–12; and Crawford's *Heart of Rome,* 3, 117–22; French translation of, 96, 104; and Gissing's *New Grub Street,* 3, 111–15; and Gissing's *Whirlpool,* 111; in Hemingway's library, 136; and James's "Crapy Cornelia," 48; and James's "Round

of Visits," 43–44; light imagery in, 48; in mystery by Joan Smith, 5; opening chapter of, 120; preface to, by Bourget, 96–97; in Raphael's *Edith Wharton Murders,* 238, 240; sales of, 96, 97; serialization of, 113; writing of, 113, 114

Howard, Richard, 1, 4, 185–91, 239

Howe, Irving, 59

Howells, William Dean, 28, 47, 116

Hudson River Bracketed (Wharton), 193

Hugh-Smith, A. John, 48, 53

Huguenots, 64

Hunt, William Holman, 155

Ibsen, Henrik, 39

Idylle Tragique (Bourget), 2, 95–96

"Impressions of a Cousin" (James), 64

incest, 77, 124, 127–28, 225

"Indicatrice" (Bourget), xii, 3, 99–103, 104

"International Scene" (James), 148

"Introducers" (Wharton), 49

Italian Backgrounds and Italian Villas and Their Gardens (Wharton), 158, 172, 173, 175, 178

James, Alice, 222

James, Henry: artworks owned by, 215; on Bourget's *Un Divorce,* 104; on Bourget's personality, 94; on cleverness of Wharton, 38–39; Collected Edition of, 35; conversational style of, 30–31, 35, 36–37, 83; criticism of Wharton's works by, 18–19 (n. 10), 29–30, 31, 38–39, 50, 60, 72, 88–89, 206; death of, 15, 33; eyes of, 53; family background of, 236; on French elements, 104–5; friendship with Wharton generally, 1–2, 14–15, 33, 35–36, 41, 55, 191; on Fullerton, 211; "hermit-like asceticism" of, 9; homoeroticism of, 53, 61, 187, 190–91, 211; and inter-

(James, Henry, *continued*)
est in art generally, 156–57; international theme of, 24; and jokes, 30–31, 35, 36, 83; library of, xiii, 5, 17, 211, 241, 246, 248 (n. 1); Lubbock's editorship of letters of, 2, 58–59, 161 (n. 7); on marital difficulties of Wharton, 12, 15, 16–17, 40, 41, 44, 51; New York Edition of, xiv, 14, 20, 32, 35, 70, 85; personality of, 11; physical appearance of, 53; Pocket Diaries of, 245; and proposed "personality paper" on Wharton, 30, 31; and "Qu'acre" group, 53–54, 61, 187; quotations from, in Magida's *Rules of Seduction,* 235–36; reading of Wharton's works by, 18–19 (n. 10), 29–30, 38–39, 52, 79, 85; relationship with brother William, 11, 14; reviews of books by, 67, 167–68; on reworking fiction by others, 79; themes in works by, 17–18, 21, 24, 77–78; trip to America in 1904–1905, 11–12, 15, 26, 35, 47–48, 113–14; trips to France by, 28–29, 31, 35, 37, 85; visits with Wharton, 11–12, 15, 28–29, 47–48, 51, 85, 113–14; Wharton on late novels of, 58, 71; Wharton's handwritten poem in Rolland's *Vie de Tolstoi,* xiii, 5, 241–48; Wharton's monetary kindness to, 102; on Wharton's personality, 36, 46, 48, 49–50, 52, 185, 187; on Wharton's divorce, 51; youth of, 11, 26. *See also specific titles of works* —in works by others: Auchincloss's "Arbiter," 198 (n. 4); Auchincloss's "They That Have Power to Hurt," 211; Hill's *Henry James's Midnight Song,* 1, 4, 190, 222–24; Howard's "Lesson of the Master," 186, 187–90; Walpole's "Mr. Oddy," 141; Wharton's "Eyes," 53–54, 61; Wharton's "Hermit and the Wild

Woman," 2, 9, 11–15, 61; Wharton's *Men and Ghosts,* 52–55; Wharton's "Ogrin the Hermit," 2, 9, 16–17, 18; Wharton's "Writing a War Story," 61
James, John, 248 (n. 1)
James, William, 11, 14, 190
James, William, Jr., 248 (n. 1)
Jarves, James Jackson, 156
Jerome sisters, 143
Johnson, Samuel, 112
"Jolly Corner" (James), 26–27, 55
Jones, Mary Cadwalader, 29–30, 38, 47, 48, 50, 60, 72, 83
Jordan, Elizabeth, 53
Julia Bride (James; 1909), 70
"Julia Bride" (James), xi, 2, 68–69, 85–89
Jung, Carl, 222
Jupiter and Antiope (Correggio), 147, 165

Kafka, Franz, 223
Kauffman, Angelica, 155, 160
Keats, John, 25, 79
Khayyám, Omar, 112
Killoran, Helen, 175, 179
Kingsgate, Lord Lawrence of, 163
Klimt, Gustav, 223
Kraus, Karl, 223

La Bruyère, Jean de, 112
La Farge, Margaret, 46
"Lamp of Psyche" (Wharton), 37
Lang, Andrew, 151
Lapsley, Gaillard, 28, 36, 39, 41, 46, 53, 59, 62, 72
Lee, Vernon, 66, 121
"Legend" (Wharton), 52–53
Lesson of the Master (Howard), 4, 185–91
"Lesson of the Master" (James), 190
Lettres à une Inconnue (Mérimée), 67
Lewis, R. W. B.: on *Age of Innocence,* 72; on *The Buccaneers,* 149; on *Custom*

"Moving Finger" (Wharton), 2, 30, 82, 95
"Mr. Oddy" (Walpole), 141
"Mrs. Mansty's View" (Wharton), 75
"Mrs. Temperly" (James), 77
Mucha, Alphonse, 201, 203, 206, 208–9, 216
Mugnier, Abbé, 218, 220
Murray, Sir James, 163
"Muse's Tragedy" (Wharton), 63
mythological references: in James's "Velvet Glove," 20, 22, 23, 24–26, 37; in Morris's *Earthly Paradise,* 167; in Wharton's works, 37, 127, 133

Nation, 67, 167–68
Nattier, Jean-Marc, 208
neoclassicism, 26, 112
Nevius, Blake, 134
New Criterion, 192
New Grub Street (Gissing), 3, 111–15
"New Novel" (James), 39, 89
New Year's Day (Wharton), 70
New York Edition (James), xiv, 14, 20, 32, 35, 70, 85
New York Historical Society, 157, 161 (n. 10)
New York Times Book Review, 192
Nietzsche, Friedrich, 223, 224
Norris, W. E., 28
North American Review, 116, 120
Norton, Charles Eliot, 28, 156
Norton, Robert, 53
Norton, Sara (Sally), 69, 85, 247
Notebooks (James), 39–40, 49

Oedipus complex, 225
"Ogrin the Hermit" (Wharton): Berry as Hermit in, 10–11; Berry as Tristan in, 11; epigraph of, 15; Fullerton as Tristan in, 18, 168; James as Hermit in, 2, 9, 16–17, 18; and James's "Velvet Glove," 17–18; plot of, 10, 15–16; publication date of, 9, 15, 17;

Wharton as Iseult in, 16–17; and Wharton's "Eyes," 53
Old Maid (Wharton), 70, 76, 124, 125–26, 127
Old New York (Wharton), 59, 70–71, 155
operas, 64
"Orpheus" (Wharton), 37
Out in the Blue (de Watteville), 134–35, 136
Outcry (James), 41, 58, 71
Outre-mer (Bourget), 93, 100, 102
"Owen Wingrave" (James), 39

"Papers" (James), 79
Partners (Auchincloss), 4, 229–32
Pater, Walter, 66
Les Paysans (Balzac), 36
"Pension Beaurepas" (James), 77
Perez Family (Aguilar), 129
Perkins, Maxwell, 135
Phillips, Steven, 116, 120
Piero de Cosimo, 158
Piero della Francesca, 71, 155, 157, 158, 160
play-within-the-box, 64
play-within-the-play, 64
"Portrait" (Bourget), 2, 95
Portrait of a Lady (James), 62, 156
Portrait of Edith Wharton (Lubbock), xii, 9, 102–3, 135, 185
Pound, Ezra, 53
poverty, 111–15
Pre-Raphaelites, 4, 155, 157, 162–68
"Pretext" (Wharton), 61
"primitives," 156–57, 158
Princess Casamassima (James), 64, 65, 66
"Princess's Secrets" (Balzac), 128
Prothero, Fanny, 45, 51
Proust, Marcel, 219, 220
Prudhon, Pierre-Paul, 26
Putt, S. Gorley, 21

"Qu'acre" group, 53–54, 61, 187

Touchstone (Wharton), 79, 82–83
Tragic Muse (James), 62–64, 79
Transport of the Holy House, 170–72
"Tree of Knowledge" (James), 80–81
Turgenev, Ivan, 211
"Turn of the Screw" (James), 20, 53, 54
Twilight Sleep (Wharton), 3, 76, 124, 127, 130–32
Two-Part Inventions (Howard), 185

Vale of Cedars (Aguilar), 129
Valley of Decision (Wharton), 121
Vanderbilt, Alva, 143–51
Vanderbilt, Consuelo, xii, 143–51
Vanderbilt, George, 147
Vanderbilt, William K., 144, 145, 147, 148, 198
"Velvet Glove" (James): and Berry, 17, 40; bird imagery in, 37; compared with James's "Mora Montravers," 42; germ of, 27, 29–30; James as Berridge in, 21, 41; as mock-epic, 20, 21–27, 37; mythological references in, 20, 22, 23, 24–26, 37; Paris in, 28, 36, 37; plot of, 21–24; publication date of, 15, 17, 20, 28; theatrical or dramatic nature of, 25; themes of, 17–18, 21; Wharton as the Princess in, xi, 9, 14, 15, 20, 29–31, 37, 38, 70; and Wharton's *Age of Innocence,* 69–70; and Wharton's *Fruit of the Tree,* 206; and Wharton's "Hermit and the Wild Woman," 15, 17; and Wharton's "Ogrin the Hermit," 17–18; Wharton's reading of, 17, 28, 52
Vice (Correggio), 165
Vie de Tolstoi (Rolland), 5, 241–48, 248 (n. 1)
Virginia reel, 146–47
Virtu (Correggio), 165

Walpole, Hugh, 1, 4, 139–42, 190
War and Peace (Tolstoi), 247

Ward, Mrs. Humphry, 89
Washington Square (James), 68, 190
"Wedding Guest" (Auchincloss), 208
Weininger, Otto, 223
Wells, H. G., 114
Westbrook, Max, 134–35, 137
Wharton, Edith: American homes of, 12, 15, 35, 46, 47–48, 51, 114–15, 175, 196; aristocratic and cosmopolitan background of, 97, 101, 146–47, 149; art history as interest of generally, 5, 6 (n. 2), 158, 215; artworks owned by, 158, 215; automobile of, 45, 46, 50, 185; and Bahlmann, 145–47; and blackmailing of Fullerton by Mirecourt, 49, 51; Bourget on intellect of, 93, 102; Bourget's criticism of works by, 96; Bourget's literary friendship with, xi–xii, 1, 2–3, 93–98, 99, 102, 104; burial of, 185, 244; clothing of, 102; Crawford's literary friendship with, 1, 3, 116–22; divorce of, 51, 85, 146, 148, 192; and Dreyfus case, 40; European winter and summer homes of, 175; friendship with James generally, 1–2, 14–15, 33, 35–36, 41, 55, 191; governess of, 145; handwritten poem by, in Rolland's *Vie de Tolstoi,* xiii, 5, 241–48; on James's conversational style, 30–31, 35, 36, 83; James's criticism of works by, 18–19 (n. 10), 29–30, 31, 38–39, 50, 60, 72, 88–89, 206; James's visits with, 11–12, 15, 28–29, 47–48, 51, 85, 113–114; library of, 101, 117, 151, 166, 167, 244–47; literary agent of, 145–46; love affair with Fullerton, 9–10, 15, 49, 85, 166–67, 168, 185, 192, 199–200, 204, 207, 209, 215, 241, 243–44, 247, 248 (n. 4); love letters to Fullerton from, 1, 4, 199–200, 204–5, 206, 211–12, 225, 226, 244; marital difficulties of, 9, 11, 12, 16–

17, 40, 41, 44, 51, 81, 85, 192, 193; maternal feelings of, 124; mother-daughter relationship in works of, 75–77, 78, 124–29; mythological references in works by, 37; notebooks of, 60; parents of, 77, 78, 132; Paris homes of, 28–29, 31, 35, 37, 42, 44–45, 46, 85, 96; in Paris hotels, 101, 102, 104; personality of, 36, 38–39, 46, 48, 49–50, 52, 102, 185, 187; "personality paper" on, to be written by James, 30, 31; physical appearance of, 12, 50, 101, 102, 206; poetry by, 37, 168, 200, 206, 244, 247; popularity of, xiii, 239; reading of James's works by, 28, 52, 85, 114; relation with Berry, 5, 9–10, 185, 187, 207, 243, 244, 248, 248 (n. 4); social circle and social life of, 28–29, 31, 36, 37, 46, 47–48, 96, 143, 146–47, 193; travels of, 12, 36; trips to England by, 28, 35–36, 39, 51; Walpole on, 139; youth of, 101, 116, 132, 146, 147, 149. *See also specific titles of works*

—in works by others: Auchincloss's "Arbiter," 192, 193–98, 204, 206, 216; Auchincloss's *Education of Oscar Fairfax,* 4, 218–21, 222; Auchincloss's "'Fulfillment' of Grace Eliot," xii, 199–209, 216; Auchincloss's "They That Have Power to Hurt," 210–17; Bourget's "L'Indicatrice," 99–103; Bourget's *Outre-mer,* 93, 102; Bourget's "Portrait," 95; Hill's *Henry James's Midnight Song,* 1, 4, 190, 222–24; Howard's "Lesson of the Master," 185–90; James's "Bench of Desolation," 48–52; James's "Crapy Cornelia," 45–48; James's *Finer Grain* tales, xi, 2, 33–54; James's "Mora Montravers," 39, 41–42; James's "Round of Visits," 43–45; James's "Velvet Glove,"

xi, 9, 14, 15, 20, 29–31, 37, 38, 70; Raphael's *Edith Wharton Murders,* 4, 238–40; Schine's *Love Letter,* 4, 222, 225–26

Wharton, Edward (Teddy): in Auchincloss's "Arbiter," 193–98, 199, 216; divorce of, 51, 85, 146, 148, 192; infidelity of, 44, 199; marital difficulties of, 9, 11, 12, 40, 41, 44, 51, 81, 85, 192, 193

Wharton Society, 239

What Maisie Knew (James), 156–57

"Wheel of Time" (James), 76

Whirlpool (Gissing), 111, 114

Whistler, James, 215

White (Wharton's butler), 50

White, Mrs. Henry, 146

White, Richard Grant, 156, 157

Whitman, Walt, 185

Wilde, Oscar, 185

Wilson, Edmund, 59, 197

Wings of the Dove (James), 83, 210, 244

Winthrop, Egerton, 194–95

Winthrop Covenant (Auchincloss), xii, 193, 199, 207

Wittgenstein, Ludwig, 223

Wolff, Cynthia, 59, 62, 132, 134, 174–75, 248 (n. 2)

Women Friendships (Aguilar), 129

World Columbian Exposition (Chicago), 26

World War I refugees, 175

"Writing a War Story" (Wharton), 59–62

Writing of Fiction (Wharton), 52, 113, 160, 219, 220

Yale University Museum, 156

Yeats, W. B., 140

Yznaga, Consuelo (Duchess of Manchester), 143, 147, 149

Zorzi, Rosella Mamoli, xii, 170, 172, 179

ADELINE R. TINTNER, the author of numerous works on Wharton, James, and their circle, is an independent scholar living in New York City.